The A-Z Guide to Federal Employment Laws

For the Small Business Owner

By Shannon Johnson
with Berit Everhart

The A-Z Guide to Federal Employment Laws
For the Small Business Owner

Copyright © 2011 Atlantic Publishing Group, Inc.
1405 SW 6th Avenue • Ocala, Florida 34471 • Phone 800-814-1132 • Fax 352-622-1875
Web site: www.atlantic-pub.com • E-mail: sales@atlantic-pub.com
SAN Number: 268-1250

Library of Congress Cataloging-in-Publication Data

Everhart, Berit, 1983-
  The A-Z guide to federal employment laws for the small business owner / by Berit Everhart.
     p. cm.
  Includes bibliographical references and index.
  ISBN-13: 978-1-60138-308-2 (alk. paper)
  ISBN-10: 1-60138-308-8 (alk. paper)
  1. Small business--Law and legislation--United States. 2. Small business--Ownership--United
States. I. Title.
  KF1659.E94 2010
  344.7301--dc22
                              2009053566

PROJECT MANAGER: Nicole Orr • FINAL EDITOR: Chris Kissell
INTERIOR DESIGN: Holly Marie Gibbs
COVER DESIGN: Meg Buchner • meg@megbuchner.com
BACK COVER DESIGN: Jackie Miller • millerjackiej@gmail.com

Printed in the United States

Printed on Recycled Paper

We recently lost our beloved pet "Bear," who was not only our best and dearest friend but also the "Vice President of Sunshine" here at Atlantic Publishing. He did not receive a salary but worked tirelessly 24 hours a day to please his parents. Bear was a rescue dog that turned around and showered myself, my wife, Sherri, his grandparents Jean, Bob, and Nancy, and every person and animal he met (maybe not rabbits) with friendship and love. He made a lot of people smile every day.

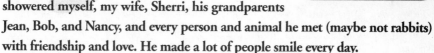

We wanted you to know that a portion of the profits of this book will be donated to The Humane Society of the United States. *–Douglas & Sherri Brown*

The human-animal bond is as old as human history. We cherish our animal companions for their unconditional affection and acceptance. We feel a thrill when we glimpse wild creatures in their natural habitat or in our own backyard.

Unfortunately, the human-animal bond has at times been weakened. Humans have exploited some animal species to the point of extinction.

The Humane Society of the United States makes a difference in the lives of animals here at home and worldwide. The HSUS is dedicated to creating a world where our relationship with animals is guided by compassion. We seek a truly humane society in which animals are respected for their intrinsic value, and where the human-animal bond is strong.

Want to help animals? We have plenty of suggestions. Adopt a pet from a local shelter, join The Humane Society and be a part of our work to help companion animals and wildlife. You will be funding our educational, legislative, investigative and outreach projects in the U.S. and across the globe.

Or perhaps you'd like to make a memorial donation in honor of a pet, friend or relative? You can through our Kindred Spirits program. And if you'd like to contribute in a more structured way, our Planned Giving Office has suggestions about estate planning, annuities, and even gifts of stock that avoid capital gains taxes.

Maybe you have land that you would like to preserve as a lasting habitat for wildlife. Our Wildlife Land Trust can help you. Perhaps the land you want to share is a backyard— that's enough. Our Urban Wildlife Sanctuary Program will show you how to create a habitat for your wild neighbors.

So you see, it's easy to help animals. And The HSUS is here to help.

2100 L Street NW • Washington, DC 20037 • 202-452-1100
www.hsus.org

Dedication

This book is dedicated to my son, Zion E. Council, the light of my life. I would also like to thank all of those friends and family members who kept me going when I was overwhelmed by the many tasks set before me, and expressed a confidence in my ability that I myself did not possess.

— Shannon Johnson

Table of Contents

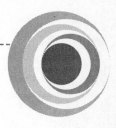

Chapter 4: The Americans with
Disabilities Act of 1990 (ADA)   49

Chapter 5: The Consolidated Omnibus
Budget Reconciliation Act of 1985 (COBRA)   69

Chapter 6: Employee Polygraph
Protection Act 1988 (EPPA)   91

Chapter 10: The Family Medical Leave Act   139

Chapter 11: The Genetic Information Nondiscrimination Act   155

Chapter 12: The Immigration Reform and Control Act of 1986 (IRCA)   157

Chapter 13: The National Labor Relations Act   165

Chapter 14: The Occupational Safety and Health Act

185

Chapter 15: Personal Responsibility and Work Opportunity Reconciliation Act

197

Chapter 16: The Pregnancy Discrimination Act (PDA)

203

Chapter 17: Title VII of the Civil Rights Act of 1964

207

Chapter 18: Uniformed Services
Employment and Reemployment Rights Act 219

Chapter 19: Worker Adjustment
and Retraining Notification Act 231

Foreword

Employment law is one of the fastest growing areas of the law. Amendments to existing legislation, as well as new legislation, require employers to undergo constant training regarding their workplace obligations. Many of the employment laws are also complex, so companies need a comprehensive understanding of their obligations to their employees. This is particularly true for small business owners whose exposure to liability is often great. Small business owners may have a general understanding of employment law, but this may not be sufficient to ensure that they are in compliance with the law. Even unintentional violations often result in employer liability.

Within the last century, America has evolved from a country with little protection for employees to one of ever-increasing protection. Employers who do not understand employment laws are at risk for liability if they fail to follow the law. While lawyers, judges, and legislators continue to work together to find ways to ensure that employees are protected in the workplace and employers are not unfairly penalized, small business owners must protect themselves by understanding employment law.

The A-Z Guide to Federal Employment Laws For the Small Business Owner is a significant contribution to the resources on employment law. The book comprises a scholarly, comprehensive resource on federal employment laws. This "one-stop shopping" manual will allow employers ease of access to further their understanding of employment law. In addition to explaining the federal laws, it is filled with helpful Web sites, recent cases, and case studies from those experienced in employment law. What is particularly helpful to small business owners is that the book provides the historical background and purpose of each law discussed. This will help employers understand why the law was enacted, which may assist employers in understanding the importance and value of complying with the law. Although the book focuses on federal employment laws, there is also an appendix to identify corresponding state statutes.

With the wealth of resources available on the subject of employment law, small business owners should reach for the most comprehensive, user-friendly guides. *The A-Z Guide to Federal Employment Laws For the Small Business Owner* is certainly one of those. Small business owners should ensure that each person in their company with supervisory duties has access to this book.

Professor Jennifer Smith
Florida A&M University
College of Law

Jennifer M. Smith is an associate professor of law at Florida A&M University College of Law. Smith received her J.D. from the University of Miami School of Law and her B.S. from Hampton University. Before joining FAMU College of Law, Smith was a partner with the international law firm of Holland & Knight LLP. During her time with Holland & Knight, she was a trial lawyer who represented clients in a variety of litigation matters, including employment law, and has experience as lead counsel in jury trials, arbitrations, and administrative hearings. Smith began handling employment matters in the mid-1990s and has represented both corporations and employees.

Introduction

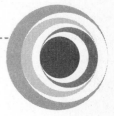

Running a small business can be an exciting task, often complicated by the many non-business concerns that face those who own a small business. Even those business owners who are graced with keen minds and sharp business senses can be daunted by this exhaustive list of concerns on a daily basis. Among these concerns are the many issues that arise related to their obligations under the various employment laws of this country. Attempting to sift through and understand the morass of rules U.S. employment laws impose on a business owner can be a task that overwhelms even the most dedicated and focused individuals. Shannon Johnson has taken a step toward alleviating some of the mystery surrounding many key employment laws relevant to small business owners with the publication of *Federal Employment Laws*.

Federal Employment Laws provides a detailed overview of some of the most relevant employment laws for small business owners. The laws covered are often dense and difficult to understand, and wading through this legalese can be difficult. *Federal Employment Laws* does this for the reader by tackling and breaking down the laws in a reader-friendly fashion — you will find the key provisions of the laws defined in layman's terms. *Federal Employment Laws* then grounds the legal concepts in concrete and accessible examples and hypotheticals that illustrate how certain everyday situations play out under the law. With *Federal Employment Laws*, the reader finds a relatable context in which to place those legal concepts.

Non-lawyers often find that their lack of familiarity with formal legal models and techniques is one of the biggest obstacles to navigating the law. A small business owner who is unfamiliar with the extensive network of employment laws can gain a general understanding of the employment law framework from *Federal Employment Laws*. Once a reader becomes more comfortable with the legal concepts presented by each law and understands the everyday situations to which they apply, the gap between the law and real life will begin to narrow.

This book provides an extensive overview of many of the key laws relevant to business owners. While it functions as a user-friendly overview of the covered material, it cannot function as the ultimate authority on all subjects that a small business owner might face in the arena of employment law. There are certain laws whose technical nature and level of detail are simply beyond the scope of this book. Business owners should, therefore, proceed with the knowledge gained from *Federal Employment Laws* with the understanding that more research may be necessary before one is able to completely answer all questions related to employment law. However, readers will find that the knowledge gained from *Federal Employment Laws* provides an important foundation for future study of employment laws and provides them with a general familiarity with concepts that will be useful going forward.

Disclaimer

The coverage in this book is intended as a general description of some laws that may be relevant to the average small business. It does not carry the force or authority of a legal opinion and is not intended to provide legal advice. The resolution of any legal matter depends on the particular facts and circumstances of that matter and cannot be determined based on any advice in this book. Any reader who believes that a specific law may be applicable to his or her situation should consult a licensed attorney before making any decisions.

Chapter 1
Overview

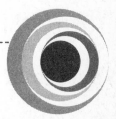

Federal employment law is an ever-evolving topic area. Each year, agencies and courts issue new rulings and regulations to address employee complaints regarding employer discrimination. It is helpful to have a resource that helps you navigate through the complexities of intertwining acts and enforcement agencies.

This book lays out the laws in a forthright manner. As an employer, it is important that you have a general understanding of employment law and its requirements and prohibitions. This book will provide you with an overview of each major employment law statute. It also highlights links to Web sites that can provide you with forms and additional compliance information.

Conflicts of Federal and State Laws

Federal law is derived from federal statutes, federal regulations, and federal court opinions. State law is derived from the same sources at the state level. When federal and state law conflict, federal law takes precedence over, or "preempts," the state law. It is important to remember this as you read through this book because each state has its own employment laws. State law can grant more power for business owners — in some areas — than federal law does, but it cannot take away rights or responsibilities given by a federal law. Therefore, depending on which state you operate your business in, you may have more legal freedoms, according to your state's law, than you would if you were operating your business in another state.

Sources of Law

Statutes are bills passed by either the U.S. Congress or a state's legislature and signed into law — either by the president at the federal level, or a governor at the state level. Regulations are rules issued by the agency that interpret a specific statute. Using the framework laid out by the statute, the regulations provide specific guidelines on how the statute will actually operate in relation to employers, employees, and any other affected individuals.

Case law is derived from lawsuits heard by judges. The judge will usually issue a written opinion that specifically states which party the court decided in favor of, the facts surrounding the lawsuit, what the court decided, and why the court made the decision it did. Courts are made up of various hierarchies at both the state and federal level. For example, U.S. Supreme Court decisions take precedence over any other court's decision on matters of federal law. For other cases, such as those that are not federal law, U.S. Courts of Appeal and District Courts have jurisdiction over their various regions. There are 94 U.S. judicial districts, which are organized by region. This breaks down into 12 regional circuits, with each circuit having its own court of appeals, along with other district courts.

Each state has a high court — usually called a Supreme Court — that makes final decisions regarding state law issues.

Application of Federal Law to Employers

A number of factors may cause an employer to be covered by a federal employment law. These include the number of employees employed by a business; whether an employer is a private entity, or a branch of federal, state, or local government; and the type of industry an employer is in.

The following chart shows how the number of workers a company employs determines whether or not a specific federal statute applies to the business:

Number of Employees	Applicable Statute
100	WARN — Worker Adjustment and Retraining Notification Act
50	FMLA — Family Medical Leave Act
20	ADEA — Age Discrimination in Employment Act
20	COBRA — Consolidated Omnibus Benefits Reconciliation Act
20	OWBPA — Older Workers Benefit Protection Act
15	ADA — American with Disabilities Act
15	GINA — Genetic Information Nondiscrimination Act
15	Title VII of the Civil Rights Act of 1964
15	PDA — Pregnancy Discrimination Act
1	EPPA — Employee Polygraph Protection Act
1	EPA — Equal Pay Act
1	FRCA — Fair Credit Reporting Act
1	FLSA — Fair Labor Standards Act
1	IRCA — Immigration Reform and Control Act
1	OSHA — Occupational Safety and Health Act
1	PRWORA — Personal Responsibility and Work Opportunity Reconciliation Act
1	USERRA — Uniform Services Employment and Reemployment Rights Act

What is Covered in This Book?

Each chapter provides you with a general framework of the specific law covered. This helps you understand your obligations under the law as an employer. Each chapter begins with a short description of the purpose of each law. After the purpose, most chapters include legal terms and definitions as laid out by the statute's regulations. The chapters go on to talk about employees who are covered by the statute, employers who are subject to the statutes defined within the chapter, and any required or prohibited employer action. There are also sections including information about enforcement agencies and proceedings and applicable penalties for violations of the statute. Near the end of most chapters is a list of Web sites that offer compliance assistance and guidance. Most chapters end with a "Delving Deeper" section that highlights an important topic under the relevant law.

The appendix features a list of the federal agencies that have oversight or enforcement powers over various federal laws. In regards to state employment laws, there is also an A-to-Z listing of each state, its labor department, and general information on state statutes and corresponding federal statutes.

CASE STUDY: LACK OF KNOWLEDGE, OR INTENTIONAL?

Rhonda Reeves
Associate Professor of Law
Florida A&M University
Tallahassee, Florida

While advocating for the management side of the situation, I discovered that a lot of times, employers simply act with a lack of understanding of applicable law, and not necessarily with the intent to discriminate. The situation usually begins with an employee getting genuinely upset, and yet not completely understanding why.

Federal laws are complicated, and it is hard to have a one-size-fits-all type of law. Most employers have a general idea of the requirements, but have little or no idea as to what you have to prove as an employer to defeat a discrimination case. When you are dealing with people, it is hard to regulate a workplace in strict adherence to laws. Every employer must adjust to the particular dynamics of his or her workplace because employment discrimination is so context-based. Employers find themselves in the position of having to investigate charges between sets of employees. Due to the large amount of time Americans spend at work, the lines often get blurred. In short, it becomes harder to police people stepping over the lines.

Recent Legal Developments

Observers have closely watched the most recent Supreme Court action in regard to the Equal Pay Act. The way the Supreme Court has interpreted the statute of limitations will preclude a number of plaintiffs from filing claims. In regard to retaliation claims, the courts have made several decisions intended to answer whether an employee can bring a retaliation claim under statutes that do not currently have specific provisions for such claims. A majority of the courts have interpreted these cases narrowly, which means it will become harder for employees to bring retaliation claims under federal statutes that do not explicitly provide for such claims.

Diversity Training and Settling – A Cost Benefit Analysis

Recent scholarship in the realm of diversity training and its effect on the workplace suggests that some legal scholars have concluded that diversity training is not as effective as employers presume. This is primarily due to the lack of "buy in" to the training at higher levels of the company.

More often than not, I have found that cases settle before they enter the actual litigation process. This is usually due to the costly nature of litigating employment law cases. Most employers will see the case through the motions stage, but after a grant of summary judgment, the employer will do a cost-benefit analysis to determine if settling is the least costly option. In most cases, it is.

In closing, employers should always take claims seriously and have sensible procedures in place. Also, employers should evaluate their procedures on a regular basis. Most of all, employers should treat their employees with respect.

Reeves graduated from Yale University in New Haven, Conn., and attended Stanford Law School in Stanford, Calif. She clerked for a federal law judge before beginning her tenure at Heller, Ehrman, White, and McAuliffe in Los Angeles. Reeves specialized in employment law defense while working at the firm, which represented employers accused of discriminatory behavior toward employees.

Chapter 2
Age Discrimination in Employment Act of 1967 (ADEA)

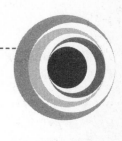

COMMON TERMS AND DEFINITIONS	
Commerce:	Trade, traffic, business dealings, transportation, transmissions, or communication among the several states, or between a state and any place outside thereof.
Compensation:	Terms, conditions, or privileges of employment; includes monetary compensation, employee benefits, and other forms as the employer sees fit.
Employee:	An individual employed by an employer. Does not include state politicians or any publicly elected officials.
Employer:	Person engaged in an industry affecting commerce that has 20 or more employees for each working day in each of 20 or more calendar weeks, in the current or preceding calendar year.
Employment agency:	Agency that matches employees with employers, usually for compensation.

Firefighter: An individual employed by a fire station whose main work functions are the control and putting out of fires.

Industry affecting commerce: Any activity, business, or industry in commerce or in which a labor dispute would hinder or obstruct commerce or the free flow of commerce.

Labor organization: Organization engaged in an industry affecting commerce, and any agent of such an organization, and includes any organization of any kind, any agency, or employee representation committee, group, association, or plan so engaged in which employees participate and which exists for the purpose (in whole or in part) of dealing with employers concerning grievances, labor disputes, wages, rates of pay, hours, or other terms or conditions of employment.

Law enforcement officer: A member of the police force or other law enforcement agency that investigates crimes and apprehends criminals; includes supervisor and administrative positions.

Person: One or more individuals, partnerships, associations, labor organizations, corporations, legal representatives, or any organized group of persons.

Prima facie: Based on the first impression accepted as correct until proven otherwise.

State: Includes any of the states of the United States, the District of Columbia, Puerto Rico, the Virgin Islands, American Samoa, Guam, Wake Island, the Canal Zone, and Outer Continental Shelf lands.

History and Purpose

The Age Discrimination in Employment Act (ADEA) was passed by Congress in 1967. (It should not be confused with the Age Discrimination Act, which was passed in 1975.) The ADEA was enacted to respond to a growing trend of employers setting arbitrary age limits for employment irrespective of job performance, making it difficult for older workers to retain their jobs. The ADEA protects both applicants and employees who are 40 years of age or older from discrimination due to their age. Congress passed the ADEA to promote the hiring and retention of workers over 40. The act prohibits the firing of or refusal to hire older employees based on their age.

PRACTICALLY SPEAKING A company might prefer to hire younger employees for a variety of reasons. For example, assume Acme Company received two applications for a single position. Julie is a 30-year-old woman with two years of relevant experience. Vivian is a 50-year-old woman with 10 years of relevant experience. Before the ADEA, Acme legally could have made its hiring decision based on the relative ages of the candidates and favored Julie solely based on her younger age. The ADEA requires Acme to disregard the ages of the applicants and weigh their respective skills when making the hiring decision.

Protected Class of Employees

The ADEA protects the following individuals:

- Employees who are at least 40 years old

- Job applicants who are at least 40 years old

- Employee and job applicants who are at least 40 years old and citizens of the United States, but are employed by an employer in a workplace in a foreign country

Employers Subject to the ADEA

The following employers must comply with the ADEA:

- Employers with 20 or more employees. (Employees must be working each day in each of the 20 or more calendar weeks in the current or preceding year.)

- Employment agencies

- Labor organizations

- Apprenticeship programs

- Interstate agencies

- States or political subdivisions of states

- Foreign companies that are controlled by American employers

NOTE: Neither the United States nor any corporations wholly owned by the United States will be governed by the ADEA.

Prohibited Discriminatory Employer Actions

Employers are barred from discriminatory acts that have an adverse effect on employment or hiring decisions. Generally, employers must not take any of the following actions:

1. Treating employees age 40 or older differently when it comes to promotion, compensation, firing, benefits, job assignments, and training.

PRACTICALLY SPEAKING For example, a company might not want to provide health insurance to older employees under the assumption that it would cost more than it would to provide such coverage to younger employees. The ADEA prohibits such action.

2. When interviewing potential employees and their age is not clear, showing any interest or asking any questions that might allude to any concern or extra interest in their age.

PRACTICALLY SPEAKING Examples of prohibited questions might include questions related to age such as "How old are you?" and indirect questions such as "Do you believe that a person of your age is capable of performing this position?"

3. Limiting, segregating, or classifying employees 40 or older in a way that deprives them of or has the potential of depriving them of employment opportunities that are available to employees under 40. This includes taking actions that would negatively affect an employee's status due to his or her age.

PRACTICALLY SPEAKING It would violate the ADEA to institute an advancement structure designed to provide promotion opportunities every two years for employees under 40 and every four years for employees over 40.

4. Reducing the pay rate of an employee because of his or her age.

PRACTICALLY SPEAKING Once you reach the age of 55, your boss decides to pay you less and reduce your hours, anticipating either your retirement or a slowed work pace and decrease in productivity.

Employment agencies must also ensure they do not refuse to refer a person for employment to a company on the basis of that person's age. Also, employment agencies should refrain from classifying or referring potential employees on the basis of their age.

Labor organizations are barred from any of the following actions if they are solely based on the employee's or member's age:

1. Excluding or expelling him or her from membership

2. Failing to refer a person for employment

3. Limiting, segregating, or classifying a person in a way that would limit his or her employment opportunities or have a negative effect on his or her status as an employee or as an applicant

4. Causing or attempting to cause an employer to discriminate against an individual in violation of the ADEA

Retaliation

Employers, labor organizations, and employment agencies will be in violation of the ADEA if they retaliate against an employee, potential employee, or member for filing a charge, openly opposing discriminatory practices, or testifying or participating in an investigation, proceeding, or trial.

Notices

All notices and advertisements that relate to employment, membership, or referral for employment are in violation of the ADEA if they indicate age preferences, limitations, specifications, or discriminations due to age.

Foreign entities

The rights granted by the ADEA do not cover American employees working for a foreign company that is not controlled by an American entity. However, if an American employee is working in a foreign country for a company that is controlled by an American entity, he or she will be entitled to all the rights and protections granted by the ADEA.

To determine whether an employer controls a corporation, the following factors will be analyzed:

1. Interrelation of operations

2. Common management

3. Centralized control of labor relations

4. Common ownership or financial control of the employer and the corporation

The more these factors are present, the more likely it will be that the American entity controls a foreign company.

EVERYDAY
ILLUSTRATION   Mark, a U.S. citizen, works for a French Company as a sales representative in its New York office. Even though Mark works in the United States and is a U.S. citizen, he does not enjoy the protections of the ADEA.

Contrast Mark's situation with that of Paul, a U.S. citizen working in the Paris office of USA Company. Because Paul works for a U.S. company, he will enjoy the protection of the ADEA. Similarly, Joe, a U.S. citizen working in the Barcelona office of Spain Sub — a wholly owned subsidiary of USA Company — would enjoy the protections of the ADEA.

Pension benefit plans

Employers, employment agencies, and labor organizations are prohibited from establishing a plan that requires or permits the ending of an employee's benefit accrual or a reduction of the rate of an employee's benefit accrual based on the employee's age.

Waivers

In some situations, an employer might ask an employee to waive his or her rights under the ADEA. Employees who agree to waive such rights under the ADEA give up the protections of the ADEA and allow the employer to discriminate against them based on their age. It is possible for employees to waive their rights and claims under the ADEA, but all waivers must be "knowing and voluntary." For a waiver to be knowing and voluntary, the employee must understand that he or she is waiving rights under the ADEA and is doing so voluntarily.

In addition to being knowing and voluntary, the waiver must comply with the following requirements:

- Entire agreement must be in writing.

- Must be drafted in plain language and written such that the party signing the waiver can easily understand it. The employer must take into account the employee's education and level of comprehension when drafting the waiver.

- Must not have a misleading or misinforming effect. All aspects of the waiver, including advantages and disadvantages, must be laid out clearly.

- Must not include rights and claims that may arise after the date the waiver is executed (i.e., an employee cannot waive his or her rights related to discrimination that occurs after the date of signing the waiver).

- Must refer to rights or claims under the ADEA by their specific names.

- Must advise the individual in writing to consult with an attorney before signing the document.

- Must be executed in exchange for something of value that is not something the individual is already entitled to (e.g., extra compensation, benefits, bonuses, etc).

- Employee must have at least 21 days to consider the agreement. If the waiver is being signed in connection with an employment termination, the employee must have 45 days to consider the waiver agreement.

- Person signing the waiver must be given a seven-day revocation period to change his or her mind. This period cannot be given or taken way.

For a more detailed discussion of the waiver requirements, see Chapter Three.

Exceptions to the general rule

The following actions by employers, employment agencies, or labor organizations do not violate the ADEA:

- Taking the actions named above to observe the terms of a bona fide seniority system that is not trying to get around the purposes for the enactment of the ADEA. The bona fide system cannot require or allow the involuntary retirement of any individual (specified by 631(c)) due to his or her age.

- Engaging in prohibited actions where age is a bona fide occupational qualification, reasonably necessary to the normal operation of an individual business.

- Treating employees who are different ages differently as long as it is based on reasonable factors other than age.

- Failing to adhere to the ADEA if the entity is an American company with American employees located in a foreign country when compliance with the ADEA violates the foreign country's laws.

EVERYDAY
ILLUSTRATION   Host Country, a European country, has a
                mandatory retirement age of 64. USA Com-
pany operates a subsidiary in Host Country. To legally operate in
Host Country, the subsidiary must comply with the mandatory
retirement age. Under these facts, the subsidiary will not be held
in violation of the ADEA because its non-compliance is required
by the laws of Host Country.

- Having a legitimate voluntary early retirement incentive plan consistent with the purpose of the ADEA.

- An employer discharging or disciplining an employee who is at least 40 years old for a good cause.

- Instituting a legitimate seniority system, as long as it does not require the involuntary retirement of any employee.

- Taking any of the prohibited actions if age is a legitimate requirement of the position and is necessary to the operation of the business of the employer.

NOTE: Benefit plans or early retirement incentive plans cannot be used to refuse to hire individuals who are 40 years of age or older, nor can they be used to force employees 40 years old or older into early retirement. Employers, employment agencies, and labor organizations will have the burden of proving that the plans are legitimate.

Bona fide Occupational Qualifications — BFOQ

A bona fide occupational qualification is a special exception for an otherwise discriminatory hiring practice. To not violate the ADEA, while employing those younger than 40, the employer will have to comply with the following:

- BFOQ must be reasonably necessary to the normal operation of the particular business.

- Employer will have to prove that either all or substantially all individuals excluded from the job involved are in fact disqualified, or that some of the individuals so excluded possess a disqualifying trait that cannot be ascertained except by reference to age.

EVERYDAY
ILLUSTRATION   Teens Company designs and manufacturers
a line of clothing specifically for teenagers.
As a result of the company's product and target demographic,
Teens Company hires only teenagers to model its clothing. Even
though Teens Company is making employment decisions based
on age and discriminating against older applicants, it is not in
violation of the ADEA because there is a BFOQ: only teenagers
are capable of effectively modeling clothes for teenagers.

State exceptions

States, state agencies, and interstate agencies are not governed by the ADEA when hiring for the positions of firefighters or law enforcement officers. Also, they will not be held to the requirements of the ADEA when hiring or firing in connection with a bona fide hiring or retirement plan.

Law in
Real Life   As an example, consider § 58(1)(a) of New
York civil service law, which does not allow
anyone older than 35 to sit for the civil service exam and become a police officer. New York found that older officers present an economic problem for the state because they leave the force at a higher rate than younger officers and utilize more sick leave than younger officers.

Enforcement Agency and Procedures

The Equal Employment Opportunity Commission (EEOC) is the agency charged with investigating ADEA claims and performing the necessary record keeping. The EEOC also has the power to file a claim against employers, employment agencies, or labor organizations in federal court. Individuals who have been discriminated against can submit complaints to the EEOC in person, by telephone, or via mail.

Filing of claims

Any action filed in federal court will take precedence over any action filed in the state court system. If an individual chooses to sue within the state court system first, he or she must wait 60 days from the date of the state court filing before filing a federal court claim.

A charge must be filed with the EEOC within 180 days of the alleged discriminatory action. If the state where the discriminatory action occurred has its own age discrimination laws, the complaining individual has 300 days to file a charge with the EEOC or 30 days after the termination of any state proceedings, whichever occurs first.

Upon receiving a charge, the EEOC will notify the respondent (employer, employment agency, or labor organization) that charges have been filed. The complaining party then must wait 60 days to file suit. However, if the EEOC decides to sue on an employee's behalf, the employee will no longer have the right to file a private suit.

PRACTICALLY SPEAKING   A person suing for personal injury, breach of contract, or other matters unrelated to ADEA can go straight to the courts without involving another party. However, claims arising out of the ADEA must go through the EEOC. Employees considering filing suit under the ADEA should be prepared for EEOC involvement in the case.

Penalties for Violations

The EEOC shall attempt to eliminate discriminatory practices and to get the employer to voluntarily comply via informal mediation methods. Courts hearing actions under the ADEA have the power to order the following remedies:

- Payment of back pay, lost benefits, and any other compensation lost due to discrimination

- Hiring, rehiring or promotion of the wronged individual

- Payment of liquidated damages (if the violation was willful)

- Payment of court costs and attorney fees

Employer Compliance and Requirements

Record keeping

Employers must keep the following records for a three-year payroll period for each employee:

- Name

- Address

- Date of birth

- Occupation

- Rate of pay

- Compensation earned each week

Employers must keep the following records for a period of one year from the date of personnel action:

- Job applications

- Résumés

- Any other form of employment inquiry submitted in response to an advertisement for a job or potential job opening, including those relating to the failure or refusal to hire any individual

- Records related to promotion, demotion, transfer, selection for training, layoff, recall, or discharge of any employee

- Job orders submitted by employer to employment agency or labor organization for recruitment of personnel for job openings

- Test papers completed by applicants for any position that shows aptitude or serves as the basis for any personnel action

- Results of any physical exam where the exam is considered by the employer before any personnel action

- Advertisements or notices to the public or employees relating to job openings, promotions, training programs, or opportunities for overtime

- Employee benefit plans (pension and insurance) copies of seniority systems, and merit systems, which are in writing, must be kept for at least one year after its termination

NOTE: If the employee benefit plan is not in writing, then the employer must keep a detailed memo that fully outlines the terms of the plan or system and how it was communicated to the affected employees. The document must also include notations relating to changes or revisions.

Employment agencies must keep the following records for a period of one year from the date of the action to which the records relate:

- Placements

- Referrals where a person is referred to an employer for a known or reasonably anticipated job opening

- Job orders from employers seeking individuals for job openings

- Job applicants' résumés, or any other form of employment inquiry; or, documents where a person identifies his qualifications for employment, whether for a known job opening or future referral to an employer

- Test papers completed by applicants or candidates that disclose agency-administered employment tests considered by an agency in connection with job referrals

- Advertisements or notices relative to job openings

Labor organizations must keep the following records:

- Current records identifying members by name, address, and date of birth. Records of the name, address, and age of any individual seeking membership in the organization must be kept for a period of one year from their creation.

NOTE: An individual seeking membership is a person who files an application for membership or who, in some other manner, indicates a specific intention to be considered for membership.

Notices and advertisements

All employers, employment agencies, and labor organizations have to post in an obvious place a notice that offers information regarding the pertinent parts of the ADEA. The location shall be in a place where it can easily be seen and read by employees.

Employers should exercise caution to ensure their help wanted ads do not include language such as: "25 to 35," "young college students," or "recent college graduates." If the position does not fall under one of the exceptions (noted in the exceptions section), the aforementioned type of language is prohibited because it has the effect of deterring older applicants. Also, phrases such as "45 to 55," or "retired person" are also prohibited because they are discriminatory against others in the protected class. The use of the phrase "state age" on advertising or applications is not automatically a violation of the ADEA; however, notices that use this language will be closely looked at to ensure the request is being used for a lawful purpose.

 **DELVING DEEPER** An employer may be liable under the ADEA when unlawfully firing an employee within the protected class, even if the employee is replaced with another member of the protected class. If the original firing was in violation of the ADEA, the status of the replacement employee will not act as a safeguard or bar charges from being brought by the EEOC. The following case illustrates this point.

O'Connor v. Consolidated Coin Caterers Corp., 517 U.S. 308 (1996)

In this case, the following question was answered: Did an employee who believed he was discharged in violation of the ADEA have to show that someone outside of the protected age group replaced him?

The Supreme Court in this case held that being replaced by someone under 40 was not a necessary element of an ADEA prima facie case.

The court ruled that the ADEA does not ban discrimination against employees because they are age 40 or older; it bans discrimination against employees because of their age, but limits the protected class to those who are 40 or older. Therefore, employees over the age of 40 are legally protected under this law and can receive benefits or have penalties incurred on their employers, although age discrimination is generally prohibited.

Facts of the Case:

Consolidated Coin Caterers operated vending machines and cafeterias throughout different regions of North Carolina. James O'Conner served as a manager for one of the regions. As a consequence of a reorganization that reduced the number of regions, Consolidated fired O'Connor, age 57, and installed two other individuals, ages 40 and 35, as managers of the new regions.

The lower court determined that O'Conner could not establish a violation of the ADEA because he was replaced by someone 40 years old. As stated above, the Supreme Court rejected this interpretation of the ADEA. Had the Supreme Court followed the lower court's interpretation, a company could have avoided an ADEA violation by simply hiring a person at least 40 years old to fill the position.

CASE STUDY: HOW CLEAR IS THE LAW?

Patricia A. Broussard
Associate Professor
Florida A&M College of Law
Tallahassee, Florida

I basically "fell" into the practice of employment law, due to clients who came to my office with employment law issues. I spent about two years handling various federal employment law cases, but for the most part I dealt with disability discrimination. The most egregious case I have handled regarded a client who had a pinched nerve, and due to the severity of the pain, had a permanent prescription for Percodan. Yet, the government denied her disability claim.

A lot of employment law cases stem from a combination of employers' willful ignorance of the law and a desire to skirt the law. The best way to avoid litigation is to ensure that everyone in your company has a clear and thorough understanding of the law, and that everyone adheres to clearly defined employment policies. Also, treating employees in a fair and equitable manner will prevent a wealth of misunderstandings. Having a competent human resources manager and an employment law attorney on retainer can prevent small issues from building into larger, unmanageable ones.

Federal employment statutes tend to be confusing and somewhat contradictory. Where specificity is needed, the law tends to lean toward ambiguity. For instance, businesses should be aware of the recent changes to the Family Medical Leave Act. There are regulations that have been issued by several states, the federal government and the military. Employers should seek clarification to avoid violating any new rules.

Patricia A. Broussard has a bachelor's of science degree from Northwestern University in Evanston, Ill., and a J.D., cum laude, from Howard University School of Law in Washington, D.C. Broussard taught legal writing at Howard University School of Law for seven years. For her last three years at Howard, she was the acting director of the Legal Writing & Research Program. At Florida A & M College of Law, Broussard teaches constitutional law, legal methods, appellate brief writing, professional responsibility, and women and the law.

Helpful Web Sites

1. Overview of law and links to statute plus regulations:
   www.eeoc.gov/policy/adea.html

2. Sections of EEOC Compliance Manual dealing with discrimination and employee benefits:
   www.eeoc.gov/policy/docs/compensation.html
   www.eeoc.gov/policy/docs/benefits.html

State law considerations

States that have their own age discrimination statutes can be found in the State Statute Tables located in Appendix B.

Chapter 3
Older Workers Benefit Protection Act (OWBPA)

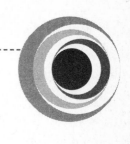

COMMON TERMS AND DEFINITIONS

Disability benefits: Any program for employees of a state or political subdivision of a state that provides long-term disability benefits, whether on an insured basis in a separate employee benefit plan or as part of an employee pension benefit plan.

Employee benefit plan: Includes compensation, terms, conditions, or privileges of employment, including benefits provided via a bona fide employee benefit plan.

Reasonable notice: With respect to notice of new disability benefits given to each employee, the notice must be sufficiently accurate and comprehensive to inform the employee of the terms and conditions of the disability benefits, including whether the employee is immediately eligible to receive such benefits; and must be written in a manner that could be understood by the average employee eligible to participate.

History and Purpose

The Older Workers Benefit Protection Act (OWBPA) was passed in 1990 as an amendment to the ADEA. The amendment establishes certain minimum requirements that must be met when an employer requests employees to waive their rights under the ADEA. If the OWBPA requirements are not satisfied, any attempted waiver of an employee's ADEA rights will be invalid and the ADEA will continue to protect that employee's rights. Additionally, the OWBPA added requirements on employers providing benefit plans.

PRACTICALLY SPEAKING The waiver provisions of the OWBPA seek to ensure that an employee's waiver of rights under the ADEA is knowing and voluntary. In other words, the employee must know and understand the rights he or she is giving up under the ADEA and enter into the agreement to waive them without being coerced to do so.

Protected Class of Employees

The OWBPA covers all employees and job applicants covered by the ADEA. Generally, this means all employees and applicants who are over 40 years old. This includes foreign workers who are over 40 years old and working for a covered employer and U.S. citizens who are over 40 years old and working in foreign countries for covered employers.

Employers Subject to the OWBPA

All employers who fall under the jurisdiction of the ADEA are also subject to the OWBOA. This will generally include private employers with 20 or more employees, state and local governments, employment agencies, and labor organization.

Waiver Requirements

Employees can only execute a waiver of rights if that waiver is entered into knowingly and voluntarily. For a waiver to be considered knowing and voluntary, it must meet the following minimum requirements:

- Must be part of an agreement between the employer and the employee written in a manner able to be understood by the employee or by an average individual.

- Must refer specifically to rights or claims arising under the OWBPA.

- Employee cannot waive rights or claims that may come about after the date the wavier is signed.

- Employee must receive new and valuable consideration in exchange for the waiver.

- Employee must be advised in writing to consult with an attorney before signing the agreement.

- Employee must be given at least 21 days to consider the agreement.

- Employee must be given at least seven days to revoke the agreement after signing it.

PRACTICALLY SPEAKING The consideration requirement means the employer must give employees something in exchange for their promise to waive rights. Think of this as payment from the employer to the employee in exchange for the employee relinquishing the right to sue under the ADEA. The consideration must be new consideration and cannot be something that the employer is already obligated to provide to the employee. For example, an employer agreeing to continue to employ the employee and pay him or her a salary in exchange for the employee's promise to waive ADEA rights would not constitute new and valuable consideration. The employer is already under an obligation to employ the employee and pay a salary.

Special requirements for exit incentive or employment termination programs

If a waiver is signed in connection with an exit incentive or other employment termination program offered to a group or class of employees, the employee must be given 45 days to consider the agreement. On the first day that the 45-day period begins, the employer must provide written notice to the employee stating the group of people covered by the exit or termination program, the eligibility factors for the program, and any time limits applicable to the program. The notice must also include the job titles and ages of all individuals eligible or already selected for the program and the ages of any individuals in the same group who are ineligible for the program.

Special requirements for EEOC charge settlements

Waivers resulting from a settlement of an age discrimination charge filed with the Equal Employment Opportunity Commission or resulting from a suit based on age discrimination filed in court by the employee must be knowing and voluntary. Also, the individual must be given a reasonable period of time to consider the settlement agreement.

Benefit Requirements

In addition to adding minimum standards for waivers of ADEA rights, the OWBPA also amended ADEA provisions related to employer-provided benefit plans. The following is a summary of some of those requirements.

Pension plan benefits

Employee pension benefit plans can require that employees reach a certain minimum age to qualify for normal or early retirement benefits. Defined benefit plans may provide for payments that are actually subsidized portions of an early retirement benefit, and may provide for Social Security supplements for plan participants that start and end before the age that employees are eligible to receive Social Security benefits.

Contingent events

An employer will be allowed to deduct the following from severance pay as long as the contingent event is not related to the employee's age:

- Value of any retiree benefits received by the employee for an immediate pension

- Value of any additional pension benefits made available to the employee solely as the result of the contingent event

Retiree health benefits

Retiree health benefits are provided via a group health plan. They must comply with the following:

- Package of benefits provided by the employer to the retirees younger than 65 must be comparable to the benefits provided by the Social Security Act.

- Package of benefits for retirees age 65 and older must be comparable to a plan with a benefits package that provides one-fourth of the benefits provided by the Social Security Act.

Limited and unlimited duration benefits

If the employer is obligated to provide retiree health benefits of a limited duration, the value of the benefits must be $3,000 a year for benefit years before age 65 and $750 a year for benefit years for ages 65 and older.

If the employer is providing retiree health benefits of unlimited duration, the value for each individual will be calculated at a rate of $48,000 for those younger than 65 and $24,000 for those 65 and older.

Long-term disability benefits

An employer can reduce long-term disability benefits by pension benefits paid to the individual as the result of a voluntary election or by pension benefits that an individual who is 62 years or older is eligible to receive.

Enforcement Agency and Procedures

The EEOC is the agency in charge of issuing rules and regulations to ensure employer compliance with the OWBPA. The EEOC also investigates OWBPA complaints. Also, the EEOC has the power to negotiate with employers and bring lawsuits against any employer for the purpose of ending the employer's discriminatory practices.

An aggrieved party may file a charge with the EEOC or maintain a private suit. If the individual decides to file a private suit, the party must notify the EEOC of the intent to sue. This intent must be provided to the EEOC within either 180 days (in states that do not have antidiscrimination laws) or 300 days (in states that do have antidiscrimination laws) from the time of the discriminatory activity. After providing the EEOC with the notice of intent, an individual must wait at least 30 days before filing a lawsuit.

Penalties for Violations

The penalties for violating the OWBPA are the same as those that apply under the ADEA.

 **DELVING DEEPER** Employers must ensure that any waiver of ADEA rights by an employee is both voluntary and knowing. Courts require strict compliance with this standard. At trial, employers will carry the burden of proving that a waiver was both knowing and voluntary. The case of *Peterson v. Seagate U.S., LLC*, 2008 WL 2230716 (D. Minn. 2008) in the U.S. District Court of Minnesota demonstrates the kind of evaluation that a court will make of circumstances surrounding waivers.

In *Peterson*, Seagate was undergoing a reduction in force and sought waiver of ADEA rights from some of its employees. A group of employees signed waivers but later challenged them, arguing that they were not "voluntary and knowing" because Seagate had failed to comply with certain requirements of the statute. Specifically, Seagate allegedly failed to disclose the job title and ages of all terminated employees and disclosed certain information related to job categories in an unintelligible and unclear form. The employees were able to identify two terminated employees who were not included in the chart provided with the notice that detailed the job titles and ages of the terminated employees. The employees also demonstrated that while Seagate reported that 154 employees were terminated, only 152 employees were terminated in fact. The employees also demonstrated that the disclosure charts listed different categories of the engineer, which produced a confusing presentation of the required information.

The court ruled that the releases were invalid and made it clear that "substantial compliance" with the OWBPA was not enough. In order for waivers to be valid, employers must strictly adhere to the requirements of the statute. In the facts of *Peterson*, this meant disclosing the job titles and ages of each individual and ensuring that information in the disclosure notices was presented "in a manner calculated to be understood by the individual employees." Seagate's failure to account for the ages and titles of the two missing employees in the disclosure notice meant that Seagate failed to comply with the requirements of the statute. Additionally, Seagate's failure to accurately report the number of employees terminated — even though only off by two employees — did not comply with the requirements of the

...cntd.

statute and was a further reason to find that the waivers were not voluntary and knowing.

Peterson demonstrates that courts will hold employers to a very strict standard in evaluating the validity of ADEA waivers. An employer should carefully consider the requirements of the statute and ensure absolute compliance with these requirements when obtaining ADEA waivers.

Helpful Web Sites

EEOC basic information on the ADEA
www.eeoc.gov/policy/adea.html

Overview of a Severance Agreement
**www.delawareemploymentlawblog.com/2009/02/best_
practices_when_considerin.html**

State law considerations

State laws regarding age discrimination can be found in Appendix B: State Statutes Tables.

Chapter 4

The Americans with Disabilities Act of 1990 (ADA)

COMMON TERMS AND DEFINITIONS	
Auxiliary aids and services:	Includes effective methods for making materials available to visually or hearing impaired individuals, including through the acquisition of equipment and devices.
Covered entity:	Such entities may include employers, employment agencies, labor organizations, or joint labor management committees.
Direct threat:	A significant risk to the health or safety of others that cannot be eliminated by reasonable accommodation.
Disability:	With respect to an individual, includes a physical or mental impairment that substantially limits one or more of the major life activities of such an individual. This will include having a record of such an impairment or being regarded as having such an impairment.

Illegal use of drugs: The use of drugs, the possession or distribution of which is unlawful under the Controlled Substances Act. This does not include drugs taken as prescribed by doctor or any other uses authorized by the Controlled Substances Act.

Qualified individual with a disability: An individual with a disability who, with or without reasonable accommodation, can perform the essential functions of the employment position that such individual holds or desires to hold. Consideration shall be given to the employer's judgment as to what functions of a job are essential. If an employer has prepared a written description before advertising or interviewing applicants for the job, this description is considered to be evidence of the essential functions of the job.

Reasonable accommodation: Includes making existing facilities used by employees readily accessible to and usable by individuals with disabilities; job restructuring, part-time, or modified work schedules; reassignment to a vacant position; acquisition or modification of equipment or devices; appropriate adjustment or modifications of examinations; training materials or policies; the provision of qualified readers or interpreters; and other similar accommodations for individuals with disabilities.

Undue hardship: An action requiring significant difficulty or expense when considered in light of the following factors:

(a) The nature and cost of the accommodation needed under this chapter

(b) The overall financial resources of the facility or facilities involved in the provision of the reasonable accommodation; the number of persons employed at such facility; the effect on expenses and resources; or the impact otherwise of such accommodation upon the operation of the facility

(c) The overall financial resources of the covered entity; the overall size of the business of a covered entity with respect to the number of its employees; the number, type, and location of its facilities

(d) The type of operation or operations of the covered entity, including the composition, structure, and functions of the workforce of such entity; the geographic separateness, administrative or fiscal relationship of the facility or facilities in question to the covered entity

History and Purpose

The Americans with Disabilities Act (ADA) was enacted in 1990. Titles I and V prevent private employers, state and local government, employment agencies, and labor unions from discriminating against American workers who have physical or mental disabilities. The legislation applies to various aspects of employment, including firing, advancement, and compensation.

More than 43 million Americans have at least one physical or mental disability. The ADA was intended to provide a clear and comprehensive national mandate for the elimination of workplace discrimination against persons with disabilities.

PRACTICALLY SPEAKING Prior to the enactment of the ADA, a private company could fire an employee based solely on the employee's disability. For example, Acme Company employs Janice, who is confined to a wheelchair, as an office manager. Janice performs her duties as an office manager satisfactorily but Acme Company decides to fire her based solely on her disability. Prior to the ADA, Janice would have no recourse against Acme Company. The ADA allows Janice to sue for wrongful termination.

Protected Class of Employees

The ADA protects all qualified individuals with a disability (according to definitions outlined in the ADA) who are applying for a job or are currently working in a position.

To qualify as having a disability, employees or individuals must have actual physical or mental impairments that substantially limit one or more of their major life activities, have a record of such impairment, or be regarded as having such impairment.

PRACTICALLY SPEAKING Examples of such physical and mental impairments include blindness, deafness, immobility, depression, anxiety disorders, and certain depressive disorders. However, not all impairments qualify as a disability. For example, courts have found that individuals with a diagnosis of attention-deficit hyperactivity disorder that is able to be controlled through the use of medication do not have the requisite mental impairment. Similarly, personality traits such as laziness or irritability are not protected.

In order for a condition to qualify as a disability, the physical or mental impairment must have the effect of substantially limiting the major life activity of the individual. There are two important parts to this test:

- *Major life activity must be impaired.* A major life activity is an activity the average person can perform with little or no difficulty. This includes actions such as caring for oneself, performing manual tasks, walking, seeing, hearing, speaking, breathing, learning, and working.

- *Major life activity at issue must be substantially impaired by the condition.* A condition substantially limits a major life activity if one of two things is true. First, the condition leaves an employee unable to perform a major life activity. Second, the condition significantly restricts the way the employee can perform a particular major life activity compared to how an average person would perform the particular activity.

There are certain factors to consider when determining whether an individual is unable to perform or is substantially limited in performing a major life activity. They include the nature and severity of the impairment, the duration or expected duration of the impairment, and the permanent or long-term impact (or the expected permanent or long-term impact) of or resulting from the impairment.

When considering a major life activity in regard to employment, "substantially limits" means an individual is significantly restricted in his or her ability to perform a broad range of jobs in various classes when compared to the average person with comparable training. However, the inability to perform a single, distinct job will not amount to a substantial limitation in a major life activity.

PRACTICALLY SPEAKING Consider blindness as an example of determining whether or not something is a disability. Blindness qualifies as a disability under the ADA because it is a physical impairment that substantially limits a major life activity. The major life activity in the case of blindness is the ability to see. The ability to see is substantially limited by blindness because it makes it impossible for an individual to perform the act of seeing.

If a condition causes an employee to be either unable to perform a major life activity or substantially restricts an employee's ability to perform a major life activity, then the condition will be a disability that falls under the ADA.

The physical or mental impairment that substantially limits the major life activity of the individual can include a physical disorder or condition, a cosmetic disfigurement, an anatomical loss affecting one or more of the following body systems (for example neurological, cardiovascular, reproductive, or digestive), or any mental or psychological disorder, such as mental retardation, organic brain syndrome, emotional or mental illness, and specific learning disabilities.

Illegal drug use

The ADA also protects individuals that have used illegal drugs in specific situations. First, the ADA will protect an individual that has successfully completed a supervised drug rehabilitation program and is no longer engaging in the illegal use of drugs, or has undergone alternate successful rehabilitation and no longer uses drugs. Second, the ADA will protect an individual that is participating in a supervised rehabilitation and is no longer using illegal drugs. Third, the ADA will protect an individual that is erroneously regarded as engaging in such use, but in reality is not. Note that only individuals who are no longer using illegal drugs are protected by the ADA. The ADA does not protect current illegal drug users.

EVERYDAY
ILLUSTRATION In 2007, Acme Company learns that Bill, a sales representative for Acme Company, successfully completed a drug treatment program in 2005. Bill has not engaged in any illegal drug use since the completion of the program and has performed all of his job responsibilities at Acme Company in an exemplary manner. The ADA prohibits Acme Company from firing Bill based on his participation in the drug treatment program.

Employers Subject to the ADA

The ADA applies to the following types of employers:

- Private employers with 15 or more employees (this includes part-time employees)

- Employment agencies

- Labor organizations

- Joint labor management committees

- State and local governments

- American employers who control corporations located in foreign countries

The ADA does not apply to an American company located in the foreign country if compliance with the ADA violates that country's laws.

Prohibited Discriminatory Employer Actions

Direct acts of discrimination

It is illegal for employers who must comply with the ADA to discriminate against people with disabilities in the following situations:

- Recruitment, advertising, and job application procedures

- Hiring, upgrading, promotion, award of tenure, demotion, transfer, layoff, termination, right of return from layoff, and rehiring

- Rates of pay or any other form of compensation and changes in compensation

- Job assignments, classifications, organization structures, position descriptions, lines of progression, and seniority lists

- Leaves of absences and sick leave

- Fringe benefits available by virtue of employment — does not matter whether or not these are administered by the entity subject to the ADA

- Selection and financial support for training, including apprenticeships, professional meetings, conferences, and other related activities — this includes selection for leaves of absence to pursue training

- Activities sponsored by an entity subject to the ADA, including social and recreational programs

- Any other terms, conditions, or privilege of employment

Indirect acts of discrimination

Employers are also barred from indirect acts of discrimination on the basis of an individual's disability such as:

- Limiting, segregating, or classifying a job applicant or employee in a way that negatively affects his or her employment opportunities or status

- Participating in a contractual relationship that effectually subjects qualified applicants or employees to discrimination (includes relationships with employment agencies, collective bargaining agreements, organizations providing fringe benefits, or training and apprenticeship programs)

- Using standards, criteria, or methods of administration that are not job-related and consistent with being necessary to the business and that have the effect of discrimination, or that perpetuate discrimination of others under administrative control

- Excluding or denying equal jobs or benefits to a qualified individual because of his or her relationship (family, business, or other social connection) with an individual with a known disability — *see this chapter's Legal Updates section for examples*

Reasonable Accommodation Requirements

Employers must make reasonable accommodations for employees who qualify as disabled under the ADA. An employer subject to the ADA must make reasonable accommodations to clear physical or mental limitations of an otherwise qualified applicant or employee with a disability *unless* the affected entity can demonstrate that the accommodation would impose an undue hardship on the operation of its business.

Entities subject to the ADA are barred from denying employment opportunities to otherwise qualified job applicants or employees with a disability.

PRACTICALLY SPEAKING Reasonable accommodations may include changes to the work environment to reduce physical barriers for individuals (e.g., installing wheelchair ramps for employees confined to a wheelchair), modifications to schedules (e.g., allowing modified or part-time schedules for individuals unable to work full time due to a disability), or altering workplace policies (e.g., permitting an employee with insulin-dependent diabetes to eat at his or her work station when company policy prohibits employees from eating or drinking at their work stations).

It is important to emphasize that the ADA does not force employers to make accommodations that would result in an undue hardship on the operation of the business. For example, an engineer works as part of a team designing a bridge. Successful completion of the job requires the team to work together. The team works daily from 8 a.m. until 5 p.m. As a result of her disability, the engineer requests that her hours be modified so that she works 11 a.m. to 8 p.m. every other day. The employer is not required to modify the work hours of the engineer because doing so would prevent the other members of the team from doing their jobs.

Qualification, Test, and Medical Standards

Employers are restricted from using qualification standards, employment tests, or other selection criteria for screening out individuals with disabilities or a class of individuals with disabilities on the basis of their disability. An exception to this rule occurs if the standard, test, or selection criteria is shown to be job-related to the position and is necessary for the business. If an employee or applicant sues to challenge the use of such qualification standards or tests, the employer will bear the burden of proving that the standard, test, or selection criterion is job-related and necessary. Therefore, employers should use caution before adopting any standard or test for screening out individuals with disabilities by making sure that such screening is related to a particular position and necessary for the business.

Administration of tests

When requiring employees or prospective employees to take certain tests, the employer must select and administer tests in the most proficient manner. Employers cannot attempt to measure certain skills or aptitudes of disabled individuals (usually those individuals with sensory, manual, or speaking impairments). As an employer, you can ask potential employees about their ability to perform certain functions, only if they are job-related. Therefore, any test that is given to measure task efficiency, or other areas of performance, must be clear in its purpose.

EVERYDAY
ILLUSTRATION Acme Company employs security guards that it places with various businesses throughout the community. As a prerequisite to employment, candidates must pass a hearing test without the use of a hearing aid. Any candidate who does not pass the test without a hearing aid is automatically disqualified. Sarah applies for a position with Acme Company. She passes the hearing test with the help of a hearing aid but is unable to pass the test without her hearing aid. Acme Company's use of the hearing test to automatically disqualify Sarah violates the ADA. *See Ruiz v. Mukasey*, 594 F. Supp. 2d 738 (S.D. Tex 2008).

Medical examinations

Employers are prohibited from conducting pre-employment examinations or inquiries if they are intended to determine whether an individual has a disability, or if they are designed to determine the nature or severity of such a disability. It is also unlawful for employers to inquire as to whether the employee has a disability, ask about the nature or severity of their disability, or make current employees undergo required medical examinations.

Law in Real Life   While an employer cannot conduct medical exams for the sole purpose of determining whether an employee is disabled, an employer can require medical exams of employees for other purposes. For example, an employer can require a medical exam to determine an employee's ability to work when the employee has a mental impairment that causes him or her to threaten others. In such a case, the employer can ask for the medical exam to determine whether the threats might actually be carried out. *See Menchaca v. Maricopa Community College District*, 595 F. Supp. 2d 1063 (D. Ariz. 2009).

Retaliation and coercion

Employers are barred from retaliating or discriminating against any individual as a result of that individual opposing any practices or acts made unlawful by the ADA. In addition, employers may not retaliate against or discriminate against an individual who makes a charge, testifies, assists, or participates in any manner in an investigation, proceeding, or hearing regarding enforcement of the ADA.

Employers will be found to be in violation of the ADA if they coerce, threaten, harass, or interfere with any individual's exercise or enjoyment of rights granted by the ADA. It is also a violation of the ADA to threaten, harass, or interfere with an individual's right to aid or encourage another individual to enjoy and exercise rights granted by the ADA.

PRACTICALLY SPEAKING   In order to be effective, the ADA must protect individuals from being discriminated against because of their disability, or for asserting their rights under the ADA. Without these protections, an employer sued by an employee under the ADA could simply fire the employee for filing suit under the ADA. The employer's actions would be based on the lawsuit, not on the employee's disability. Therefore, the protections are necessary to prevent employers from finding a way around the protections of the ADA.

Exceptions to the general rule

The following individuals are not considered to have a disability and are not protected under the ADA:

- Those with an ongoing illegal drug habit

- Transvestites, transsexuals, pedophiles, exhibitionists, voyeurists, or people with gender identity disorders not resulting from physical impairments or any other sexual behavior disorders

- Those with compulsive gambling, kleptomania, or pyromania disorders

- Individuals with psychoactive substance use disorders resulting from ongoing illegal use of drugs

- Homosexuals and bisexuals

Entities Specifically Excluded

A few organizations are not required to adhere to the provisions of the ADA. Private membership clubs exempt from ordinary tax rules are not covered by the ADA. Also, the federal government is not covered by the ADA, but instead by the Rehabilitation Act (29 U.S.C.A. sec 791, 793, and 794) that prohibits federal agencies, federal contractors having contracts of $10,000 or more with the federal government, and recipients of federal financial assistance from discriminating on the basis of disability. Finally, foreign entities that are controlled by foreign employers are not subject to the ADA, even if the employee is an American citizen.

A private membership club must qualify for tax-exempt status under §501(c) of the tax code and be a "bona fide private membership club (ADA Compliance Manual § 2-III(B)(4)(a)(ii))." Factors to consider in determining whether an organization is an exempt private club are:

- Selectivity in membership

- Member control over the operations of the establishment

- Exclusion of non-members from core activities of the club

- Purpose of the organization

- Limits to the size of the organization

EVERYDAY
ILLUSTRATION   A golf course that qualifies under § 501(c) for
tax-exempt status, severely restricts member-
ship, and opens its facilities only to members would qualify as a
private membership club.

Medical exams

There are certain medical examination situations in which employers subject to the ADA may engage. An affected employer may engage in the following:

- Pre-employment inquires about the ability of an applicant to perform job-related functions.

- Asking an applicant to describe or even demonstrate (with or without reasonable accommodations) the applicant's ability to perform job-related function.

- Requiring a medical exam or inquiry after offering employment to a job applicant before that applicant begins employment. It will also be permissible for the employer to make employment conditional on the exam or inquiry if all employees entering that job category are subject to the same exam or inquiry regardless of disability.

EVERYDAY
ILLUSTRATION As a part of its application process, Acme
Company, a construction company, asks can-
didates about any medical conditions that would prohibit them
from operating the different types of equipment that are used
by its employees on the job site. Because of the cumbersome
nature of the equipment, Acme Company asks these questions
to ensure that it is hiring employees who will be able to operate
the equipment. Such an inquiry would not violate the ADA.

Permissible activities

The following activities are not considered to be in violation of the ADA:

- Religious entities giving preference to people with the same religious affiliation as the entity itself

- Entities subject to the ADA prohibiting the use of illegal drugs and alcohol by all employees

- A company requiring employees to undergo drug tests

- Entities subjected to the ADA prohibiting or placing restrictions on smoking

Restaurants and food service employers

An employer can refuse to assign an individual to a food handling position if reasonable accommodations cannot eliminate the risk of an employee with an infectious or communicable disease from transmitting the disease. The employer must determine whether there is a reassignment available in a position that does not require food handling.

Under a straight application of the ADA, food service employers are caught between the position of having to avoid discrimination under the ADA while also maintaining strict adherence to public health rules. When a food service employer has an employee with a communicable disease, any action taken to segregate that employee may be seen as violating the ADA's prohibition against discriminating against an employee because of his or her disability.

To fix this problem, section 12113(e) (2) of the ADA specifically carves out an exception for food service employers for those instances when discrimination is in the best interests of public health. An employer may refuse to hire or may fire a person who poses a direct threat to the health or safety of others in the workplace. A direct threat is defined as a significant risk of substantial harm. The risk has to be such that it cannot be avoided or reduced with reasonable accommodations. While employers are allowed to take these actions, it is not permissible to ask medical questions regarding transmittable diseases in an interview. An employer must wait until an offer of conditional employment has been extended.

EVERYDAY
ILLUSTRATION   Betty, who is infected with HIV, is a surgical technician working for Acme Hospital. Betty's responsibilities as a surgical technician require her to place her hands upon and into surgical incisions. These responsibilities create a risk that Betty will be pricked with a needle or sustain minor cuts. Because of the risk that Betty's disease presents to patients under her care, Acme Hospital can reassign or unassign Betty from her position as a surgical technician without violating the ADA. *See Estate of Mauro v. Borgess Medical Center*, 137 F.3d 398 (6th 1998).

Enforcement Agency and Procedures

The Equal Employment Opportunity Commission (EEOC) is the enforcement agency for the ADA. The Office of Federal Contract Compliance Programs (OFCCP) acts as an agent of the EEOC for the purposes of the ADA. Charges filed with the OFCCP are considered to be simultaneously filed with the EEOC. If charges are filed with the OFCCP, the agency will alert the contractor that it has received a complaint of discrimination. *Charges filed with the EEOC will be handled in the same manner as Title VII charges, which can be found in Chapter 18 of this book.*

Penalties for Violations

An employer who violates the ADA may face one or more of the following sanctions:

- Reinstatement of the employee who was unlawfully fired

- Payment of back pay to the employee who was unlawfully fired

- Promotion of the employee if the employee was wrongfully denied a promotion

Intentional violations of the ADA carry stiffer penalties. This is because intentional violations mean the employer knew or should have known that its behavior was in violation of the ADA. Penalties can consist of any one or more of the following:

- Compensatory damages for future monetary losses, emotional pain and suffering, inconvenience, mental anguish, loss of enjoyment of life, and other non-monetary losses

- Punitive damages as follows (employer must have the number of employees noted for each of the 20 or more calendar weeks in the current or preceding year):

  - 15 to100 employees — $50,000

  - 101 to 200 employees — $100,000

  - 201 to 500 employees — $200,000

  - More than 500 employees — $300,000

- Attorney fees are also available for compensation under most circumstances

NOTE: The above limits on damage awards do not include interest on back pay.

PRACTICALLY SPEAKING The increased penalties for intentional violations highlight an important point: Even those employers who do not intend to commit acts prohibited by the ADA can be found in violation of the ADA. Employers are advised to both avoid adopting new employment practices that violate the ADA and re-evaluate current practices to ensure they are in compliance.

Employer Compliance and Requirements

Employers are required to make the following reasonable accommodations to disabled employees. This list is not comprehensive or meant to be the only reasonable accommodations you are required to make.

- Acquiring or modifying equipment or devices

- Job restructuring

- Part-time or modified work schedules

- Reassignment to a vacant position

- Adjusting or modifying examinations, training materials, or policies

- Providing readers and interpreters

- Making the workplace readily accessible to and usable by people with disabilities

Posting of notices

Employers must post a notice describing the provisions of the ADA. This notice must be accessible to applicants, employees, and members of labor organizations. Employers may obtain the poster by contacting the EEOC.

Employers will not violate the ADA if they follow any state, county, or local food handling law that is designed to protect the public from infectious and communicable diseases.

 **DELVING DEEPER** As mentioned above, the ADA prohibits employers from discriminating against an individual because of that person's relationship to an individual with a known disability. This provision, known as the ADA association provision, states that employers violate the ADA by "excluding or otherwise denying equal jobs or benefits to a qualified individual because of the known disability of an individual with whom the qualified individual is known to have a relationship or association." The courts have been responsible for defining what kind of relationship must exist between the employed individual and the disabled individual to trigger the protections of the association provision.

The association clearly covers individuals who have a family relationship, but courts have also found that a relationship can exist without familial ties. In Dollinger v. State Insurance Fund, 44 F. Supp. 2d 467 (N.D.N.Y. 1999), the court accepted that the required relationship existed when a plaintiff alleged he was denied promotions based on his unspecified "association with people with HIV/AIDS." Additionally, the plaintiff in Innovative Health Systems, Inc. v. City of White Plains, 117 F.3d 37 (2nd Cir. 1997) established a sufficient relationship when the plaintiff alleged discrimination based on relationships with individuals suffering from drug and alcohol dependency. Specifically, the plaintiff, an outpatient of a drug and rehabilitation center, alleged that "various governmental agencies discriminatively blocked . . . [its] construction of a drug and alcohol treatment center because the intended beneficiaries of the center, the corporation's clientele, suffered from drug and alcohol dependency."

In addition to providing an employee with a cause of action against an employer who discriminates against the employee based on her relationship or association with a disabled individual, the ADA also protects the employee from retaliation from the employer based on that cause of action. These protections do not, however, extend to the individual with the disability. The disabled individual, however, will not be able to bring an action against the employer because he or she lacks legal standing, as the disabled individual is not directly associated with the employer — the disabled individual, in this case, is not employed by the employer, and only knows the employer through a relationship with someone else.

Consider the facts of Morgenthal v. AT&T Co., 1999 WL 187055 (S.D.N.Y. 1999). In Morgenthal, Jay Morgenthal sued his employer, AT&T, when the company's employer-administered health care plan refused to cover autism treatment for Morgenthal's son, Daniel. Morgenthal alleged that AT&T's

...cntd.

refusal to cover the treatment amounted to discrimination based on disability in violation of the ADA. The court determined that because Daniel was not an employee of AT&T, he lacked standing to sue. However, the court determined that Morgenthal, as an employee of the company, had the required standing to sue under the association provision of the ADA.

Helpful Web Sites

1. General Information about the ADA
   www.eeoc.gov/facts/fs-ada.html

2. Language of the Statute:
   www.eeoc.gov/laws/statutes/ada.cfm

3. Regulations
   www.eeoc.gov/laws/regulations/index.cfm

4. EEOC Compliance Manual
   www.eeoc.gov/laws/guidance/compliance.cfm

5. Employer Responsibilities
   www.eeoc.gov/facts/ada17.html

6. Job Applicants and the ADA
   www.eeoc.gov/facts/jobapplicant.html

7. Small Employers and Reasonable Accommodation
   www.eeoc.gov/facts/accommodation.html

8. How to Comply with the ADA: Guide for Restaurants and Food Service Employers
   www.eeoc.gov/facts/restaurant_guide.html

State law considerations

Any state laws regarding disability discrimination can be located in Appendix B: State Statute Tables.

Chapter 5

The Consolidated Omnibus Budget Reconciliation Act of 1985 (COBRA)

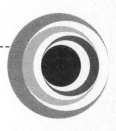

COMMON TERMS AND DEFINITIONS	
COBRA continuation coverage:	Coverage under a group health plan that satisfies COBRA continuation provisions.
Condition:	Medical condition.
Covered employee:	An individual who now has or previously had coverage under a group health plan as an employee benefit.
Dependent:	Any individual who is or may become eligible for coverage under the terms of a group health plan because of a relationship to the participant.
Enroll:	To become covered for benefits under a group health plan, without regard to when the individual may have completed or filed any required forms that are required to become covered under the plan.
Genetic information:	Information about genes, gene products, and inherited characteristics that may derive from an individual or family member.

Group health plan: An employee welfare benefit plan that provides medical care to participants or beneficiaries directly or through insurance, reimbursement, or another method. The term does not include any plan under which almost all of the coverage is for qualified long-term care services.

Group market: Market for health insurance coverage offered in connection with a group health plan.

Health insurance coverage: Benefits consisting of medical care under any hospital or medical service policy or certificate, hospital, or medical service plan contract, or HMC contract offered by a health insurance issuer.

Health insurance issuer: An insurance company, insurance service, or insurance organization (including HMOs) required to be licensed to engage in the business of insurance in a state. A health insurance issuer is subject to state law that regulates insurance.

Health maintenance organization (HMO):   A federally qualified health maintenance organization; an organization recognized under state law as a health maintenance organization; or a similar organization regulated under state law to the same extent as such a health maintenance organization.

Individual health coverage: Health insurance coverage offered to individuals in the individual market; does not include short-term or limited-duration insurance, but may include dependent coverage.

Individual market: Market for health insurance coverage offered to individuals not connected to a group health plan.

Insurer:	Health insurance issuer.
Optional extension of required periods:	A group health plan shall not be treated as failing to meet the requirements of COBRA solely because the plan provides both (a) that the period of extended coverage begins with the date of the loss of coverage and (b) that the applicable notice period commences with the date of the loss of coverage.
Plan year:	Year that is designated as the plan year in the plan document of a group health plan. If there is no plan document it will be the deductible; if there is no deductible, it will be the limit year used in the plan; if there is no limit year, then it will be the policy year; if there is no policy year, then it will be the employer's taxable year.
Qualified beneficiary:	Spouses and dependent children of covered employee under a group health plan. If employee was terminated or had his or her hours reduced, this term will also include the employee. This term also applies to a covered employee who retired on or before the date coverage terminated.
Short-term limited duration insurance:	Health insurance coverage provided pursuant to a contract with an issuer that has an expiration date specified in the contract.

History and Purpose

COBRA was passed in 1985 and then amended in 2004. Generally, CO-BRA gives employees and their families who are subject to a group health insurance plan the opportunity to decide whether to temporarily continue that coverage (at their own expense) after the occurrence of certain events (usually the loss of employment) that would otherwise result in the loss of coverage.

PRACTICALLY SPEAKING Before COBRA, any employee whose relationship with a company ended would lose health insurance coverage. COBRA allows employees to retain insurance coverage for themselves and their families even after they are no longer working. This can provide significant assistance to those who have family members who are already sick when the employee's job ends and would be otherwise unable to qualify for new health insurance.

Temporary health insurance coverage is usually available for a period of 18 to 36 months. COBRA sets forth the minimum requirements for group health care plans offering continuous coverage. The congressional purpose behind enacting COBRA was to address the growing number of uninsured Americans and the corresponding problem of hospitals reluctant to treat individuals without health insurance. COBRA was meant to provide families with a less expensive method of temporarily maintaining health insurance while undergoing life-altering events, such as job loss, divorce, or death.

Protected Class of Employees

For employees to become eligible for COBRA benefits, they must be considered to be a qualified beneficiary within the meaning of the statute and they must also experience a qualifying event.

There are three main requirements that must be met before an employee can fall within the protection of COBRA:

- Employer's group health insurance must meet the requirements of COBRA

- Employee must be a qualified beneficiary

- Employee must experience a qualifying event

Meeting the requirements of COBRA

The first requirement means the group health plan the employee was under when employed must have been one that had 20 or more employees employed more than 50 percent of the typical business days in the previous calendar year. Both full-time and part-time employees will be counted when determining this number. Part-time employees will count as a fraction of an employee. The fraction will be equal to the number of hours the part-time employee worked divided by the hours a person must work to be considered full time.

EVERYDAY
ILLUSTRATION   Acme Company provides a group health plan that covers 40 part-time employees who work 10 hours a week and nine full-time employees who work 40 hours a week. Acme Company's plan does not meet COBRA requirements. The 40 part-time employees count as 10 for purposes of COBRA. The number is figured by taking the actual number of employees multiplied by the ratio of actual hours worked per part-time employee over the number of hours worked by each full-time employee — 20 x (10/40). Ten part-time employees plus the nine full-time employees equals 19 employees for the purposes of COBRA — one less than required. Beta Company provides a group health plan that covers 20 part-time employees who work 20 hours a week and 10 full-time employees that work 40 hours a week. Beta Company's plan meets COBRA requirements. The 20 part-time employees count as 10 for purposes of COBRA. This number is figured by taking the actual number of employees multiplied by the ratio of actual hours worked per part time employee over the number of hours worked by each full-time employee — 20 x (20/40). Ten part-time employees plus the 10 full-time employees equals 20 employees for the purposes of COBRA.

Qualified beneficiary

The second requirement is that the person claiming COBRA coverage must be a qualified beneficiary. The term "qualified beneficiary" includes any individual covered by a group health plan the day before the qualifying event that caused the loss of coverage. Any child born to or adopted by the covered employee during the COBRA period of continued coverage is also a qualified beneficiary. Agents, independent contractors, and directors who participate in the group health plan may also be qualified beneficiaries.

PRACTICALLY SPEAKING Common examples of qualified beneficiaries are the previously covered employee, the employee's spouse or former spouse, or the employee's dependent children.

The final requirement is that there be a qualifying event. A qualifying event is the event that causes the employee to lose his or her health coverage. Qualifying events are important because they determine who the qualified beneficiaries are and the minimum length of the COBRA period.

PRACTICALLY SPEAKING COBRA sets a minimum period of time, known as the qualifying event. It is important to remember that employers can always increase this period of time (allowing employees to continue to take advantage of the group health plan for a time period longer than that mandated by COBRA) but cannot decrease the period of time.

Examples of Qualifying Events (from **www.dol.gov**):

For Employees:

- Voluntary or involuntary termination of employment for reasons other than gross misconduct
- Reduction in the number of hours of employment

For Spouses:

- Voluntary or involuntary termination of the covered employee's employment for any reason other than gross misconduct

- Reduction in the number of hours worked by spouse of the employee

- Spouse of the employee becoming entitled to Medicare

- Divorce or legal separation

- Death of the covered employee

Dependent Children:

- Loss of dependent child status per the plan rules

- Voluntary or involuntary employment termination of the parent other than for gross misconduct reasons

- Parent/employee becoming entitled to Medicare

- Parent/employee's working hours reduced

- Divorce or legal separation of the parent/employee

- Death of the parent/employee

PRACTICALLY SPEAKING It may help to think of these examples in terms of termination events. In each case, the occurrence of the event would end the health coverage of the affected individual without COBRA protection. For example, if a health plan covers dependent children under the age of 21, the 22nd birthday of that child would end his or her benefits and, therefore, be a triggering event. Similarly, if a health plan covers employees and spouses, the divorce of the spouse from the employee would be a qualifying event that ends his or her (the spouse's) coverage.

Types of Businesses the Act Covers

COBRA only applies to private employers who have maintained more than 20 employees on more than 50 percent of an employer's typical business days during the prior calendar year. State and local governments also fall under the umbrella of COBRA. However, churches and the federal government do not.

Both full- and part-time employees are counted when determining whether a health care plan is subject to COBRA, but part-time employees are counted as a fraction of a person based on the number of hours they work in relation to full-time employees. The following formula illustrates the calculation:

FORMULA: each part-time employee counts as a fraction of one full-time employee, with the fraction being equal to the number of hours that the part-time employee worked divided by the hours an employee must work to be considered full time. See the previous examples for illustrations of this formula.

Employer Compliance and Requirements

There are a number of employer requirements under COBRA. This chapter only addresses the major ones of notices, election procedures, and coverage periods.

The sponsor of each group plan is required to provide the option to continue coverage under the plan to every qualified beneficiary who stands to lose coverage as a result of a qualifying event. The beneficiaries must make this election within a certain time period. Also, employers must follow certain procedures regarding cancellations, extensions, and payments made under COBRA.

Notices

There are five relevant types of notices: general notice, COBRA qualifying event coverage notice, election notice, notice of unavailability of continuation coverage, and notice of early termination of continuation coverage. Each notice differs in its purpose and content.

General notice

The administrator of the group health insurance plan must provide written notice to each covered employee and spouse of the right to continue coverage under the existing health plan in the event of a qualifying event. This notice is meant to generally describe COBRA rights to employees and potential qualified beneficiaries.

Timing of notice

The timing of notice shall be no later than the earlier of the following occurrences:

1. 90 days after the date on which the individual's coverage under the plan starts, or 90 days after the date on which the plan first becomes subject to the continuation coverage requirements

2. The first date on which the administrator is required to furnish (or supply) the covered employee, spouse, or dependent child of such employee notice of a qualified beneficiary's right to elect continuation coverage

Content of notice

The notice must be written in a manner that the average plan participant can comprehend, and it must provide the following information:

- The name of the plan offering the continuation coverage. Also, the name, address, and telephone number of the person or persons who can provide additional information regarding the plan and its continuation coverage.

- A general description of the continuation coverage under the plan, including: identification of the classes of individuals who may become qualified beneficiaries, the types of qualifying events that may give rise to the right to continuation coverage, the obligation of the employer to notify the plan administrator of the occurrence of certain qualifying events, the maximum period for which continuation coverage may be available, when and under what circumstances continuation coverage may be extended beyond the applicable maximum period, and the plan's requirements applicable to the payment of premiums for the continuation coverage period.

- An explanation of the plan's requirements in regard to the responsibility of a qualified beneficiary to notify the administrator of the plan of a qualifying event (such as divorce, legal separation, and so forth) and a description of the plan's procedures for handling such notice.

- An explanation of the plan's requirements regarding the responsibility of a qualified beneficiary who becomes disabled to notify the plan administrator of such a change in status, and how such notice should be given.

- An explanation of the importance of ensuring the plan administrator has a record of all current addresses of participants or beneficiaries under the plan who are, or who may become, qualified beneficiaries.

- A statement that explains the notice is not a full description of continuation coverage and rights and that a full explanation can be obtained from the plan administrator.

NOTE: Under the single notice rule, one notice addressed to the covered employee and the spouse of the covered employee will be sufficient to provide notice to both persons.

COBRA Qualifying Event Coverage Notice

Upon the occurrence of a qualifying event, the employer or the employee must give notice to the group health coverage plan of the qualifying event.

This notice is designed to alert the plan to the fact that an event has occurred that may trigger COBRA benefits for the employee.

The employer is required to give notice of the qualifying event to the plan within 30 days of the qualifying event if the qualifying event was any of the following:

- Termination of the covered employee's employment

- Reduction in hours of the covered employee

- Death of the covered employee

- Qualification of the covered employee for Medicare

- Bankruptcy of the employer

The employee is required to give notice of the qualifying event to the plan within 60 days of the qualifying event if the qualifying event was any of the following:

- Divorce or legal separation

- A child's loss of dependent status under the plan

Election notice

After receipt of notice of a qualifying event, the plan must provide qualified beneficiaries with an election notice. This notice will give a basic summary of the rights to COBRA coverage, and how to make the election. This notice must be provided within 14 days after the plan administrator's receipt of the notice of qualifying event.

Election notices must have the following information:

- Name of plan

- Name, address, and telephone number of the plan's COBRA administrator

- Qualifying event details

- Name or status of each qualified beneficiary

- Explanation of the qualified beneficiary's right to elect continuation coverage

- Date coverage will terminate if said coverage is not elected

- Procedure by which continuation coverage is chosen

- What happens in the event continuation coverage is waived

Sample election notices are available at **www.dol.gov/ebsa**. Use of this model election is considered in good faith compliance with this section of COBRA.

Notice of continuation coverage unavailability

In the event a group health plan denies a request for continuation of or an extension of coverage, the plan must provide individuals with a notice of denial of coverage within 14 days of the receipt of the request. The notice should give a detailed explanation as to the reason for denying the request.

Notice of early termination of continuation coverage

The typical coverage periods are 18, 29, and 36 months. However, the group health plan may decide to end continuation coverage before the applicable period expires. The plan must notify the qualified beneficiary as soon as possible after it decides to terminate coverage. The notice must include the following information:

- Date when coverage will terminate

- Reason for termination

- Any rights the qualified beneficiary has under the plan or applicable law to elect alternative group or individual coverage

There are a number of reasons that COBRA coverage can terminate early. They include the following:

- Employee does not pay the premiums on time

- Employer no longer has a group health plan

- Qualified beneficiary begins coverage under another group health plan

- Qualified beneficiary becomes entitled to Medicare benefits after electing continuing coverage

- Qualified beneficiary engages in conduct that justified terminating coverage, such as fraud

PRACTICALLY SPEAKING

The following is an example of a notice timeline:

Day 1   Employee and dependents become covered by a group health plan and the administrator of the plan sends the employee a general notice explaining the right to COBRA continuation.

Day 10   Employee is fired, resulting in a qualifying event. Employer has until day 40 (30 days from the qualifying event) to send the plan qualifying event coverage notice.

Day 40   The plan receives the qualifying event coverage notice and has 14 days to send election notice to the qualifying beneficiary notifying him or her of the right to request continuation and how to request the continuation.

Day 54   The qualified beneficiary receives the election notice and formally requests a continuation of benefits under COBRA. Upon receiving this request, the plan must determine whether a continuation is available. If the plan determines the continuation is not available, it must send the qualified beneficiary a notice of continuation coverage unavailability within 14 days of receiving the request from the qualified beneficiary.

PRACTICALLY SPEAKING   ...cntd.

Day 100   Assume that the plan allows continuation. Sometime after granting the continuation, circumstances change so that the employer no longer has a group health plan. The plan must send the qualified beneficiary a notice of early termination of continuation of coverage.

COBRA Election Procedures

Qualified beneficiaries have 60 days to decide whether to elect COBRA benefits. The qualified beneficiary shall have either 60 days from when the election notice was received or 60 days from when coverage would be lost due to a qualifying event — whichever happens latest.

EVERYDAY ILLUSTRATION   An employee was terminated on June 1, 2007. The employer immediately provided the plan with a qualifying event coverage notice that it received on June 2, 2007. On June 10, 2007, the plan provided the employee with election notice. Because the date of election notice is later than the date of the qualifying event, the employee has 60 days from the date of election notice to decide whether to elect COBRA benefits.

Each qualified beneficiary must be given a chance to elect continuation of coverage. However, a parent or legal guardian can elect continuation of coverage on behalf of any minor children.

NOTE: Qualified beneficiaries who waive continuation of coverage during the election period can change their minds and decide to elect coverage as long as it is done before the end of the election period. The coverage will begin on the date the waiver was revoked.

Summary plan description

Employers are also required to send a summary description of the applicable COBRA plan to the qualified beneficiaries. This document provides the qualified beneficiaries with plan information including:

- Benefits available

- Rights of participants and beneficiaries under the plan

- Explanation of how the plan works

Each member of the plan must receive the summary plan description, usually within 90 days of becoming a participant of a plan. This period can be extended up to 120 days if the plan falls under alternative ERISA rules.

In the event that material changes are made to the plan, employers are required to send members a summary with the changes no later than 210 days after the end of the plan year within which the changes become effective. If material changes affect services or benefits, the employer must provide notice within 60 days after the changes take place.

Minimum benefit requirement

There are minimum requirements that must be met by the employer when offering COBRA coverage. In general, a COBRA participant is entitled to the same rights and regulations that similarly situated active employees and their families receive. For instance:

- Continuation coverage must be identical to coverage that the qualified beneficiary had immediately before the qualifying event

- The qualified beneficiary's benefits, choices, and services must be the same as current employees

- The qualified beneficiary must be subject to same plan rules and limits, including filing of benefit claims and appealing denials

- Any changes made to plans' terms must apply equally to current employees as well as to qualified beneficiaries

PRACTICALLY SPEAKING A qualified beneficiary who elects continuation coverage must receive coverage identical to that available under the plan to similarly situated current employees and their families. Typically, this means the qualified beneficiary is entitled to receive the exact same coverage he or she was receiving before the qualified event that resulted in a termination of coverage.

Maximum periods of coverage

Qualified beneficiaries are entitled to COBRA coverage for a maximum of 18 or 36 months. The time period will depend upon the type of qualifying event that caused COBRA to be available.

Most qualifying events will result in 36 months of continuation coverage from the time of the qualifying event. There are two exceptions. First, when the qualifying event is the termination of employment or a reduction of hours and the employee became entitled to Medicare less than 18 months before the qualifying event, COBRA coverage will last 36 months from when the employee became entitled to Medicare. Second, if the qualifying event is the termination of the covered employee or the reduction of the covered employee's hours worked, the continuation coverage will be 18 months.

EVERYDAY
ILLUSTRATION Bob, a covered employee at Acme Company, becomes entitled to Medicare on June 1, 2008. On May 21, 2009, Bob stops working for Acme Company The end of Bob's employment is the qualifying event for COBRA and COBRA coverage for Bob and his spouse and children would last 36 months from June 1, 2008 (the date that Bob became entitled to Medicare). Measured another way, Bob's CO-BRA coverage will last 24 months from the date of termination (36 months minus 12 months, the number of months that Bob has been entitled to Medicare).

Mandatory extensions of coverage

Qualified beneficiaries are entitled to an extension of the maximum coverage period if one of the qualified beneficiaries becomes disabled or if a second qualifying event occurs.

Disability

If a family member is disabled and meets the following requirements, all of the qualified beneficiaries in that family group are entitled to an 11-month extension.

- The disability must be determined by the Social Security Administration (SSA) during the first 60 days of continuation coverage.

- The disability must continue during the remainder of the 18-month period of continuous coverage.

- The disabled, qualified beneficiary must notify the plan of the Social Security Administration determination. This notice must be given within 60 days from the latter of a) the date on which the SSA issues the disability determination, b) the date on which the qualifying event occurs, or c) the date on which the qualified beneficiary receives the COBRA general notice.

NOTE: If the SSA makes the determination that the qualified beneficiary is no longer disabled, the extension can be terminated.

Second qualifying event

Qualified beneficiaries receiving an 18-month continuation period may qualify for an 18-month extension due to a second qualifying event. The second event is considered a second qualified event only if it would have caused the beneficiary to lose coverage under the plan independent of the first plan. Simply put, the second qualifying event must amount to a qualifying event on its own merit. Additionally, the qualified beneficiary must experience one of the following:

- Divorce or legal separation of the covered employee and spouse

- Death of covered employee

- Entitlement of the covered employee to Medicare

- Loss of dependent child status under the plan

Payment requirements

The maximum amount employers can charge qualified beneficiaries for continuation of coverage is 102 percent of the cost to the plan for similarly situated individuals (i.e., current employees).

PRACTICALLY SPEAKING If coverage under the plan costs $200 per covered employee, the maximum charge for a qualified beneficiary is $204. This cost is meant to cover any costs paid to maintain the plan, plus a 2 percent charge for administrative costs.

Exhaustion of COBRA continuation coverage

Exhaustion occurs when coverage ceases: (a) due to failure of the employer or other responsible entity to remit premiums on a timely basis, or (b) when the individual no longer resides, lives, or works in the service area of an HMO or similar program and there is no other COBRA continuation coverage available to the individual, or (c) when the individual incurs a claim that would meet or exceed a lifetime limit on all benefits and there is no other COBRA continuation coverage available to the individual.

Enforcement Agency and Procedures

COBRA is enforced by several agencies, including the Department of Labor and the Department of the Treasury. The Department of Labor has interpretative responsibility concerning disclosure and notification requirements. The Treasury Department is responsible for defining the requirements of continuation coverage.

The Internal Revenue Service and the Treasury Department both issue regulations on COBRA provisions regarding eligibility, coverage, and payment. The Department of Health and Human Services administers the continuation coverage law that affects state and local government health plans.

Penalties for Violations

There are a number of penalties that an employer will face for violation of COBRA. These penalties will differ based upon whether the employer is in the public or private sector.

Private sector

A private employer will be subject to excise taxes of $110 for every day that it fails to comply with COBRA. The tax will apply for each separate qualifying beneficiary that the employer fails to provide with the required coverage. The noncompliance period will begin on the date of the first day of the violation and will end on the earlier of the date the employer corrects the violation or six months after the last day of the qualified beneficiary's coverage period.

No excise tax will be assessed if the failure is not intentional and the employer has a reasonable application, or if the employer corrects the violation within 30 days of finding out about the violation.

Also, an employer faces fines, civil liability to individuals who incur damages as a result of not receiving coverage they were entitled to, and attorney's fees.

DELVING DEEPER Recall that COBRA does not normally apply to an employer employing fewer than 20 full-time employees on a typical business day. For this reason, it is crucial to calculate the number of employees in your company.

This fact was illustrated in Giddens v. University Yacht Club, 2006 WL 508056 (N.D. Ga. 2006). Giddens, an employee of University Yacht Club, was fired. After his termination, he received no medical continuation coverage. Giddens sued University Yacht Club, alleging a violation of COBRA.

University Yacht Club responded that it was not required to provide benefits under COBRA because it fell under the small-employer exception. While Gidden and University Yacht Club both based their calculation on the company's payroll records, each focused on different relevant numbers resulting in significantly different results.

Gidden determined that University Yacht Club employed at least 20 employees for 29 out of 52 weeks of the previous year while University Yacht Club determined that it employed 20 employees for only 11 out of the 52 weeks of the previous year.

Several factors explained the discrepancy. First, Gidden and University Yacht Club used different definitions of full-time employee. Gidden counted any employee working at least 30 hours as working full time while University Yacht Club only counted those employees working at least 32 hours as full-time employees. Second, Gidden included vacation, holiday, and sick time hours in determining whether an employee worked the requisite number of hours to be considered full time. Third, Gidden double counted employees who worked in multiple capacities for University Yacht Club, thereby inflating the number of employees.

Gidden illustrates the potential confusion surrounding the counting of em-

DELVING DEEPER ...cntd.

ployees and shows that employers should clearly define who is considered full time and base their calculations off these numbers. Even if an employer believes it is justified in refusing to provide COBRA benefits because of its calculations, those calculations must accurately reflect the reality of the situation. An inadvertent violation of the statute based on a mistaken calculation will still subject an employer to penalties.

Helpful Web Sites

1. An Employer's Guide to Group Health Continuation Coverage under COBRA
   www.dol.gov/ebsa/pdf/cobraemployer.pdf

2. An Employee's Guide to Group Health Continuation Coverage under COBRA
   www.dol.gov/ebsa/pdf/cobraemployee.pdf

3. General Information regarding COBRA
   www.dol.gov/dol/topic/health-plans/cobra.htm

4. Compliance Assistance
   www.dol.gov/ebsa/compliance_assistance.html

State law considerations

Any state laws regarding COBRA can be located in Appendix B: State Statute Tables.

Chapter 6
Employee Polygraph Protection Act 1988 (EPPA)

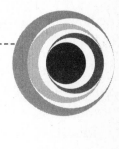

COMMON TERMS AND DEFINITIONS	
Employer:	Any person acting directly or indirectly in the interest of an employer in relation to an employee or prospective employee. A polygraph examiner either employed by a company or whose services are retained for the sole purpose of administering polygraph tests who ordinarily would not be deemed an employer with respect to the examinees.
Lie detector:	Polygraph, deceptograph, voice stress analyzer, psychological stress evaluator, or similar device (whether mechanical or electrical) used to give a diagnostic opinion as to the honesty or dishonesty of an individual's responses to questions.
Polygraph:	An instrument that records changes in cardiovascular, respiratory, and electrothermal patterns to render a diagnostic opinion as to the honesty or dishonesty of an individual's response to certain questions.

History and Purpose

The Employee Polygraph Protection Act of 1988 (EPPA) was enacted for the purpose of preventing most private employers from using lie detector tests for pre-employment screening or during a person's employment. As a general rule, employers are prohibited from administering polygraph tests to potential and current employees. A few exceptions apply to permit federal, state, and local governments to administer the tests under restricted circumstances.

Protected Class of Employees

The following individuals are protected from illegal polygraphs:

- All employees of affected employers, regardless of citizenship status

- Employees of foreign corporations operating in the United States

- Employees who are located within the territorial jurisdiction of the United States

Types of Employers Covered by the EPPA

The EPPA applies to all employers engaged in interstate commerce. Employers violate the EPPA when they directly request or require perspective or current employees to take polygraph tests. Employers also violate the EPPA by indirectly suggesting a polygraph test may be required of perspective or current employees.

PRACTICALLY SPEAKING "Engaged in interstate commerce" is known as a legal term of art. Generally, it covers most businesses and exempts only a small number of businesses with extremely localized operations. Unless instructed otherwise by an attorney, a company should assume it is "engaged in interstate commerce" and must comply with the EPPA.

Prohibited Discriminatory Employer Actions

The extensive coverage of the EPPA will bar employers from taking the following actions:

- Requesting, suggesting, or causing an employee or a prospective employee to take any lie detector test.

- Accepting, referring to, or asking about the results of any lie detector test that an employee or prospective employee has taken.

- Taking or threatening to take any negative employment action against an employee or prospective employee on the basis of results of a test, or for the employee's refusal to take a test, filing a complaint regarding a test, testifying in a proceeding, or exercising any rights given by the Act.

Examples of negative employment action include discharging, disciplining, discriminating against, or denying employment or promotion.

Waivers

The examinee/employee rights provided by the EPPA cannot be waived by contract or in any other manner unless it is part of a written settlement agreement agreed to and signed by the parties in a pending action or complaint under the EPPA.

Exceptions to the general rule

Government exception:

The EPPA does not apply to the United States government, any state or local governments, or any political subdivisions of state or local governments.

National defense and security exception:

When performing counterintelligence inquires, the federal government is not prohibited from administering a lie detector test to:

- Any expert, consultant, or employee of an expert or consultant that has a contract with the Department of Defense.

- Any expert, consultant, or employee of an expert or consultant that has a contract with the Department of Energy in connection with atomic energy defense.

The federal government is not prohibited in any way when performing intelligence or counterintelligence functions from administering a lie detector test to the following individuals or employees of the National Security Agency, the Defense Intelligence Agency, or the Central Intelligence Agency:

- Any individual employed by, assigned to, or acting for any of the previously mentioned organizations.

- Expert or consultants under contract.

- Any individual applying for a position.

- Any individual assigned to a space where sensitive cryptology information is produced, stored, or processed.

Note: This exception allows only the federal government to administer the test. Private contractors that have contracted with the federal government and employ the above mentioned individuals cannot rely on this exception to administer a lie detector test to that employee.

FBI contractor exception:

The FBI may administer a lie detector test to any employee of a contractor who is involved in any way with the performance of any counterintelligence function.

Ongoing investigation exception:

While the above mentioned exemptions apply to federal, state, and local governments, the EPPA also provides a narrow exemption for private employers. Under the ongoing investigation exemption, an employer may request that an employee submit to a polygraph test upon the satisfaction of all of the following conditions:

- Test is administered in connection with an ongoing investigation involving economic loss or injury to the employer's business, such as theft, embezzlement, misappropriation, or acts of unlawful industrial espionage or sabotage

- Employee being tested had access to the property that is the subject of the investigation

- Employer has reasonable suspicion that the employee was involved in the incident or activity under investigation

- Employer executes a statement that must be given to the employee (before the test) that gives the details about the incident being investigated

- Statement gives the basis for why the employee is being tested — along with the specific loss or injury of the employer, and a statement detailing that the employee had access to the property — and describes the basis for the employer's reasonable suspicion that the employee was involved

- Statement is kept by the employer for at least three years and is signed by a person legally authorized to bind the employer

EVERYDAY
ILLUSTRATION   Bakery Company produces and sells birthday cakes. The exact recipe of the cakes
is a closely guarded trade secret. Last month, the only written copy of the recipe was stolen from the company safe. An
investigation of the crime scene suggests that the theft was
accomplished by someone with access to the safe. Larry and
Jim, both employees of Bakery Company, were the only two
people who had access to the safe during the time period of the
theft. A month after the theft, Larry's wife decides to start up her
own cake-making business and begins producing cakes almost
identical to those of Bakery Company. In light of these facts,
Bakery Company can require Larry to take a polygraph after
executing the required statement and arranging to keep the
statement for at least three years.

Security services exception:

The EPPA will also allow private employers to use polygraph tests on certain
prospective employees. In order to fall under this exemption, the employer's
business must be one of the following:

- The provision of armored car personnel, or personnel engaging in the design, installation, and maintenance of security
  alarm systems.

- Other uniformed or plainclothes security personnel.

- Facilities, materials, or operations that have a significant
  impact on the health or safety of any state or political subdivision, or the national security of the United States. This
  will include facilities engaged in production, transmission, or
  distribution of nuclear power; public water supply facilities;
  shipments or storage of radioactive or other toxic waste materials; and public transportation.

Drug security, drug theft, or drug diversion exception:

Employers authorized to manufacture, distribute, or dispense a controlled
substance listed in schedules I, II, III, or IV of the Controlled Substance

Act may administer polygraph tests to prospective employees and current employees under specific circumstances. For prospective employees, the test may only be administered if the prospective employee "would have direct access to the manufacture, storage, distribution, or sale of any such controlled substance (29 U.S.C. §2006(f)(1), (2)(A))." Tests administered to current employees must be in connection with an ongoing investigation of criminal conduct or any other misconduct involving or potentially involving loss or injury to the manufacture, distribution, or dispensing of any controlled substance. The employee must have also had access to the person or property that is the subject of the investigation.

Restrictions on the use of exceptions

1. There will be no exception relating to ongoing investigations if the employee suffers any of the following as a result of his or her refusal to take a test without proper evidence or on the basis of an analysis of a polygraph test:

   - Termination

   - Disciplined

   - Denied employment or promotion

   - In any way discriminated against

NOTE: Evidence required is located on page 62 under the subheading Ongoing Investigations Exception.

2. The exceptions for security services and drug security, drug theft, or drug diversion investigations will not apply if the results of the analysis of the polygraph test chart are used as the basis for an adverse employment action.

Examinee rights under exception circumstances

For employers to qualify for the ongoing investigation, security services, and the drug security, theft, and drug diversion investigation exceptions, they must strictly adhere to the following rules regarding the examination of the employee.

1. During all phases of the test:

   - The employee must be able to terminate the test.

   - No questions should be asked in a manner that would degrade or needlessly intrude on the examinee.

   - The examinee cannot be asked any questions regarding religious beliefs or affiliations; beliefs or opinions regarding racial matters; political beliefs or affiliations; any matter relating to sexual behavior; and beliefs, affiliations, opinions, or lawful activities dealing with unions or labor organizations.

   - The examiner cannot conduct the test if there is sufficient written evidence by a doctor that the examinee is suffering from a medical or psychological condition or undergoing treatment that might cause abnormal responses during the actual testing phase.

2. During the pretest phase, the prospective examinee:

   - Must be provided with reasonable written notice of the date, time, and location of the test, and also of his or her right to obtain and consult with legal counsel or an employee representative before each phase of the test.

   - Must be informed in writing of the nature and characteristics of the tests and the instruments involved.

- Must be informed of the remedies available if the test is not conducted in the correct manner and the legal rights and remedies of the employer under the EPPA.

- Must be provided an opportunity to review all questions to be asked during the test and re-informed of his or her right to terminate test at any time.

3. During the actual testing phase:

- The examiner is barred from asking any questions that were not in writing before the test began.

- The examiner is required to disclose to the employee whether the testing area contains a camera or other observation device, whether recording devices will be used for recording or monitoring the test, and that the employer examinee can make a recording of the test.

- The employee must read and sign a written notice that informs the employee that the test is not required as a condition of employment, and that statements made during the test could be used as additional supporting evidence for an adverse employment decision.

- The employee must be notified of the limitations on the test if the employee's rights are terminated.

- The employee cannot be asked any questions regarding religious beliefs, racial beliefs, political beliefs, anything dealing with sexual behavior, or labor organization and union beliefs.

- The employee cannot be tested for more than 90 minutes.

4. During the post-test phase, the employer cannot take any adverse employment action until the employer has:

- Interviewed the examinee on the basis of the results of the test.

- Provided the examinee with a written copy of any opinion or conclusion given because of the test and a copy of the questions asked during the test and the corresponding charted responses.

NOTE: The examiner cannot conduct and or complete more than five polygraph tests a day.

Qualifications and requirements of examiners

Any polygraph test administered under an exception must be conducted by a qualified examiner. The examiner conducting the test must meet the following requirements:

- Hold a valid and current license from the licensing authority

- Have a minimum of $50,000 bond or professional liability coverage

- Give opinions in writing that are based only upon the polygraph test charts

- Maintain all opinions, reports, charts, written questions, and other records relating to the test for a minimum period of three years after the administration of the test

The examiner's opinion cannot contain any information, case facts, and interpretation of the charts relevant to the purpose and stated objectives of the test. The examiner is also barred from including any employment recommendations concerning the employee.

Enforcement Agency and Procedures

The Employment Polygraph Protection Act is enforced by the Department of Labor (DOL). The agency within the DOL that handles complaints is the Wage and Hour Division of the Employment Standards Administration. The secretary of labor is in charge of distributing the act's notices, issuing rules and regulations, and enforcing provisions of the EPPA. The secretary of labor is also vested with the following powers:

- To bring injunctive actions in U.S. district courts to restrain violations.

- To assess civil money penalties against employers who violate any provision of the EPPA.

- To cooperate with state, local, and other agencies and to cooperate with and furnish technical assistance to employers, labor organizations, and employment agencies to aid in bringing about the purposes of the EPPA.

- To make investigations and inspections and require the keeping of records necessary or appropriate for the administration of the EPPA.

- Subpoena authority for the purpose of investigations carried out under the EPPA.

Penalties for Violations

The high cost of violating the EPPA is one that can be avoided by ensuring that your company has a clear understanding of the requirements. Employers face civil liability and fines as follows:

- Civil penalties of up to $10,000. The previous record of the employer regarding compliance with the EPPA will be taken into account when determining the amount of the fine.

- The employer also faces being served with a temporary or permanent restraining order or injunction to require compliance with the EPPA.

- The employer could be ordered to reinstate or promote the employee, employ the prospective employee, and pay lost wages and benefits.

- The employer also is civilly liable to the employee or prospective employee. The legal and equitable relief available in such suits is employment, reinstatement, promotion, and the payment of lost wages and benefits.

Employer Compliance and Requirements

Posting of notices

Employers must post and maintain in a conspicuous place on its premises the notice provided by the secretary of labor that contains excerpts and summaries of the pertinent provisions of the EPPA. A copy of the current notice can be found at the Department of Labor's Web site **www.dol.gov/esa/whd/regs/compliance/posters/eppa.htm**.

Disclosure of test information

To maintain compliance with the EPPA, an employer can disclose, either directly or indirectly, the information gathered during a polygraph test (with the exception of the examinee) only to the following:

- The examinee or an individual specifically designated in writing by the examinee to receive such information

- The employer requesting the polygraph test, and only if the disclosure is relevant to the carrying out of job responsibilities

- Any court, governmental agency, arbitrator, or mediator as a result of a court order requiring the production of said information

- The secretary of labor, or one of the secretary's representatives, when designated in writing by the examinee to be in receipt of the information

NOTE: If the information obtained is admission of criminal conduct, an employer can disclose the information without permission from the examinee to the appropriate governmental agency.

Record keeping requirements

The following records must be kept three years from the date of testing or from the date the employee was asked to take the test:

- Copies of all opinions, reports, or other records the examiner gives to the employer.

- A copy of the employer's written correspondence to the examiner identifying the person to be examined.

- If the test was being administered as part of the ongoing investigation exception, a copy of the detailed statement giving the specific incident being investigated and the reasonable basis for testing the particular employee.

- If the test was administered to a current employee under the drug testing exception, the records must state with specificity the loss or harm under investigation and the detailed mode of access of the employee to the person or property damaged.

 DELVING DEEPER As an employer, it is imperative to understand how easily the protection of the EPPA can be triggered. The case of Campbell v. Woodard Photographic, 433 F. Supp. 2d 857 (N.D. Ohio 2006) presents an illustration of this point. In Campbell, the employer (Woodard) experienced a theft of some equipment and cash. Before Woodard conducted its investigation, a meeting was held where employees were told, "an investigation was going to begin and that there was a possibility that polygraph exams would be given." Woodard also required all

 **DELVING DEEPER** ...cntd.

employees to fill out a questionnaire regarding the theft. After its investigation, Woodard fired Dwayne Campbell in connection with the theft. Campbell sued Woodard, claiming it violated the EPPA when it told employees that polygraph exams might be administered. Woodard defended the EPPA claim, arguing that the company never required Campbell to take a polygraph test.

The court found that Woodard's alleged statement regarding the possibility of polygraph testing was enough to establish a violation of the EPPA. The court focused on the language of the EPPA, stating "that an employer can be liable for directly or indirectly requiring, requesting, suggesting, or causing any employee or prospective employee to take or submit to any polygraph examination."

This case is a clear statement to employers that any communication regarding polygraphs to employees and/or prospective employees should be carefully crafted. Any reference to or threat of the potential use of polygraph exams should be avoided unless the employer is confident that it qualifies for one of the exceptions discussed above.

Helpful Web Sites

Compliance Assistance Materials
www.dol.gov/compliance/laws/comp-eppa.htm

Employment Law Guide- Lie Detector Tests
www.dol.gov/compliance/guide/eppa.htm

State law considerations

Any state laws regarding employee polygraph testing can be located in Appendix B: State Statute Tables.

Chapter 7
Equal Pay Act of 1963

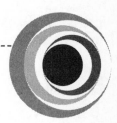

COMMON TERMS AND DEFINITIONS

Competitive service: Jobs in the executive branch of the federal government subject to federal civil service laws. This does not include jobs at certain agencies, such as the Federal Bureau of Investigation and the Central Intelligence Agency, that are not part of competitive service.

Effort: The amount of physical or mental exertion needed to perform the job.

Employee: Any individual employed by an employer.

Employer: Any person acting directly or indirectly in the interest of an employer in relation to an employee (includes public agency).

Establishment: A distinct physical place of business rather than an entire business or enterprise consisting of several places of business. The prohibition against compensation discrimination under the EPA applies only within an establishment.

No appropriated fund instrumentalities: Federal organizations under the jurisdiction of the armed forces whose activities are conducted for the support, pleasure, recreation, or improvement of the members of the armed forces.

Responsibility: The degree of accountability required in performing the job.

Skill: Measured by factors such as experience, ability, education, and training required to perform the job. The key issue is what skills are required for the job, not what skills the individual may have.

Wages: All payments made to or on behalf of an employee as remuneration for employment. Includes all forms of compensation, irrespective of the time of payment, whether paid periodically or deferred until a later date, and whether called wages, salary, profit sharing, expense account, monthly minimum, bonus, uniform cleaning allowance, hotel accommodations, use of company car, gasoline allowance, or some other name. Fringe benefits are also included in wages.

Wage rate: Standard or measure by which an employee's wage is determined. It is considered to encompass all rates of wages whether calculated on a time, commission, piece, job incentive, profit sharing, bonus, or other basis. It also includes the rate at which overtime compensation or other special remuneration is paid as well as the rate at which straight time compensation for ordinary work is paid. It also includes the rate at which a draw, advance, or guarantee is paid against a commission settlement.

Willful violation: When an employer violates the law knowingly or with reckless disregard as to the illegality of such conduct.

Working conditions: Made up of two factors — the physical surrounding (e.g., temperature, fumes, and ventilation) and the hazards themselves.

History and Purpose

The Equal Pay Act (EPA) was enacted in 1963 as an amendment to the Fair Labor Standards Act of 1938. It prohibits wage discrimination on the basis of sex. By passing the EPA, Congress was attempting to remedy the disparity in pay and job mobility between men and women in the workplace. The EPA seeks to ensure that women are paid the same wages as men who work in the same company and perform the same job or jobs requiring substantially the same skill, effort, and responsibility under similar working conditions.

Protected Class of Employees

The EPA protects the following employees:

- All executive, administrative, and professional employees exempt from coverage under the FLSA (*for more information about the FLSA, see Chapter 9*).

- All state and local government employees.

- Private employees whose employers are engaged in commerce, goods that have moved in commerce, or the production of goods for commerce.

- The majority of employees of the federal government.

Types of Employers Covered by the EPA

The EPA applies to almost all government and private employers, including unions.

Private employers will usually consist of any employer engaged in interstate commerce, commerce, and the production of commerce. Practically speaking, this will cover almost every private employer. Labor organizations can be employment organizations, agencies, or committees in which employees participate and which exist for the purpose of dealing with employers on matters such as grievances, labor disputes, wages, rates of pay, hours of employment, or conditions of work.

> EVERYDAY
> ILLUSTRATION   The following are examples of governmental employers subject to the EPA:
>
> - Executive agencies
> - U.S. Postal Service
> - Library of Congress
> - Military departments that employ civilians
> - Judicial and legislative branches that have positions in the competitive service

Prohibited Discriminatory Employer Actions

The EPA requires that men and women working in the same company be paid equal pay when performing equal work. Employers are prohibited from paying unequal wages to men and women who perform substantially similar jobs. Jobs are substantially similar when they require similar skill, effort, and responsibility and are performed under similar working conditions within the same company.

EVERYDAY
ILLUSTRATION Acme Company employs three individuals:
Bruce, John, and Mary. Bruce and John hold
the position of manager at Acme Company Mary holds the position of supervisor at Acme Company All three individuals have worked for Acme Company for two years. Acme pays Bruce and John an annual salary of $50,000 in their capacity as managers and pays Mary an annual salary of $40,000 in her capacity as supervisor. Managers and supervisors are each responsible for overseeing a team of 20 individuals. Both managers and supervisors must have master's degrees. Managers and supervisors are required to work 50 hours a week and are entitled to the same benefits. Managers and supervisors are both provided with a private office in the company headquarters.

In light of these facts, the positions of manager and supervisor are substantially similar. They require similar skills (master's degrees), entail the same responsibilities (supervision of a team of 20 individuals), and require similar effort (50 hours a week). Because these positions are substantially similar, Acme Company violates the EPA by paying Mary less than her male counterparts.

An employer does not have to act "knowingly" to actually violate the EPA. To establish a violation, an employee must only demonstrate that the employer allowed the employee to perform the equal work without equal pay. As previously mentioned, the work does not have to be identical but only substantially similar as to skill, effort, and responsibility. For this reason, job title is not dispositive of the issue and any court assessing unequal treatment will analyze the facts and circumstances of each job to determine if they are substantially similar.

Wage classification systems

There are certain wage structures or fact patterns that almost always violate the EPA. Employers should understand these structures and seek to avoid them. First, when jobs are denoted as "male jobs" and "female jobs," it is usually an indicator of a pay practice based on sex. Unless sex is a bona fide occupational qualification for the job, the EPA prohibits such classifications because they amount to discrimination in wage setting based on sex. Second, when an employee of one sex is removed and replaced with an employee of the opposite sex at a lower pay rate, this will raise the presumption of an EPA violation. Under this situation, the employer must justify the difference in payment using one of the defenses discussed later in this chapter.

Retaliation

In addition to prohibiting wage discrimination, the EPA also prohibits employers from firing or in any other way discriminating against an employee because that employee files a complaint or any other proceeding under the EPA.

Defenses to alleged violations

Because the EPA is focused on preventing wage discrimination based on the sex of the employee, the simple fact that a man and women performing a similar job are being paid different amounts does not alone violate the EPA. Pay must be based on the sex of the individual to violate the EPA. For this reason, there are four common defenses to an allegation that an employer is engaging in wage discrimination on the basis of sex. An employer is justified in paying men and women different wages for substantially similar jobs if payment is made pursuant to one of the following:

- Merit system.

- System which measures earnings by quantity or quality of production.

- Seniority system.

- Differential based on any other factor other than sex (29 U.S.C. § 206(d)(1)(i)-(iv)).

EVERYDAY
ILLUSTRATION   John and Betty are both sales representatives
                for Acme Company. A sales representative at
Acme Company is paid based on the total revenue he or she
generates each month. In March 2009, John sells 100 units at
$1 per unit. In that same month, Betty sells 200 units at $1 per
unit. Both John and Betty are paid 10 percent of their respective
gross sales. While John and Betty are making different wages,
they are paid the same way and the reason for the difference
in pay is based on the amount each person sells and not his or
her gender.

Mary and Paul are each branch managers for Acme Company
Mary has been a branch manager for 10 years. Paul has been
a branch manager for eight years. Mary makes $100,000 as a
branch manager. Paul makes $80,000 as a branch manager.
Branch manager pay is based on the number of years a person
has held the position of branch. A person makes $10,000 for
every year he or she has been a branch manager. The pay structure in this case does not violate the EPA because it is based on
a system of seniority and not sex.

Enforcement Agency and Procedures

The Equal Employment Opportunity Commission (EEOC) is the enforcing agency of the EPA. The EEOC has the right to investigate and gather
data regarding the wage, hours, and other conditions and practices of employment of any employer covered by the EPA. The right to investigate will
include the right to:

- Enter and inspect an establishment

- Make records and transcriptions of the records

- Question employees

- Investigate facts, conditions, practices, or matters that are
  necessary to make a determination on whether any person has
  violated the EPA

Employees have 180 days from the last discriminatory act of the employer to file a charge with the EEOC if they feel they have a claim against their employer.

Penalties for Violations

Willful violators of the EPA face fines of up to $10,000 and/or imprisonment for up to six months. Only those violators who have prior convictions for violations of the EPA will face imprisonment.

Employers that violate the act will be liable to the prevailing employee or employees for unpaid wages, unpaid overtime, and an amount equal to the unpaid wages and unpaid overtime as liquidated damages. Also, employers are liable for any legal or equitable relief that is required to reinstate the employee to the place they would have been in had the discrimination never occurred. This can include employment, reinstatement, promotion, and payment of wages lost.

The applicable statute of limitation is that the complaining party file an action within two years after the cause of action accrued. If the violation by the employer was willful, the employee shall have three years to sue. Employees who do not sue within this time frame shall forever be barred from bringing suit. Actions can be maintained against any employer (this includes public agencies) in federal or state court.

Employer Compliance and Requirements

Equal work

To maintain compliance with the EPA, employers are required to pay male and female employees at the same establishment equal wages for work that requires the same skill, effort, responsibility, and that is carried out under similar working conditions. It should be noted that the positions do not have to be identical for liability under the act to be incurred — only substantially equal.

This standard will not be dependent upon job classifications or titles, but on the actual job requirements and performance. For example, two employees who have the job title "front clerk" may be asked to perform different duties — an employee of one sex spends most of the time doing the duties of a front clerk, while the employee of the other sex spends most of the time working in the inventory room. In this situation, the differential in pay might be allowed due to the variance in the actual duties of the employees.

However, if you have two employees of different sexes, both with the job title of administrative assistant, and they are essentially performing the same duties for different managers in the same company, yet are being paid differing rates, you have entered the realm of being in violation of the EPA.

 It is critical to determine when the statute of limitations begins to run for EPA violations because that moment determines how long the employee has to file an action. President Obama extended the 180-day statute of limitations for EPA violations with the first bill he signed into law, the Lilly Ledbetter Fair Pay Act. Before the law, the 180-day statute of limitations started to run at the occurrence of the last discrete discriminatory act – e.g.,. the moment of the actual decision to pay an employee less because of his or her sex. Subsequent nondiscriminatory measures related to the pay discrimination but which themselves were not intentionally discriminatory (such as issuing the paychecks) were not considered new discriminatory events and would not extend the 180-day period. This limited the amount of time that an employee had to discover the discrimination.

This problem was highlighted in *Ledbetter v. Goodyear Tire & Rubber Co.*, 500 U.S. 618 (2007). In *Ledbetter*, a woman sued her former employer, Goodyear Tire, alleging that she received poor performance reviews because she was a woman and, therefore, received lower pay than her male

colleagues. The Supreme Court held that discrete discriminatory acts that trigger the time limit for filing EEOC charge could only be discriminatory pay decisions and not the occurrence of subsequent nondiscriminatory acts. In order for her claim to be timely, the employee must have filed the EEOC claim within 180 days of the latest discriminatory act that led to the difference in pay between herself and her male colleagues (i.e., the most recent bad performance review). The court focused on the intentionally discriminatory acts of the employer and ignored subsequent nondiscriminatory acts.

With the Lilly Ledbetter Fair Pay Act, any act in furtherance of the pay discrimination resets the 180-day period whether the act itself is discriminatory or not. This has the effect of extending the time period during which an employee may file a claim by providing a fresh 180 days each time a paycheck is issued or another measure related to the pay discrimination occurs.

Helpful Web Sites

Full Text of the EPA
www.eeoc.gov/laws/statutes/epa.cfm

Facts About Equal Pay and Compensation Discrimination
www.eeoc.gov/eeoc/publications/fs-epa.cfm

State law considerations

Any state laws regarding equal pay can be located in Appendix B: State Statute Tables.

Chapter 8

The Fair Credit Reporting Act (FCRA)

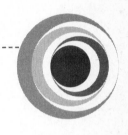

COMMON TERMS AND DEFINITIONS	
Adverse action:	Consists of any one or more of the following:
	• Any denial, cancellation, increase in charge for, reduction of, or any other adverse or unfavorable change in the terms of coverage or the amount of any insurance, existing or applied for, in connection with the underwriting of insurance.
	• A denial of employment or any other employment decision that has a negative effect on a current or prospective employee.
	• Any action that is adverse to the interest of the consumer.
Consumer report:	Written, oral, or electronic communication of any information by a credit reporting agency that has an effect on a consumer's credit worthiness, credit standing or credit capacity. It is sometimes used for employment purposes.

Consumer reporting agency:	A company that for fees, dues, or on a cooperative nonprofit basis, assembles and evaluates consumer credit information or other information on consumers for the purpose of furnishing consumer reports to third parties. This will include any company that uses any aspect of interstate commerce for the purpose of preparing or furnishing consumer reports.
File:	All information on a consumer that is recorded and retained by a consumer reporting agency.
Identity theft:	Fraud committed using the identifying information of another person.
Investigative consumer report:	A consumer report where the information contained within includes a consumer's character, general reputation, personal characteristics, or mode of living. This information is gathered via personal interviews with neighbors, friends, or associates of the consumer. This report will not contain specific factual information from creditors or from a consumer reporting agency if the factual information was obtained directly from the creditor or consumer reporting agency.
Medical information:	Information or data created by or taken from a health care provider or consumer that details the past, present, or future physical, mental, or behavioral health or condition of an individual; the provision of health care to an individual; or the payment for providing health care to an individual. The following consumer information will not fall within this category: age, gender, demographics, or any other information that does not directly relate to the physical, mental, or behavioral health or condition of a consumer.

National security investigation:	Any official inquiry by an agency or department of the U.S. government to determine the eligibility of a consumer to receive access or continued access to classified information or to determine whether classified information has been lost or compromised.

History and Purpose

The Fair Credit Reporting Act (FCRA) protects the privacy of consumer credit information. Since credit reporting has an enormous effect upon consumers, Congress wanted to ensure consumer reporting agencies exercise their responsibilities of assembling and evaluating consumer credit with fairness, impartiality, and respect for the consumer's right to privacy. When employers want to run credit reports or background checks, they must comply with certain requirements of the FCRA.

PRACTICALLY SPEAKING An employer may want to run a credit check on applicants in order to eliminate those with poor credit histories. Similarly, an employer may want to run credit checks on employees to determine whether they are financially responsible before awarding promotions. Generally, an employer may use credit reports in hiring or employment decisions as long as the employer complies with the requirements of the FCRA.

Protected Class of Employees

The FCRA will apply to any employee or prospective employee about whom an employer obtains a consumer report for the purpose of making any employment related decisions.

Employers Subject to the FCRA

The FCRA applies to both public and private employers seeking a consumer report covering an applicant or employee.

Employer Obligations

Before an employer can obtain a consumer report to be used for employment purposes, the employer must notify in writing the applicant or employee whose consumer report the employer seeks. The employer must also obtain the applicant's or employee's written consent before seeking the report.

Once the employer has provided notice and obtained written consent, the employer has additional obligations if it wishes to rely on the information in the report to take an adverse action. First, the employer must give the individual pre-adverse action disclosure. This disclosure must include a copy of the person's consumer report and a copy of "A Summary of Your Rights Under the Fair Credit Reporting Act." Second, after the employer takes the adverse action, it must provide the person with notice of the adverse action taken. This notice must include:

- Name, address, and phone number of the credit reporting agency (CRA) that supplied the report.

- Statement that the CRA supplying the report did not decide to take the adverse action and cannot provide specific reasons for it.

- Notice of the person's rights to contest any information the CRA furnished and to seek a free consumer report for the CRA within 60 days of a request for such an additional report.

Medical information

When it comes to consumer reports that contain medical information about a consumer, employers are barred from obtaining and consumer agencies are barred from supplying the consumer report.

Employer compliance

Before an employer can obtain a consumer report from a consumer reporting agency for employment purposes, the employer must certify to the agency the following:

- Information from the consumer report will not be used in violation of any applicable federal or state equal employment laws or regulations

- Clear and conspicuous disclosure has been made in writing to the employee or applicant before the report is procured that the consumer report may be obtained for employment purposes

- Employee or applicant has authorized in writing their permission for the employer to obtain the report

Disposal of records

Employers that maintain or possess consumer information (or any compilation of consumer information taken for consumer reports for business purposes) must properly dispose of such information. Proper disposal can include burning, pulverizing, or shredding papers that contain consumer report information so that the information cannot be read or reproduced. Also, it is a good idea to destroy or erase electronic files or media that contain consumer report information so that the information is undiscoverable.

Enforcement Agency and Procedures

Federal

The governing agency that ensures compliance with the FCRA is the Federal Trade Commission (FTC). The FTC will have procedural, investigative, and enforcement powers. This will include the authority to issue procedural rules to enforce compliance with the FCRA, including filing of reports, production of documents, and requiring the appearance of witnesses. The FTC can also bring an action against any person who has a pattern or practice of violation of the FCRA.

Enforcement actions under the FCRA must be brought in the appropriate U.S. district court. The action will be limited in time, meaning a lawsuit must be brought within the following time periods:

- The earlier of two years after the date of discovery by the plaintiff of the violation that forms the basis for liability

- Five years after the date on which the violation actually occurred

State

If the chief law enforcement office of a state or such official or agency designated by the state has any reason to believe that any person within the state has violated the title, the state can bring an action to enjoin the violation or bring an action on behalf of the residents of the state to recover damages, meaning the state can prohibit this particular action regarding the consumer report. The Federal Trade Commission retains the right to intervene in the action and to be heard. This will include the right to file petitions. States will be barred from filing suit if a suit is pending in federal court.

Penalties for Violations

Civil

For willful noncompliance with the FCRA, an employer can face the following penalties:

- Civil liability to a consumer for actual damages suffered as a result of the failure in an amount not less than $100 or more than $1,000

- If a person obtains a consumer report under false pretenses or knowingly without a permissible purpose, he or she will be liable for the actual damages sustained by the consumer or for $1000, whichever is greater

- Punitive damages as allowed by the court

- Reasonable attorney's fees as determined by the court

Employers who are negligent in failing to comply with the requirements of the FCRA will be liable to the consumer in an amount equal to the sum of the following:

- Actual damages sustained by the consumer as a result of the failure

- Costs of the action, including reasonable attorney's fees

Criminal

If an employer knowingly and willingly obtains information on a consumer from a consumer reporting agency under false pretenses, the resulting penalty is up to two years in prison.

 **DELVING DEEPER** As noted above, penalties for violating the FCRA will vary depending on whether the failure to comply with the FCRA was due to willful or negligent conduct. Non-willful violations of the FCRA only subject an employer to liability for actual damages suffered by the employee as a result of the violation. Willful violations of the FCRA, however, subject an employer to the possibility of actual damages, statutory damages, punitive damages, and reasonable attorney's fees and court costs.

While the definition of willful clearly covers employer actions intentionally made in violation of the FCRA, it also covers actions that are committed in reckless disregard of the notice obligations of the FCRA. See Safeco Insurance Co. of America v. Burr, 551 U.S. 47 (2007). In Safeco, the court found that an action is committed with reckless disregard of the FCRA obligations when it is done in a manner that creates "an unjustifiably high risk of harm that is either known or so obvious that it should be known." Therefore, even if the employer does not know that its actions violate the FCRA, it will be found to have willfully violated the law if a reasonable, average employer should have known that its actions violated the FCRA. This standard ensures that employers cannot avoid willful liability by simply keeping themselves ignorant of the obligations of the FCRA.

Helpful Web Sites

Federal Trade Commission's site on the FCRA
www.ftc.gov/credit

Summary of employee rights under the FCRA
www.yale.edu/hronline/careers/screening/documents/Fair-CreditReportingAct.pdf

State law considerations

Any state laws regarding fair credit reporting can be located in Appendix B: State Statute Tables.

Chapter 9

The Fair Labor Standards Act

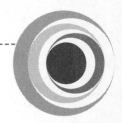

COMMON TERMS AND DEFINITIONS	
Collective bargaining:	Negotiation of wages and other conditions of employment by an organized body of employees.
Employee in fire protection activities:	Firefighter, paramedic, EMT, rescue worker, ambulance driver, or hazardous materials worker who is trained in fire suppression and employed by a fire department of a city, county, fire district, or state.
Industry:	Includes trade, business, industry, or other similar activity.
Goods:	Wares, products, commodities, merchandise, or articles or subjects of commerce.
Engaged in production of goods:	Employees employed in producing, manufacturing, mining, handling, transporting, or working on goods or in a closely related process.

Oppressive child labor:	Employment conditions where any employee under the age of 16 is employed by an employer in an occupation that has been found by the secretary of labor to be particularly hazardous or detrimental to the health and well-being of children between the ages of 16 to 18.
Public agency:	The government of the United States or a state; any agency of the United States or a state; any political subdivision of state; or any interstate governmental agency.
Sale or sell:	Exchanging, selling, contracts for sale, consignment for sale, shipment for sale, or other disposition.
Tipped employee:	Employee engaged in an occupation where he regularly receives more than $30 a month in tips.
Wage:	The money paid to any employee for hours worked. It can include the furnishing of board, lodging, or other facilities to an employee if that is a common practice of the employee.

History and Purpose

The Fair Labor Standards Act (FLSA) establishes standards related to overtime pay, minimum wage, record keeping, and child labor. The FLSA applies to both public and private employers. Almost every private employer will be required to comply with the standards set out under FLSA.

Employers Subject to the FLSA

Almost every employer in the United States will fall within the purview FLSA, including:

- The federal government

- State and local governments

- Companies with annual gross sales of at least $500,000

- Enterprises engaged in commerce or in the production of goods for commerce

- Retail and service employers

- Hospitals and establishments that provide care for the ill, elderly, or mentally disabled

- Educational facilities for pre-kindergarten schools, elementary schools, high schools, and schools that are specifically for physical or mentally disabled children

Whether an enterprise is subject to the FLSA depends on the nature and size of the business. Enterprises are considered to be businesses if they have related activities, performed under unified operation or common control, for a common business purpose. Further, an enterprise subject to the FLSA must fall within one of the three following categories:

- An enterprise that has employees engaged in commerce or in the production of goods for commerce or employees handling, selling, or otherwise working on goods or material that have been moved in or produced for commerce with an annual business volume must be more than 500,000

- An enterprise that conducts one of the several listed types of businesses, including schools and hospitals

- An enterprise that is an activity of a public agency

Employer Compliance and Requirements

Minimum wage

Employers are required to pay all employees at a rate equal to federal minimum wage. The current federal minimum wage is $7.25 an hour. In addition to the federal minimum wage, most states have a state minimum wage. While the majority of states that have a minimum wage law have set the state rate at the same rate as the federal rate, states may set their minimum wage at a rate higher than the federal minimum wage. For this reason, employers should check with the labor board in the state in which they do business to make sure they comply with both federal and state minimum wage requirements.

Law in Real Life Texas, Utah, and North Carolina have state minimum wage rates that are equal to the federal minimum wage rate. Alabama and South Carolina have no state minimum wage rate and simply rely on the federal minimum wage rate to set the standard throughout the state. California, Oregon, and Michigan have minimum wage rates that are higher than the federal minimum wage rate. California's minimum wage rate is currently $8 an hour. Oregon's minimum wage rate is currently $8.40. Michigan's minimum wage rate is currently $7.40 an hour.

Regular rate of pay

An employer cannot attempt to inflate the rate of pay to comply with the minimum wage rate requirement by including in the rate of pay items given to the employee in addition to his or her base pay. The following items will not be considered to be within an employee's regular rate of pay, nor will they be considered payment for overtime worked by an employee:

- Money paid to employees as gifts for Christmas or other special occasions. The amounts cannot be based on factors such as hours worked, production, or efficiency.

- Money paid to employees for random periods where the employee is not working, such as vacation, holidays, or illness. Also, amounts paid for traveling expenses or any other expenses that the employee should be reimbursed due to their being incurred on behalf of the employer.

- Amounts paid to the employee at the sole discretion of the employer not connected with any prior promise or contract with the employee.

- Contributions to a trustee or third person connected to a retirement, life, accident, or health insurance plan.

- Overtime pay received by employee for time worked over the standard 40-hour work week.

- Amounts paid to an employee at a premium rate one and a half times the rate paid on regular days for time worked on Saturdays, Sundays, or holidays.

- Amounts paid to an employee at a premium rate for work done outside of an established collective bargaining agreement.

- Amounts paid to an employee as a result of stock option or stock appreciation rights, or employer-provided grants.

PRACTICALLY SPEAKING These provisions are meant to prohibit an employer from escaping the minimum wage requirements by including certain extras in overall compensation. For example, assume that Acme Company pays its employees $5 an hour, an amount below the federal minimum wage rate. Each employee works eight hours a day and due to the responsibilities of the position, incurs $40 of travel expenses a day. Acme Company reimburses each employee for this amount. Without the above provisions, Acme Company could argue it actually pays each employee $10 an hour because each employee receives $5 an hour base pay plus $5 an hour in travel expenses ($40 a day/eight hours a day). The above provisions prohibit Acme Company from trying this end run around the minimum wage requirement by excluding the $40 of travel expenses from the overall compensation calculation.

Exceptions to Minimum Wage Requirements

Tipped employees

Employees who are tipped by customers may not qualify for minimum wage. This can include a wide range of occupations such as food servers and certain hotel positions. Employees who receive tips must receive a minimum wage of at least $2.13 an hour from the employer and receive at least $30 in tips a month. Additionally, the base pay plus the tips must equal or exceed the minimum wage rate. To qualify for this exemption, an employer must inform employees of the tip credit allowance and be able to show that employees are being paid at least minimum wage when their tips are added to the base pay. Employers also must permit employees to keep all the tips earned.

EVERYDAY ILLUSTRATION Greg works as a waiter at BB'Q House. As required by the FLSA, BB'Q house pays Greg $2.13 an hour. During Week 1, Greg works 20 hours and makes $200 in tips. During Week 2, Greg works 20 hours and makes $100 in tips. For Week 1, BB'Q House can legally pay Greg $2.13 under the FLSA because he made at least $30 in tips during the month and his overall compensation rate is greater than the federal minimum wage rate. He made a total of $242.60 — ($2.13 x 20 hours) + $200 — over a 20-hour period for a compensation rate of $12.13 an hour ($242.60/20). However, BB'Q House will have to pay Greg more than $2.13 an hour during Week 2 because his total compensation rate was lower than the federal minimum wage rate. He made a total of $142.60 over a 20-hour period for a compensation rate of $7.13 an hour. BB'Q House will have to pay Greg an additional 12 cents an hour, for a total compensation rate of $2.25 an hour, so that he will make at least $7.25 an hour.

Special certificates

Certain employees may be paid less than minimum wage if certain requirements are first met. Employers must obtain special certificates before qualifying to pay the following employees less than the federal minimum wage:

Full-time students

If an employer is a college or university, or is in the retail, service or agricultural industries and hires a full-time student, there are certain exceptions to the minimum wage requirement. Full-time students can be paid 85 percent of minimum wage.

However, full-time students who are paid less than minimum wage can work no more than eight hours a day and 20 hours a week while school is in session. When school is not in session, full-time students can work up to 40 hours a week. Employers must obtain a certificate from the Department of Labor to be able to qualify for this exception.

Vocational students

Employers who hire high school students who are at least 16 years old and are enrolled in vocational education courses can obtain a certificate from the Department of Labor. The certificate will allow the employer to pay the student at least 75 percent of minimum wage for the period of time that the student is enrolled in the vocational education program.

Disabled workers

Employers must receive a certificate to pay special minimum wages (wages lower than federal minimum wage) to employees who have certain disabilities. The employee must have a disability for the job being performed or have one that will impair his or her earning or productive capacity. For instance, blindness, mental illness, mental retardation, cerebral palsy, alcoholism, and drug addiction will qualify an employee to receive a reduced wage. However, disabilities such as educational disabilities, chronic unemployment, welfare recipients, parole, or probation will not qualify.

Employees under the age of 18

The FLSA includes special youth employment provisions specifically designed to protect young workers. These provisions generally limit the types of jobs young workers can perform and the number of hours they may work. The limitations depend on the age of the minor worker. Once an employee turns 18, he or she is no longer subject to these provisions and only the general provisions of the FLSA will apply.

General age requirements

In most cases, employees who are at least 16 years old can work for an unlimited number of hours. Employees who are 14 to 15 years old may be employed in most jobs but are subject to the following hours restrictions. The employee cannot work:

- More than three hours on a school day
- More than 18 hours in a week
- More than eight hours on a non-school day
- More than 40 hours in work not related to school

The employee's working hours must be between the hours of 7 a.m. and 7 p.m. However, during the summer (June 1 to Labor Day) employees can work until 9 p.m.

Law in Real Life In addition to the federal standards of the FLSA, many states further restrict the number of hours and times of day that minor employees may work. Employers should check with the state department of labor of the state in which they conduct business to learn about those rules. In most cases, a simple Internet search for the specific state's department of labor will produce the state department of labor Web site and the relevant state rules.

14-year-olds and 15-year-olds may not work in the following positions:

- Communication or public utilities

- Construction or repair

- Driving a motor vehicle or helping a driver

- Manufacturing, mining, or processing

- Power-driven hoisting apparatus or machinery, other than typical office machines

- Public messenger

- Transporting people or property

- Workroom where products are manufactured, mined, or processed

- Warehousing and storage

- A hazardous job

Generally, children under 14 are prohibited from working. However, children under the age of 14 can be employed in the following positions:

- Newspaper deliveries

- Babysitting

- Actor or performer in motion pictures, television, theater, or radio

- Employee in a business solely operated/owned by his or her parents

- On a farm owned or operated by his or her parents

Hazardous jobs

Employers with positions that fall within the Department of Labor's definition of hazardous cannot hire employees under the age of 18. The secretary of labor has noted the following positions and job actions as being hazardous:

- Manufacturing or storing explosives

- Driving a motor vehicle (by employees 16 years old or younger); certain driving for 17-year-olds

- Coal mining and other forms of mining

- Logging and saw milling

- Power-driven wood working machines

- Exposure to radioactive substances

- Power-driven hoisting apparatus

- Power-driven metal forming, punching, and shearing machines

- Meat packing or processing

- Power-driven bakery machines

- Power-driven paper product machines

- Manufacturing brick, tile, and related products

- Power-driven circular saws, band saws, and guillotine shears

- Wrecking, demolition, and ship-breaking operations

- Roofing operations and all work on or about a roof

- Excavation operations

Limited exemptions are available for some of these positions for interns or apprentices under strict specified standards. An employer engaged in one of these hazardous jobs who is interested in hiring a minor apprentice should contact the Department of Labor to discuss those exemptions in detail.

Overtime

Unless exempt, employees who work more than 40 hours a week are entitled to overtime pay. The rate paid must be one and a half times the employee's regular pay rate and is paid for any time worked over the standard 40 hours.

EVERYDAY
ILLUSTRATION   Betsy works 47 hours the second week of August. Her normal rate of pay is $10 an hour. Betsy's employer is required to compensate her $505 for the second week of August. This is the total of 40 hours at $10 an hour ($400) plus seven hours of overtime at $15 an hour ($105).

Certain employees are exempt from the overtime pay requirement. These exemptions are narrowly defined and employers should contact their local wage and hour division office within the Department of Labor's Employment Standards Administration to check the exact terms for each exemption. The following are examples of employees who are exempt from the overtime pay requirements:

- Executive, administrative, and professional employees

- Certain seasonal and amusement or recreational establishments

- Certain small newspapers and switchboard operators of small telephone companies

- Employees engaged in newspaper delivery

- Certain commissioned employees of retail or service establishments

- Certain employees in the tobacco industry

Employer Obligations

Record keeping

Employers must keep payroll records for at least three years. Employers must retain records used in wage computation for two years. Examples of such records include time cards, work schedules, additions to or deductions from wages, and work tickets. These records must also be open for inspection by DOL representatives and must include:

- Full name

- Home address, including ZIP code

- Date of birth, if under 19

- Sex

- Occupation in which employed

- Time and day of week on which employee's work week starts

- Rate of hourly pay

- Hours worked each day, and total number of hours worked each week

- Total daily or weekly earning

- Total amount of overtime pay

- Any additions or deductions from wages

- Total amount of pay for each pay period

- Date of payment and the pay period covered by payment

Posting of Notices

All employers subject to FLSA must place a poster in a clear and obvious place that explains the FLSA such that any employee can easily access, view, and read it. The official poster is available at **www.dol.gov/osbp/sbrefa/poster/main.htm**.

Retaliation

Employers are prohibited from firing or discriminating against any employee because of his or her filing a complaint, filing a suit, or testifying in a proceeding under FLSA.

Enforcement Agency and Procedures

The Wage and Hour Division of the Department of Labor (DOL) is the administrative agency in charge of ensuring compliance with FLSA. The DOL or any designated representatives can investigate and gather data regarding the wages, hours, and other conditions and practices of employment for any employer covered by the FLSA. The investigators also have the right to enter and inspect places, question employees, and investigate facts, conditions, practices, or other matters that will assist in determining whether the company is in violation of FLSA.

Employees can file a complaint with the agency or they can choose to file a lawsuit in state or federal district court. An employee must file within two years of the employer's violation or within three years if the violation was willful. If an employer violates the child labor provisions of FLSA, only the DOL will have the right to file a complaint.

In the event that the DOL determines there has been a violation or a repeated willful violation of FLSA and decides to assess a civil penalty, the employer will be entitled to a notice of the decision. The notice will include the amount of the penalty, the reasons the penalty was imposed, and the employer's right to request a hearing. Hearings must be requested within 15 days of an employer's receipt of the notice or the decision by the DOL will become final and not subject to appeal.

If an employer does request a hearing, the complaint will be forwarded to an administrative judge who will make a decision. The employer will have the right to appeal the administrative judge's decision to the secretary of labor. The secretary of labor will make a final decision (not subject to appeal) regarding the violation and penalty to be assessed.

Penalties for Violations

Civil

Employers who willfully and repeatedly violate the minimum wage or overtime provisions of FLSA are subject to a penalty of $1,100 per violation. A repeat violator is an employer who has previously violated the minimum wage or overtime provisions of the act and has received notice of violations from the DOL's Wage and Hour Division or has been found in violation in a court of law. Willful violations are found when the employer knew that his or her conduct was prohibited by the act, and the employer recklessly disregarded the provisions of the act.

If an employer violates the child labor provisions of FLSA, there will be a penalty of not more than $11,000 for each child employee who is the reason for the violation. The following factors will be considered when determining the amount of the penalty:

- Size of the business

- Number of employees

- Dollar volume of sales or business done

- Amount of capital investment and financial resources

- Gravity of the violations

- History of prior violations

- Number of minors illegally employed

- Occupations in which the minors were employed

- Exposure of minor to hazards and whether any minors were injured

- Time frame of the minor's employment (e.g,, school hours and hours of the day)

Helpful Web Sites

1. Questions and answers about minimum wage. Includes the addresses and phone number of regional offices.
   http://www.dol.gov/dol/topic/wages/minimumwage.htm

2. List of employees who are exempt.
   www.dol.gov/elaws/esa/flsa/screen75.asp

3. Information on how FLSA applies to workers with disabilities.
   www.dol.gov/elaws/esa/flsa/docs/sec14.asp

4. Chart showing all of the states minimum wage laws.
   www.dol.gov/esa/minwage/America.htm

5. Link to required FLSA poster and guidelines on how it is to be posted.
   http://www.dol.gov/compliance/laws/comp-flsa. htm#posters

6. Instructions for applying for the certificate to employ employees who receive less than minimum wage.
   http://www.dol.gov/whd/regs/compliance/whdfs22.htm

7. FLSA fact sheets for employers. Some sheets are available in multiple languages.
   http://www.dol.gov/compliance/laws/comp-flsa.htm#factsheets

8. General requirements of FLSA.
   www.dol.gov/elaws/esa/flsa/screen5.asp

9. Contains fact sheets for certain types of employees, along with fact sheets dealing with almost every area of FLSA that applies to employers that fall within the guidelines of FLSA.
   http://www.dol.gov/whd/offtheclock/index.htm

State law considerations

Any state laws regarding state minimum wage can be located in Appendix B: State Statute Tables.

Chapter 10

The Family Medical Leave Act

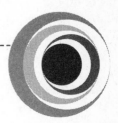

COMMON TERMS AND DEFINITIONS

Employment benefits:
Benefits provided to employees by an employer, including group life insurance, health insurance, disability insurance, sick leave, annual leave, educational benefits, and pensions.

Health care providers:
Includes doctors of medicine or osteopathy authorized to practice medicine or surgery by the state in which they practice. It also includes any other person determined by the Department of Labor (DOL) to be capable of providing health care services.

Parent:
Either the biological parent of an employee or the individual who stood in as a parent (without having the legal rights of a parent) when the employee was his or her son or daughter.

Reduced leave schedule:
Employee's leave schedule that reduces his or her usual number of work hours per week or per day.

Secretary:
The secretary of the Department of Labor.

Serious health condition:	An illness, injury, impairment, or physical or mental condition that involves in-patient care in a hospital, hospice, or residential medical care facility or continuing treatment by a health care provider.
Son or daughter:	This term will include the following, who must be under 18 years of age or — if over 18 — unable to take care of themselves due to a mental or physical disability:

- Biological child
- Adopted child
- Foster child
- Stepchild
- Legal ward
- Child of a person who is standing in as a parent

Spouse:	A husband or wife.
State:	For the purposes of this section, this includes any state of the United States, the District of Columbia, and any territory or possession of the United States.

History and Purpose

The Family Medical Leave Act (FMLA) was passed in 1993 and requires employers subject to the FMLA to provide eligible employees up to 12 weeks of unpaid leave a year to address certain familial responsibilities. The FMLA provides employees with a period of time in which they are able to take care of family responsibilities. This alleviates the pressure of having to choose between employment responsibilities and family responsibilities.

Many states had and continue to have similar provisions governing family medical leave. In addition to understanding and complying with the provisions of the FMLA, employers should also consult the department of labor located in the state in which they do business to ensure compliance with any different state provisions.

Protected Class of Employees

Employees eligible for coverage under FMLA are those who have worked for an employer subject to the FMLA (as defined below) for at least 12 months and who during the previous 12-month period worked at least 1,250 hours. For purposes of satisfying the 12 months of employment period, the time of employment does not need to be consecutive. Additionally, the employee must have worked at a location in the United States or any territory of the United States where at least 50 employees are employed by the employer within 75 miles of the location.

EVERYDAY
ILLUSTRATION   It is Sept.1, 2009. Julie works in the Atlanta office of Acme Company. The office employs 70 people. Julie has worked at Acme Company. since May 1, 2008, but took a three-month period of leave starting Oct. 1, 2008, and ending Dec. 31, 2008. During the past 12 months, Julie worked a total of 1,300 hours for Acme Company. Assume that Acme Company is a covered employer. In light of these facts, Julie is entitled to coverage under the FMLA. She satisfies all the requirements because she:

- Works for an employer subject to FMLA
- Worked for Acme Company for a total of 13 months
- Worked at least 1,250 hours over the previous 12-month period
- Works in a U.S. location that employs at least 50 people

Employers Subject to the FMLA

The FMLA applies to private sector employers who employ 50 or more employees in 20 or more work weeks during the current or preceding calendar year. This includes joint employers and successors of covered employers. The FMLA also applies to the federal government, state governments, and federal agencies.

Employer Compliance and Requirements

General requirements

Employers are required to provide eligible employees up to 12 weeks of unpaid leave during any 12-month period. Employees can take leave for any of the following reasons:

- Birth of child and care of new child

- Adoption of a child or receipt of a foster care child

- Care of a spouse, child, or parent suffering from a serious health condition

- Employee's inability to work due to his or her suffering from a serious health condition

If an employee takes leave for the birth and care or adoption of a child, the leave must end within 12 months of the birth or placement of the child.

Reduced schedule and intermittent leave

Under certain circumstances, employees may work a reduced schedule or take leave on an intermittent basis instead of taking full leave. A reduced schedule or intermittent leave may be taken when necessary to care for a seriously ill family member or when necessary due to the employee's own serious health condition. Additionally, an employee may work a reduced schedule or take intermittent leave to care for a newborn or adopted child, but only with the employer's permission. FMLA leave time includes only the actual amount of leave taken while on a reduced schedule or intermittent leave schedule.

The employer can require the employee to move to an available alternative position within the company when an employee requests intermittent leave or reduced leave. The alternative position must:

- Be a position for which the employee is qualified.

- Offer equivalent pay and benefits.

- Offer better accommodations for the recurring periods of leave than the employee's regular position.

Military leave requirements

Employers subject to the FMLA must also grant up to 26 work weeks of unpaid leave during a 12-month period to an eligible employee who is a spouse, son, daughter, parent, or next of kin of a current member of the armed forces (including the National Guard or Reserves) with a serious injury or illness.

Additionally, employers subject to the FMLA must provide eligible employees a total of 12 work weeks of unpaid leave during a 12-month period if they have a spouse, son, daughter, or parent on active duty or who has been notified of a pending order to active duty. The leave is intended to help employees deal with qualifying exigencies arising out of the active duty or pending active duty, including:

- Issues arising from the service member's deployment on seven or fewer days of notice.

- Military events and activities related to the active duty or call to active duty (official ceremonies or events).

- Childcare issues related to active duty (arranging alternative childcare or school options).

- Making or updating financial and legal arrangements to address the service member's absence.

- Attending counseling.

- Taking five days of leave to spend with service members on short-term leave.

- Attending post-deployment activities (arrival ceremonies).

- Any other event agreed to be a qualifying exigency between the employee and employer.

PRACTICALLY SPEAKING These provisions are meant to ensure that employees with family serving active duty in the military are able to attend to issues related to deployment. While the above discussion provides specific examples of qualifying exigencies that may trigger 12 weeks of unpaid leave, employers should not consider the list exhaustive. Other issues related to active duty service may arise and employers and employees should attempt to discuss these within the purpose and design of the FMLA.

Substituting paid leave

If employers are required to provide employees with 12 weeks of unpaid leave, employees can choose to use accrued paid vacation or personal or family leave for part of the FMLA leave period. If an employee does not choose to do so, the employer may require the employee to use his or her accrued leave. If the accrued leave is substituted for the unpaid leave, the accrued leave and the unpaid FMLA leave will run concurrently. This substitution can only be made if the company's leave policy would otherwise cover the circumstance.

Spouses employed by the same employer

If an employer is employing both a husband and wife and both are eligible for FMLA, the employer is not required to give both spouses 12 weeks of unpaid leave for certain circumstances. Spouses employed by the same employer are limited to a combined total of 12 weeks of unpaid leave for the birth of a child, the adoption of a child, and to care for an employee's parent with a serious health condition. The employer can provide one or the other with the required 12 week of unpaid leave or can split the leave between the two spouses. However, if the husband, wife, their child, or one of their parents is suffering from a serious medical condition that prevents the employee from performing his or her position, the employer is required to give each employee the required 12-week leave.

EVERYDAY
ILLUSTRATION Wanda and Harry are married and work for
Acme Company. Wanda and Harry decide to
adopt a child. In anticipation of the adoption, both Wanda and
Harry ask for 12 weeks unpaid leave to prepare for the adoption
and arrival of the child. Acme Company is not required to provide
both employees with 12 weeks unpaid leave. FMLA requires that
Acme Company provide 12 weeks unpaid leave total to both
Wanda and Harry, which they may divide as they see fit.

Benefit protection

Employers are required to keep group health care coverage for the employee while he or she is on leave. Also, an employer cannot withdraw any benefit that the employee had before taking FMLA leave.

Restoration to position

With the exception of highly compensated employees, employees who take FMLA leave must be restored to their original position or a position of equal benefits, pay, and other terms of employment. The employee will not be entitled to the accrual of any seniority or employment benefits during leave or any right, benefit, or position of employment other than the original one.

Employer Obligations

Notice requirements

Employers that fall within the requirements of the FMLA are required to post and to keep posted in an obvious place on the workplace premises a notice prepared by or approved by the DOL. The notice must include FMLA's pertinent provisions and information on how to file complaints. The DOL has prepared a notice poster that satisfies these requirements. The poster can be found at **www.dol.gov/esa/whd/regs/compliance/posters/fmla.htm**.

Record keeping requirements

Certain records must be kept to comply with FMLA. The DOL may require any employer to submit to the DOL any books or records. This submission is not required more than once every 12 months unless the DOL has reason to believe that an employer is in violation of the FMLA.

Employers must make, keep, and preserve any records of employees that relate to the employee's wages, hours, and other conditions and practices of employment. Also, these records must be preserved and the employer must provide certain reports to the DOL.

Employee Requirements

Notice

Employees must provide their employers with sufficient notice of their intent to take time under the FMLA if the reason the leave is being requested is foreseeable. In general, an employee must provide his or her employer with a minimum of 30 days notice for leave due to the birth of a child, the placement of an adopted child, or a foster care placement. Similarly, an employee must provide 30 days notice to his or her employer if the leave is due to a planned medical treatment on behalf of a spouse, child, parent with a serious medical condition, or for the employee's serious health condition. In addition to these notice requirements, employees must make reasonable efforts to schedule the treatment as to not unnecessarily disrupt the employer's operations.

Medical certifications

Employers have the right to request certification that an employee actually qualifies for unpaid leave under the FMLA. If an employer makes such a request, the employee should provide certification from a doctor that supports or verifies the time requested off under the FMLA. An employee may be required to get medical certification from a doctor or the doctor of a child, spouse, or parent if an employee requests time under the FMLA to care for his or her own or a loved one's medical condition. Information must be provided to the employer in a timely manner.

Contents of certifications

When the employee requests leave to care for a spouse, child, or parent with a serious medical condition, the certification must include the following information:

- Date the serious medical condition was first diagnosed

- Potential duration of the illness

- Medical facts within the doctor's knowledge regarding the condition

- Statement that the employee is needed to care for the child, spouse, or parent

- Estimate of the time the employee will be needed to take care of spouse, child, or parent

Employees requesting leave due to their own medical condition that prevents them from doing their job functions must have a certification that includes:

- Date the serious medical condition was first diagnosed

- Potential duration of the illness

- Medical facts within the doctor's knowledge regarding the condition

- Statement that the employee is unable to perform his or her job functions

An employer can require an employee have an original certification recertified if reasonably necessary to reassess qualification for leave under the FMLA. An employer may request recertification no more frequently than every 30 days.

Medical certifications for intermittent or reduced leave

When an employee is obtaining medical certifications for intermittent leave or reduced leave schedules to care for a loved one with a serious health condition, he or she must include a statement that the condition specifically requires intermittent or reduced leave to provide the required care to the family member. The certificate should also provide the expected leave duration and schedule.

When an employee takes intermittent or reduced leave for his own planned medical treatment, he or she must provide the employer with a certification that includes the dates on which the treatment is expected to occur and the duration of the treatment.

In the event that the intermittent or reduced leave is for the employee's serious medical condition that prevents the employee from performing his or her job function, the certification must include a statement of the medical necessity for the leave and the leave's expected duration.

Second opinion

Employers with suspicions regarding the information contained in the first medical certification can require the employee to obtain a second opinion. The employer will be entitled to a second opinion regarding the date on which the serious health condition commenced, the condition's probable duration, and the appropriate medical facts within the health care provider's knowledge regarding the condition. The employer must pay the expense for getting the second opinion, but may also designate who provides the second opinion, as long as the person providing the second opinion is not a regular employee of the employer.

If the second opinion contradicts the information in the first opinion, the employer can require that the employee get a third opinion at the employee's expense. The third opinion must be from a professional decided upon jointly by the employer and employee. The third opinion must contain the same information requested in the second opinion. The third opinion is considered the last opinion and both employee and employer are bound by the findings in that opinion.

Medical certification for position restoration

Employees who have been on FMLA leave due to a serious health condition that prevented the employee from performing his or her job functions must obtain medical certification before returning to work. The employer must have a uniformly applied practice or policy that requires each employee to provide this certification. This provision of the FMLA will not override a state or local law that governs the employee's return to work.

Medical certification for failure to return to work

If an employee is unable to return to work because of the continuation, reoccurrence, or onset of a serious health condition of a child, spouse, parent, or the employee, the employee will have to provide the employer with a medical certification. The certification must be issued by the heath care provider of the ill party. It must state that the employee is still needed to care for spouse, child, or parent on the date that the FMLA leave will expire, or that the serious medical condition of the employee continues to prevent him or her from performing job functions on the date that FMLA leave will expire.

Repayment of employer cost of maintaining health coverage

As previously discussed, an employer must maintain an employee's health coverage during the unpaid leave period. This requires the employer to continue to pay the cost of maintaining certain group health plans for the benefit of the employee. An employee must repay the employer's cost for maintaining group health coverage for the employee if the employee:

- Fails to return from FMLA leave after the FMLA leave has expired.

- Fails to return to work for any reason other than the continuation, reoccurrence, or onset of a serious health condition of the spouse, child, parent, or the employee (that prevents the employee from performing job functions).

- Fails to return to work for circumstances beyond the employee's control.

Periodic reporting

Upon the employer's request, employees who are out on FMLA will have to report periodically on the status of the illness and on the employee's intention to return to work.

Prohibited Discriminatory Employer Actions

Employers are prohibited from taking any action meant to interfere with an employee's exercise of any right provided under the FMLA. Employers are also prohibited from firing or in any way discriminating against an employee for opposing practices that are unlawful under the FMLA. Finally, employers are prohibited from firing or discriminating against an employee for filing a charge or initiating proceeding under the FMLA, giving or preparing to give information dealing with any investigation or proceeding relating to any right under the FMLA, or testifying or preparing to testify in any investigation or proceeding under the FMLA.

Exceptions to the general rule
Highly compensated employees

An employer is not required to restore highly compensated employees to their former position or to an equivalent position. Highly compensated employees are those who are among the top 10 percent highest paid employees of the employer within a 75-mile radius of the workplace at which the employee is employed. When an employee is a highly compensated individual, an employer may deny reinstatement when it is necessary to prevent substantial and grievous economic injury to the employer's operations. The employer must have notified the employee of the intent to deny restoration and the employee must have elected not to return to employment after receiving the notice.

Enforcement Agency and Procedures

The DOL has the power to subpoena individuals to serve as witnesses; to require the production of books, papers, and other documents; and investigative authority, which includes the following:

- Entering and inspecting locations and inspecting records

- Making transcriptions of records

- Questioning employees

- Reviewing facts, conditions, practices, or matters necessary to determine whether any violation has been committed

Statute of limitations

If the violation of the FMLA is willful, the employee has three years to bring suit after the last event that was in violation of the FMLA. If the violation was not willful, the employee will have two years after the last event that was in violation of the FMLA to bring suit.

Employee right to sue

Employees can sue employers for damages or for equitable relief for violations of the FMLA in any federal or state court. Employees can also sue on behalf of other employees in the same situation. The employee's private action shall terminate if the DOL picks up the case and files a complaint for damages or complaint for injunction.

Penalties for Violations

The penalty for failure to properly post a notice is a fine for not more than $110 per offense. Employers found in violation of the FMLA are subject to the following types of damages:

- General damages which will be equal to the amount of wages, salary, employment benefits, or other compensation denied or lost by the employee

- Interest on the general damage amounts

- Liquidated damages — an additional amount equal to the sum of the general damages and interest if the violations are deemed to be willful

- Actual monetary loss — where the amounts available under general damages were not lost or denied the employee, this will provide for the employee to be able to recover any actual losses suffered by the employee

- Equitable relief that the court finds appropriate

- Payment of the employee's reasonable attorney's fees, expert witness fees, and any other costs of the action

The DOL can seek injunctive relief against an employer that can require the employer to refrain from interfering with, denying the exercise of, or attempting to deny the exercise of rights provided by the FMLA. The injunction can also prevent an employer from terminating an employee for opposing unlawful practices, or from terminating or discriminating against an employee for taking part as a witness or otherwise in any proceeding under the FMLA.

DELVING DEEPER Employers subject to the FMLA are required to allow employees to take FMLA leave as long as the employees are eligible and they have a condition that falls within the meaning of the statute. Questions have arisen about what kinds of conditions qualify for FMLA leave. For example, although the statute does not specifically state that substance abuse is a covered condition, DOL regulations include treatment of substance as a serious health condition.

In *Darst v. Interstate Brands Corp.*, 512 F.3d 903 (7th Cir. 2008), the Seventh Circuit — which covers Wisconsin, Indiana, and Illinois — came to the conclusion that although FMLA is available for treatment of substance abuse, it is not available for employees who take FMLA leave because of incapacity caused by the substance abuse itself.

In *Darst*, an alcoholic employee missed work from July 29, 2000, to Aug.14, 2000. During this period, the first four days were spent at home and not in a hospital or treatment facility. All other days were spent in an alcoholism treatment facility. The employee sought FMLA leave to cover the period.

The missed work, claiming he was entitled to FMLA because the leave was used to treat his alcoholism, amounted to a serious health condition.

DELVING DEEPER ...cntd.

The employer denied FMLA leave for the first four days that the employee was not in treatment and fired him for exceeding the allowable number of days under the company's absentee program. The employee sued for denial of FMLA benefits, claiming he was illegally denied FMLA leave to cover the first four days of his absence.

The Seventh Circuit disagreed with the employee's allegations and held that FMLA leave can only be taken for *treatment* of substance abuse. Because the first four days of the absence period were not used for treatment, they did not qualify for FMLA leave. The Seventh Circuit distinguished an absence from work due to the treatment of a serious health condition and absence from work due to the use of a substance. Under the facts of the case, the employee's absence during the first four days amounted to absence due to the use of alcohol and not the treatment of his substance abuse.

Helpful Web Sites

Main DOL Web site for the FMLA–
http://www.dol.gov/whd/fmla/index.htm

Detailed overview of the FMLA in a compliance guide form
www.dol.gov/whd/regs/compliance/1421.htm

Analysis/comparison of federal FMLA laws and state employee family medical leave laws
www.dol.gov/esa/programs/whd/state/fmla/index.htm

Employment law guide for FMLA
www.dol.gov/compliance/guide/fmla.htm

State law considerations

Any state laws regarding family and medical leave can be located in Appendix B: State Statute Tables.

Chapter 11
The Genetic Information Nondiscrimination Act

History and Purpose

The Genetic Information Nondiscrimination Act (GINA) was passed in May 2008. GINA has two titles. Title I prohibits discrimination based on genetic information in health coverage and Title II prohibits employment discrimination based on an individual's genetic information. Title II is the relevant provision for purposes of this book and any subsequent reference to GINA refers only to Title II unless otherwise specified. GINA was passed due to increased genetic testing and reliance of that testing for employment decisions and became effective in November 2009.

PRACTICALLY SPEAKING Before GINA, there were concerns that employers would obtain results from previously administered genetic tests (or require employees and applicants to undergo genetic testing) to determine if there was a latent condition that would impact the individual's job performance in the future. GINA prevents employers from making an employment decision based on genetic tests. For examples, employers might want to know whether an applicant covers a pre-disposition for certain cancers, Alzheimer's disease, or ALS before committing to hire the person. GINA prevents the employer from obtaining this information.

PRACTICALLY SPEAKING   It is important to consider the overlap between GINA and the ADA (previously discussed). While the ADA permits an employer to require an applicant to submit to a medical exam in order to determine if the applicant is physically able to perform a job, employers must be careful to comply with GINA when administering the exam. Under GINA, the exam may not include inquiries into the applicant's medical history and genetic testing.

Enforcement agencies and procedures

The EEOC is responsible for administering Title II of GINA. Individuals may either file a complaint with the EEOC or pursue private litigation through the civil courts.

Helpful Web Sites

1. Article that examines GINA and genetic testing
   writ.news.findlaw.com/colb/20080514.html-

2. Basic information regarding the new law and its provisions
   **www.laborlawyers.com/shownews.
   aspx?Show=10579&Type=1122 -.**

Chapter 12

The Immigration Reform and Control Act of 1986 (IRCA)

COMMON TERMS AND DEFINITIONS

Admission/admitted: With respect to this chapter, this is the lawful entry of an alien into the United States after inspection and authorization by an immigration officer.

Administrator: The official designated by the secretary of state.

Advocates: Term used for an action that advises, recommends, or furthers by overt act.

Alien: A person not a citizen or national of the United States.

Application for admission: Application for admission into the United States (not the application for the issuance of an immigrant or non-immigrant visa).

Attorney general: The attorney general of the United States.

Border crossing identification card: Identification issued to an alien who is lawfully admitted into the United States for permanent residence or to an alien who is a resident in a foreign country that borders the United States. The identification card must contain a fingerprint or handprint that is electronically readable.

Clerk of Court: Clerk of naturalization court.

Consular officer: Any consular, diplomatic, or other officer or employee of the United States given the authority to issue non-immigrant or immigrant visas.

Crewman: Person serving in any capacity on board a boat or airplane.

Diplomatic visa: Non-immigrant visa that carries the titles.

Doctrine: Policies, practices, purposes, aims, or procedures.

Foreign state: Outlying possessions of a foreign state.

Immigrant: Every alien except an alien who falls within one of the exempt classes.

Independent contractors: Individuals or entities that have an independent business and are only subject to control on their results. Determined on a case-by-case basis, factors that are looked at include whether they supply their own tools and materials, work for a number of clients at the same time, and make the majority of decisions regarding their work.

Pattern/practice: Regular, repeated, and intentional activities. This term does not include random, isolated acts.

Recruit for a fee: Act of soliciting a person, directly or indirectly, and referring that person with the intent of securing employment for that person.

Refer for a fee: Sending or directing a person with the intent of obtaining employment in the United States. This will include employment on a contingency basis or on retainer.

Unauthorized alien: Alien who is not lawfully admitted for permanent residence or is not authorized to be employed.

History and Purpose

The Immigration Reform and Control Act (IRCA) was enacted to prevent employers from hiring and recruiting illegal aliens. Under the IRCA, it is illegal for an employer to knowingly hire or recruit illegal immigrants. The IRCA requires employers to verify the immigration status of their employees. The IRCA also granted amnesty to certain illegal immigrants who had continuously resided in the United States and who had entered the country prior to Jan.1, 1982.

The main provisions of the IRCA require employers to verify that employees are authorized to work in the United States, and to maintain records of employee authorization to work in the United States. Also, the IRCA prohibits employers from discriminating against individuals on the basis of citizenship or national origin. With respect to the verification and record keeping requirements of the IRCA, all employees who are U.S. citizens and nationals and all aliens legally authorized to work in the U.S. are covered. Lawful aliens, aliens entering the United States as refugees, aliens who were granted asylum from another country, and citizens and nationals of the United States are covered by the anti-discrimination provision of the IRCA. All private employers must comply with the verification and record keeping requirements of the IRCA. Private employers with four or more employees must comply with the anti-discrimination provisions of the IRCA.

Employer Compliance and Requirements

Verification

Whenever an employer hires an individual or when a recruitment agency signs a person up for referral for employment, the employer or recruitment agency must verify that the individual is authorized to work in the United States. The required form used to document the verification process is the Form I-9. An employer or recruiter must also swear (under penalty of perjury) that they have examined the documents that show an employee's eligibility and identity. Form I-9 can be used in paper or electronic format, and can be located at **www.uscis.gov/i-9**.

Form I-9 — Employer Considerations to Keep in Mind

The employer must have the employee complete and sign the Employee Information and Verification section of Form I-9 no later than the date of hire. Even though the employee must complete this section, it is the employer's responsibility to make sure this section is completed and signed in a timely manner.

Within three business days of the date the employee begins work, an employer or recruiter must physically examine the following documentation and complete the employer review and verification section of Form I-9.

    a. Documents that establish employment authorization and identity

    b. Documents that evidence employment authorization

    c. Documents establishing the identity of the individual

If the employee is being hired on a temporary basis that will last less than three days, the above mentioned documents must be examined before the end of the employee's first working day.

Record keeping

Employers must keep records of all of their employees' original I-9s and photocopies of supporting documents (noted in the verification section above) for a period of three years after the date of hiring the employee, or one year after the date the employee is fired, whichever date is later.

Recruiters must keep the original I-9 and photocopies of supporting documents for a period of three years from the hiring date.

Employers will be required to make all I-9 forms available for inspection by officers of authorized agencies, and shall be provided three days notice before inspection.

EVERYDAY ILLUSTRATION Acme Company hires Rachel on June 1, 2006. Rachel fills out the Form I-9 and provides photocopies of all required documents. Acme Company places the original I-9 and the photocopies in a file. On May 1, 2004, Acme Company fires Rachel. In light of these facts, Acme must retain Rachel's I-9 and the photocopies of the required documents until April 30, 2011.

Prohibited Discriminatory Employer Actions

Employment verification

Under the IRCA, it is illegal for an employer to hire or recruit for a fee any unauthorized alien for the purposes of employment. It is also illegal to hire an employee without complying with documentation requirements of the IRCA. Employers are barred from asking employees for additional documentation once they have presented the documents required by the IRCA. Employers must fire any employee who was an authorized alien when hired but lost that status during the course of the employment relationship.

Discrimination based on national origin or citizenship status

An employer is barred from discriminating against an employee on the basis of citizenship status or national origin. This will include refusing to hire an individual authorized to work due to his or her citizenship or firing an employee due to his or her being born in a foreign country. Also, an employer must refrain from retaliating against an individual for asserting rights under the IRCA.

Law in Real Life These provisions of the IRCA do not prohibit an employer from preferring a U.S. citizen over a non-U.S. citizen for other reasons. While an employer is prohibited from making employment decisions based on citizenship or national origin, an employer may take other factors into account when evaluating candidates with different citizenship or national origins. For example, an employer faced with a candidate who is a U.S. citizen with three years of experience and another candidate who is a Canadian citizen with one year of experience may justifiably prefer the U.S. candidate based on his or her increased level of experience without violating the anti-discrimination provisions of the IRCA.

Enforcement Agency and Procedures

The Department of Homeland Security (DHS) enforces the IRCA. The Office of Special Counsel-Immigration (OSC) (a division of the Department of Justice) and the EEOC are also vested with certain enforcement powers.

The DHS investigates discrimination complaints and inspects employers' I-9 forms. The OSC is in charge of investigating employee and applicant complaints that an employer has violated the IRCA. If a reasonable basis is found, the OSC can file an administrative complaint. The OSC can also conduct independent investigations of employers. The EEOC can investigate claims and file a complaint in a district court. The EEOC also is vested with the power to conduct independent investigations.

Verification

A person with knowledge of an employer verification violation may submit a signed written complaint in person or by mail to the service office that has jurisdiction over the business. The complaint must include the name and addresses of the person complaining and the alleged violator. Also, the complaint must contain detailed facts about the violation, including the date, time, and place of violation and the specific conduct that resulted in a violation of the act.

The DHS can conduct investigations for violations with or without receiving a complaint. If an entity has been found to be in violation of the IRCA, the DHS may issue a notice of intent to fine or a warning notice.

Penalties for Violations

Employers who fail to comply with the IRCA may be subject to civil and criminal fines. If an employer violates the IRCA by hiring unauthorized aliens, it will have to pay fines based on the number of previous offenses. If it is the first offense, the fine will be between $37 and $3,200 for each unauthorized alien employed.. If it is the second offense, the fine will be between $3,200 and $6,500 for each unauthorized alien employed. If the employer has more than two previous offenses, the fine will be between $4,300 and $16,000 for each unauthorized alien employed.

In addition to the above fines, an employer can be fined between $110 and $1,110 for each individual who they failed to examine, or for whom they failed to procure proper documentation before employing.

From a criminal standpoint, employers with a pattern or practice of violating the IRCA provisions can be fined no more than $3,000 for each unauthorized alien, and/or imprisoned for no more than six months.

 E-Verify is the Department of Homeland Security's electronic employment eligibility verification system. The system allows employers to electronically verify that newly hired employees are eligible to work in the United States. Since Sept. 8, 2009, all federal contractors and subcontractors have been required to use E-Verify

DELVING DEEPER ...cntd.

to verify their employee's eligibility to work in the United States. Federal contracts will only be awarded to employers using E-Verify to check employee authorization within 30 days of the award of the contract.

E-Verify is a free system operated by the DHS in partnership with the Social Security Administration. It takes information from Form I-9 and compares it to the federal government databases to ensure that workers are eligible to work in the United States.

For more information on E-Verify, visit **dhs.gov/e-verify.**

Helpful Web Sites

Main employer information site maintained by Department of Immigration
www.uscis.gov/portal/site/uscis/menuitem.eb1d4c2a3e-5b9ac89243c6a7543f6d1a/?vgnextoid=91919c7755cb901 0VgnVCM10000045f3d6a1RCRD&vgnextchannel=9191 9c7755cb9010VgnVCM10000045f3d6a1RCRD

Helpful examples of how to avoid discriminating against an employee based on their immigration status
www.aflcio.org/issues/jobseconomy/workersrights/ rightsatwork_e/disc_immigrants.cfm

Answers to frequently asked questions about immigration related unfair employment practices
www.usdoj.gov/crt/osc/htm/facts.htm

Department of Homeland Security Immigration Site.
www.dhs.gov/ximgtn/

State law considerations

If your state has any laws regarding immigration, you can get more information regarding the law from the Department of Labor listed in the State Statutes Table in Appendix B.

Chapter 13
The National Labor Relations Act

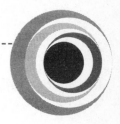

COMMON TERMS AND DEFINITIONS

Affecting commerce: In commerce, or burdening or obstructing commerce or the free flow of commerce, or having led or tending to lead to a labor dispute burdening or obstructing commerce or the free flow of commerce.

Commerce: Trade, traffic, commerce, transportation, or communication among the several states, or between the District of Columbia or any territory of the United States and any other state or territory. It also includes any such action between any foreign country and any state, territory, or the District of Columbia, or within the District of Columbia or any territory.

Heath care institution: Includes any hospital, nursing home, health maintenance organization, health clinic, extended care facility, or any other institution devoted to the care of sick, disabled, or aged individuals.

Labor dispute: Any controversy concerning the terms or conditions of employment or dealing with the representation of persons in negotiating, fixing, changing or seeking to change terms or conditions of employment.

Labor organization: Any organization of any kind, agency, or employee representation committee, in which employees participate and which exists for the purpose of dealing with employers concerning grievances, labor disputes, wages, rates of pay, hours of employment, or conditions of work.

Professional employee: Any employee engaged in work that is mainly intellectual and varied in character instead of routine mental, manual, mechanical, or physical work. This type of work typically requires education of an advanced type that includes specialized instruction and study in an institution of higher learning.

Representatives: Any individual or labor organization.

Supervisor: Any individual having authority in the interest of the employer to hire, transfer, suspend, fire, promote, or discipline other employees. This person has the authority to direct other employees or to address their concerns and grievances.

History and Purpose

The National Labor Relations Act (NLRA) was enacted in 1935 to address ongoing problems between employers, employees, and labor organizations (29 U.S.C. § 151 et. seq.). Congress found that these problems, which resulted in strikes and employee walkouts, interfered with the flow of interstate commerce. The NLRA prohibits employers from interfering with employees' rights to organize and participate in labor unions. Prior to the NLRA, employees could join labor unions and strike, but employers retained the right to fire employees or otherwise retaliate against them for such actions. The NLRA regulates the relationship between employers, employees, and labor unions and designates the rights of both employers and employees in their working relations. It also establishes and secures the role of unions within this relationship.

Protected Class of Employees

The NLRA covers all employees of private employers with the exception of the following:

- Agricultural laborers

- Domestic service workers who work inside a home

- Persons employed by a parent or a spouse

- Independent contractors

- Supervisors

- Employees subject to the Railway Labor Act (airline and railroad employees)

- Employees of any other person who does not fall within the NLRA's definition of employer

Employers Subject to the NLRA

The NLRA applies to any private employer involved in interstate commerce. This covers any employer whose employees deal with goods, information, or services that cross state lines. The following employers are the only ones not covered by the NLRA:

- Federal, state, or local governments

- Religious schools

- Any employer subject to the Railway Labor Act, which covers labor relations in the airline and railroad industries

Employee Rights and Responsibilities

Section 7 rights

Those rights provided under Section 7 of the law make up the core of the NLRA. Section 7 provides that "employees shall have the right to self-organization, to form, join, or assist labor organizations, to bargain collectively through representatives of their own choosing, to engage in concerted activities for the purpose of collective bargaining or other mutual aid and protection (29 U.S.C. § 157). Section 7, therefore, grants employees four specific rights.

- The right to self-organization (e.g., forming or attempting to form a union among the employees of a company)

- The right to form, join, or assist labor organizations (e.g., joining a union whether or not the union is recognized by the employer)

- The right to bargain collectively via representatives of their own choosing (e.g., assisting a union to organize the employees of an employer)

- The right to engage in concerted activities for the purpose of collective bargaining (e.g., going out on strike to secure better working conditions)

Additionally, employees have the right to refrain from all of the above activities, unless the employee is hired by a company that requires membership in a labor organization as a condition of employment and this condition is based on the employer's contract to that effect with a labor organization.

Strikes

Employees have the right to strike under the NLRA. Whether a strike will be deemed lawful is dependent upon the following:

- The object of the strike

- The timing of the strike

- The conduct of the striking workers

The object of the strike can be thought of as the purpose of the strike. There are two lawful objects of a strike. The first is an economic strike and the second is an unfair labor practice strike. Employees engaged in either type of strike remain employees of the employer during the strike.

PRACTICALLY SPEAKING

As the name suggests, employees engaged in an economic strike are seeking some kind of economic benefit from the employer, such as higher wages, shorter hours, or better working conditions. Similarly, employees engaged in an unfair labor practice strike are protesting some kind of unfair labor practice engaged in by the employer.

However, there are significant differences as to rights of reinstatement depending on which kind of strike the employee engages in. In both types of strikes, an employer can replace the striking employees with bona fide replacements in order to fill the jobs and continue operations.

While strikers participating in an unfair labor practice strike are entitled to be reinstated in their jobs once they make an unconditional request for reinstatement, even if replacements were used to temporarily fill their positions, strikers participating in an economic strike are not entitled to be reinstated if bona fide replacements are filling the positions when the strikers ask to be reinstated. However, if the economic strikers are unable to find regular and substantially similar work, they are entitled to be recalled for jobs that open up at the employer for which they are qualified.

EVERYDAY
ILLUSTRATION   Acme Company employs 40 service technicians and 30 machine operators. All of the
service technicians go on strike to protest the low wages Acme
Company pays its service technicians. All of the machine operators go on strike to protest Acme Company's extremely long
work hours. In order to continue operations, Acme Company
hires bona fide replacements to fill the service technician positions and the machine operator positions left empty by the strike.
After months of striking, the service technicians and the machine
operators unconditionally request reinstatement. The temporary
replacements still hold the previously vacated positions.

Under the NLRA, Acme Company is required to reinstate the machine operators in their old jobs. They were protesting unfair labor
practices and are entitled to be reinstated regardless of whether
Acme Company hired replacements. However, Acme Company is
not required to reinstate the service technicians. They engaged in
an economic strike and do not retain the right to be reinstated to
their old jobs if replacements hold those positions at the time the
strike ends. Any service technician who is unable to find similar
work retains the right to be recalled to a position that opens at
Acme Company for which he or she is qualified.

Economic strikers and unfair labor strikers may be entitled to back pay if
they have made unconditional requests for reinstatement that are denied. If
back pay is awarded, the employer will have to pay back pay from the time
the employees should have been reinstated.

Unlawful strikes

Strikes that are for an improper purpose, occur at an improper time, or
entail misconduct on the part of the strikers are considered unlawful. Employees do not have a right to engage in an unlawful strike, and an employee
who engages in an unlawful strike cannot rely upon the protections of the
NLRA strike provisions. Such employees run the risk of losing their jobs.
The following lays out reasons that a strike may be unlawful and examples
of a specific kind of strike that is unlawful for that particular reason:

- Strikes that are unlawful because of purpose (e.g., those that are in support of a union with unfair labor practice or that would cause an employer to commit an unfair labor practice)

- Strikes that are unlawful because of timing (e.g., those that violate a no-strike provision of a contract)

- Strikes that occur at the end of a contract period (e.g., strikes to change or terminate a contract)

- Strikes that are unlawful because of misconduct of strikers (e.g., refusing to work and refusing to leave the plant, physically blocking persons from entering or leaving a plant, threatening violence against nonstriking employees, or attacking management representative)

Picketing

In addition to the right to strike, the NLRA grants employees the right to picket. The NLRA puts object, timing, and misconduct limitations on the right to picket just as it puts them on the right to strike. Additionally, employees are prohibited from picketing for certain purposes that would amount to unfair labor practices under Section 8, discussed below.

Collective Bargaining and Representation Rights of Employees

Collective bargaining requirements

Collective bargaining is another key provision of the NLRA. Collective bargaining "requires that the employer and the representative of its employees meet at reasonable times to confer in good faith about certain matters, and to place in writing any agreement reached if either party requests it (29 U.S.C. § 158(d)). Employers and employees must come together in good faith to discuss matters related to wages, hours, other terms and conditions of employment, the negotiation of an agreement, or any questions arising under an agreement.

Duty to bargain

Both the employer and the union are under an affirmative duty to bargain. It is an unfair labor practice for either party to refuse to bargain with the other. However, the duty to bargain does not require that either party agree to a proposal or make concessions that they would not otherwise agree to.

EVERYDAY
ILLUSTRATION Acme Company and the union representing its mechanics disagree about the amount of wages Acme Company should pay its mechanics. Acme Company believes that a rate of $20 an hour is appropriate. The union believes that a rate of $55 an hour is appropriate. Both parties have made it clear that the numbers are firm. Even though there is a huge disparity in the two different numbers proposed and both parties have publicly said that the numbers are firm, the NLRA requires Acme Company and the union to sit down together and discuss the wage dispute in good faith. The requirement of good faith does not require either Acme Company or the union to accept a number it considers unreasonable.

Steps required to change a bargaining agreement

If the parties have reached a bargaining agreement and either party wishes to change or end the contract, the following steps must be taken by the party wishing to change the agreement:

- The party must notify the other party to the contract in writing about the proposed termination or modification 60 days before the contract is set to expire.

- The party must offer to meet with the other party for the purpose of negotiating a new contract or a contract containing the proposed changes.

- Within 30 days after notice to the party, the other party must notify the Federal Mediation and Conciliation Service of a dispute if no agreement has been reached by that time.

- The party must continue to adhere to all the terms and conditions of the existing contract with no strikes or lockouts until 60 days after the notice regarding the termination or modification was given, or until the date the contract will expire, whichever comes last.

NOTE: The time periods will be different for health institutions.

Employee representatives

Each group of employees who share common concerns and interests may elect an employee representative to speak on their behalf during collective bargaining. This person is called an employee representative. The NLRA states that employee representatives that have been "designated or selected for the purposes of collective bargaining by the majority of the employees in an appropriate bargaining unit will be the exclusive representatives of all the employees in such unit for the purposes of collective bargaining (29 U.S.C. 159(a))."

For the purposes of the NLRA, a "bargaining unit" is the group of employees who share similar interests concerning employment conditions such as wages, hours, and working conditions. Only those employees within the bargaining unit are represented by the employee representative.

Selection of bargaining representatives

Typically, bargaining representatives are elected via a secret ballot election conducted by the National Labor Relations Board (NLRB). The NLRB will only conduct an election if a petition has been filed requesting one. An employee, a group of employees, any individual, or any labor organization acting on behalf of the employees can file the petition. An employer can also file a petition.

If the petition is filed by or on behalf of employees, it must be supported by a substantial number of employees who want to be represented for collective bargaining and must state that the employer declines to recognize the representative.

PRACTICALLY SPEAKING   Note that the election of the bargaining representative is conducted by an outside third party, the NLRB.

Duties of bargaining representative and employer

The employee representative has the duty to equally and fairly represent all employees within the bargaining unit irrespective of their union membership or activities. Once the employee representative has been selected, the employer is barred from bargaining with individual employees, a group of employees, or with another employee representative.

Bars to an election

If there is already an existing collective bargaining contract, the NLRB will not hold an election. However, if any of the following factors are present, the existence of the contract will not bar an election:

- Contract is not in writing or not signed

- Contract has not been ratified by the members or the union (if this is required)

- Contract does not contain substantial terms or conditions of employment sufficient to stabilize the bargaining relationship

- Contract can be terminated by either party at any time for any reason

- Contract contains an illegal union-security clause

- Bargaining unit is not appropriate

- Union that entered into the contract is no longer in existence or is unable or unwilling to represent the employees

- Contract is racially discriminatory

- Contract covers only union members

- Contracting union is unstable due to internal high level conflict

- Employer's operations have changed substantially since the contract was executed

The election

Only employees who have worked in the bargaining unit during the eligibility period set by the NLRB and those who are employed in the bargaining unit on the day of the election can vote. Elections are usually held within 30 days after they are directed. Elections will be set aside if the NLRB finds an atmosphere of fear of reprisals or confusion that is interfering with the employees' free choice.

Prohibited Discriminatory Employer Actions

Under the NLRA, employers are prohibited from engaging in unfair labor practices. Section 8(a) of the NLRA lists the unfair labor practices of employers. Section 8(a)(1) prohibits an employer from interfering with, restraining, or coercing employees in relation to the exercise of the rights provided under Section 7 of the NLRA. As mentioned above, these rights include the right to join, form, or assist a labor organization; to bargain collectively; to engage in other concerted activities for mutual aid or protection; and to refrain from any or all of these activities. Employers must not interfere with an employee's right to exercise any of these rights.

Examples of employer actions that might violate Section 8(a)(1) include the following:

- Implementing a company policy that prohibits collective bargaining

- Threatening to close down facilities if a union is organized

- Implying that employees who join unions will suffer reduced pay or loss of benefits

Section 8(a)(2) prohibits employers from dominating or interfering with the formation or administration of any labor organization. Domination or interference can arise when any employer financially supports or otherwise contributes to a labor organization. The following discussion provides a more detailed discussion of what it means for an employer to dominate or interfere with a labor organization.

Dominating

For NLRA purposes, an employer dominates a labor organization when the employer interferes with its formation and assists and supports its operation and activities in a way that makes it look as if it being ruled by the employer and not the employees. Labor organizations are meant to be run by employees for the benefit of employees. When an employer provides support to a labor organization or gets involved in the operations of the labor organization, there is the risk that the organization will be controlled by the employer. For this reason, employer contributions and assistance are prohibited.

PRACTICALLY SPEAKING   An employer illegally dominates a labor organization if it does any of the following:

- Forms the labor union
- Has management participate in running the meetings of the labor union
- Provides the key financial backing and support for the labor organization

Illegal assistance and support

In addition to being prohibited from engaging in actions that amount to dominating a labor organization, an employer is also barred from providing a union with direct payments or indirect financial aid. Also, an employer cannot give privileges to the union it favors and deny those same privileges to another union that is disfavored.

PRACTICALLY SPEAKING An employer might have the motivation to prefer one union over another when multiple unions are attempting to organize the same group employees. In such a case, an employer may prefer one of the unions over the other because of reputation or other reasons. In that case, an employer must remain neutral. An example of improper preference would be if the employer opened up company facilities to one union for the purpose of soliciting members while denying access to those facilities to the other union.

Discrimination against employees

Under section 8(a)(3), an employer's discrimination against an employee for the purpose of encouraging or discouraging affiliation with a labor organization is considered an unfair labor practice and is prohibited. This section of the NLRA also prohibits discrimination against an employee because the employee refrains from joining a union or taking part in union activities.

PRACTICALLY SPEAKING Examples of such discrimination include refusing to hire, firing, or demoting an employee who chooses to engage in a labor organization. It also includes failing to promote an employee because of his or her affiliation with a labor organization or assigning employees who are members of a labor organization to a less desirable job or shift than nonmembers. Section 8(a)(3) does not prevent an employer from firing an employee who fails to pay required dues in the event that there is an existing lawful union security agreement, or for economic reasons such as good cause, disobedience, or bad work.

Discrimination for NLRB activity

Under section 8(a)(4) of the NLRA, it is an unfair labor practice for an employer to fire or in any other manner discriminate against an employee because he or she files charges or gives testimony under the NLRA. Section 8(a)(4) protects the employees right to protect themselves and their rights under the NLRA by ensuring they are free to file claims without fear of retribution for such action.

Refusal to bargain in good faith

Section 8(a)(5) requires that employers must bargain in good faith about wages, hours, and other conditions of employment with the collective bargaining representative selected by a majority of the employees in an appropriate unit. For a bargaining representative to enforce his rights under this section, he or she must show:

- The representative was designated by a majority of the employees

- The unit is appropriate

- There has been a demand that the employer bargain and the employer has refused to do so

The following duties are associated with the bargaining between an employer and a representative:

- Duty to meet and confer

- Duty to supply information

- Duty to refrain from unilateral action

NOTE: Employers that purchase or acquire the business of another will most likely be obligated to recognize and bargain with the union that represented the employees before the business was transferred.

Hot cargo agreements

Under section 8(e) of the NLRA, it is an unfair labor practice for an employer and labor organization to enter into a "hot cargo" agreement. A hot cargo agreement is an agreement where a labor organization's employer agrees that employees are not required to handle or work on goods or materials going to or coming from an employer designated by the union as unfair.

Such agreements have the effect of exerting pressure on secondary neutral employers because the agreement will often cause the employer to stop doing business with other employers who supply the prohibited goods or materials. Therefore, section 8(e) prohibits employers from agreeing with labor organizations that the employer will not do business with another employer. These agreements are unenforceable under section 8(e). There are certain exceptions to this prohibition for construction industries and garment industries.

Enforcement Agency and Procedures

The NLRB was established to administer and enforce the NLRA. The NLRB has the authority to direct elections and certify results. It can also act to prevent unfair labor practices in cases involving labor disputes that affect or would affect commerce. The NLRB, however, will not get involved in all types of cases. The following are those cases that fall within the jurisdictional standards of the agency:

- Non-retail business (must have revenue of at least $50,000 a year)

- Office buildings (total annual revenue must be $100,000)

- Retail enterprises (at least $500,000 annual volume)

- Public utilities (with at least $250,000 total annual volume of business or $50,000 direct or indirect outflow)

- Newspapers ($200,000 total annual volume)

- Radio, telegraph, television, and telephone enterprises (at least $100,000 total annual income)

- Hotels, motels, and residential apartment houses (at least $500,000 total annual volume of business)

- Privately owned health care institutions (at least $250,000 annual volume of business)

- Transportation enterprise, links and channels of interstate commerce (at least $50,000 total annual income derived from furnishing passenger and freight transportation services)

- Transit systems (at least $250,000 total annual volume of business)

- Taxicab companies (at least $500,000 total annual volume of business)

- Associations (these are regarded as a single employer in that the annual business of all association members is totaled to determine whether any of the standards apply)

- Enterprise in the territories and District of Columbia

- National defense (all enterprises affecting commerce when their operation has a substantial impact on national defense)

- Private universities and colleges (at least $1 million gross annual revenue from all sources, excluding contributions with limitations imposed by grantor)

- Symphony orchestras (at least $1 million gross annual revenue from all sources, excluding contributions with limitations imposed by grantor)

- Law firms and legal assistance programs (at least $250,000 gross annual revenues)

- Employers that provide social services (at least $250,000 gross annual revenues)

- United States Postal Service

- Legally run gambling casinos (total annual revenue is at least $500,000)

NOTE: At its discretion, the NLRB can decline to exercise jurisdiction over any class or category of employees when a labor dispute is not sufficient to cause the board to exercise jurisdiction.

Procedures for complaints

The complaining party must file a petition in the regional office where the unit of employees is located. The petition must be signed, sworn to, or affirmed under oath. If the NLRB investigates and finds reasonable cause to believe a question affecting commerce does exist, the NLRB shall grant a hearing. If the issue is dealing with a question of representation, the NLRB will direct a secret ballot election.

Unfair labor practice cases

A charge must be filed to invoke the authority of the board on an unfair labor practice case. An employee, employer, labor organization, or any other person can file a charge. The charge must be signed, sworn to, or affirmed under oath, and filed at the appropriate regional office. If an investigation shows there is a reasonable basis to believe an unfair practice has taken place, the NLRB will file a complaint stating the charges and notifying the charged party of a hearing to be held.

A NLRB administrative judge will preside over the hearing. The judge will make a finding and recommendations to the NLRB. At that point, the board is authorized to issue an order to cease and desist from illegal practices. The time limit on issuing a complaint is six months.

Power of the Board

The NLRB has the power to:

- Examine and copy any evidence of any person being investigated or proceeded against that relates to any matter under investigation or in question

- Issue subpoenas on the application of any party to the proceeding, requiring the attendance of witnesses or the production of evidence

- Administer oaths and affirmations, examine witnesses, and receive evidence

- Obtain a court order to compel the production of evidence or the giving of testimony

Penalties for Violations

Employers and unions can incur the following penalties for their failure to comply with the NLRA. The NLRA is remedial in nature rather than criminal, which means that it seeks to restore employees to the position they were in before the NLRA was violated and not to penalize the employer.

Employers:

- Disestablish an employer-dominated union

- Offer individuals immediate and full reinstatement to their former positions; or if the former positions no longer exist, offer substantially equivalent positions without harm to their seniority and other rights and privileges, including back pay with interest

Labor unions:

- Notify the employer and the employees that the union has no objection to the reinstatement of certain employees or the employment of certain applications whose discriminatory discharge or denial of employment was caused by the union

- Refund dues or fees illegally collected, plus interest

CASE STUDY: DO THE LAWS REALLY PROTECT THE EMPLOYEES?

Erick Trivedi

I believe that most employment law claims stem from lack of knowledge and to a degree, misinformation, instead of from a purposeful intent to discriminate against a particular employee. However, my most extraordinary case was with an employer who refused to pay an employee overtime. When the employee complained, the employer fired her, and then retroactively deactivated her health insurance the week before she had to undergo surgery.

Federal employment laws as they stand are insufficient in providing guidance to employers and in providing protection for employees. The best way to stay out of the litigation system is to maintain meticulous records on salaried employees, and to fully document every situation that arises within the context of complaints. Also, it is a good idea to build a relationship with an employer or small business lawyer before you need one.

It is true that most employment law cases settle before litigation. This is mainly due to the high cost of litigating to employers, and the fear of the liberal application of attorney's fees. One of the most challenging aspects of the practice of employment law is when your clients are businesses and they fail to understand that paying an attorney for preventative advice and assistance is much more cost-effective than the alternative.

Erick Trivedi has practiced in the employment law arena for the past two years. Trivedi handles mainly labor cases, representing small businesses.

Helpful Web Sites

NLRB Web site
www.nlrb.gov/index.aspx

Basic guide to NLRA
www.nlrb.gov/nlrb/shared_files/brochures/basicguide.pdf

NLRB details on NLRA and the board
**www.nlrb.gov/Workplace_Rights/employees_or_employ-
ers_not_covered_by_nlra.aspx**

List of examples of NLRA violations
www.nlrb.gov/workplace_rights/nlra_violations.aspx

State law considerations

Certain states will have right to work laws. Refer to the State Statutes Table
in Appendix B for more information.

Chapter 14

The Occupational Safety and Health Act

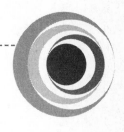

COMMON TERMS AND DEFINITIONS

Established federal standard: Any operative occupational safety and health standard established by any agency in the United States that is currently in effect.

National consensus standard: Any occupational safety and health standard or modification thereof that:

- Has been adopted by a nationally recognized standard-producing organization where interested parties have reached an agreement on the scope or provisions of the standard

- Has a standard that was formulated in a manner allowing an opportunity for diverse views to be considered

- Has been designated as a standard by the secretary of labor

Occupational safety and health standard: Standard that requires conditions, or the adoption or use of one or more practices, means, methods, operations, or processes reasonably necessary to provide a safe and healthy work environment.

Serious violation:	If there is a substantial probability that death or serious physical harm could result from a condition that exists or from one or more practices, means, methods, operations, or processes that have been adopted or are in use in a place of employment (unless the employer did not and could not, with using reasonable diligence, know the presence of the violation).
Workman's Compensation Commission:	National Commission on state workmen's compensation laws under OSH Act.

History and Purpose

The Occupational Safety and Health Act (the OSH Act) was enacted to address frequent occurrences of injuries and illnesses in the workplace and the subsequent burdens placed on commerce in the form of lost production, lost wages, medical expenses, and disability compensation payments. The OSH Act encourages employees and employers to reduce safety and health hazards at their places of employment by providing employers and employees with certain rights and responsibilities intended to promote safe working conditions. The OSH Act covers all employers, excluding federal, state, and local governments, and protects the employees of such employers. The OSH Act does not protect independent contractors or immediate family members of a farm operator.

NOTE: Most chapters in this book refer to the act in question by an acronym. The agency charged with administering the Occupational Safety and Health Act is the Occupational Safety and Health Administration, commonly referred to as OSHA. To avoid confusion between the act and the agency, this chapter will simply refer to the Occupational Safety and Health Act as the "OSH Act" and will use OSHA to refer only to the agency.

Employer Compliance and Requirements

Under the OSH Act, employers are required to furnish an employment environment free from recognized hazards that can cause or have caused serious physical harm or death to employees. Employers are also required to comply with the workplace standards set by OSHA and must also comply with record keeping, reporting, and notice requirements.

OSHA standards

There are four major categories for OSHA standards. The categories are general industry, construction, maritime, and agriculture. Some OSHA standards will apply to all four categories and some will apply only to specific categories. Standards that relate to employee access of medical and exposure records, personal protective equipment, and hazard communications are examples of some standards that apply to all four categories. Under the first standard, employees and OSHA representatives are guaranteed the right to access relevant medical records. These may include records detailing employee exposure to toxic substances. OSHA standards are expansive and often complex and detailed coverage of them is beyond the scope of this book.

Record keeping

Under the OSH Act, all employers, without consideration of any exceptions, are required to report the work-related death of any employee or the hospitalization of three or more of its employees. Additionally, employers who have 11 or more employees are required to prepare and maintain all records of occupational illnesses and injuries. Employers in most retail trade, finance, insurance, real estate, and service industries are exempt from this second requirement. A complete list of the industries that are exempt can be found at **www.osha.gov/pls/oshaweb**. If an employer owns more than one establishment and one of them is classified as a nonexempt industry, the employer must keep OSH Act injury and illness records for all of the companies.

Before an employer has a duty to keep records, the fatalities, injuries, or illnesses at issue must be work-related new cases that meet one or more of the general recording criteria.

An injury, fatality, or illness is work related if an event or exposure in the work environment either caused or contributed to the resulting conditions or greatly aggravated a pre-existing injury or illness. Work relatedness is presumed when injuries and illnesses occur in the work environment.

An injury, fatality, or illness is a new case if the employee has not had a prior recorded experience of the injury or illness of the same type that affects the same part of the body. It is also a new case if the employee has experienced the injury or illness but recovered completely and an event or exposure in the work environment caused the signs or symptoms to reappear.

An injury or illness meets the general recording criteria if it results in any of the following:

- Death
- Days away from work
- Restricted work or transfer to another job
- Medical treatment beyond first aid
- Loss of consciousness
- Significant injury or illness diagnosed by a physician or other licensed health care professional (even if it does not result in the symptoms listed above)

EVERYDAY
ILLUSTRATION Amy works at Acme Company, a manufacturing plant that employs 35 individuals. One
day at work, Amy slips and falls on a spill generated by one of
the machines, breaking her leg. Amy has never had any medical condition related to her leg. This injury must be reported by
Acme Company. It is work-related because it occurred at work
and was caused by working conditions. It is a new case because Amy has no history of any medical condition related to her
leg. Finally, it meets at least two of the general recording criteria:
the injury requires medical treatment beyond first aid and must
be diagnosed by a physician.

Any incident required to be reported should be reported using the injury
and illness record keeping forms. These forms are Form 300, Form 300A,
and Form 301. They may be located at **www.osha.gov/recordkeeping/
RKforms.html.**

All forms must be kept for five years and they must be available for inspection and copying by designated government agencies. The name of the
employee is normally used on the forms, unless there is an issue regarding
privacy. If so, it is acceptable under the act for the term privacy case to be
used instead of the employee's name.

Toxic substances

Employers must keep accurate records of employee exposure to potentially
toxic materials or harmful physical agents regulated by a standard that requires monitoring or measuring.

Employees and employee representatives will have rights to access and view
the exposure records. The records must include the following:

- Environmental monitoring data

- Biological monitoring results

- Material safety data sheets

- Any other record disclosing the identity of a toxic substance or harmful physical agent

Exposure records must be preserved for at least 30 years, and medical records must be preserved for the duration of the employee's employment plus 30 years. The information can be kept on microfilm, microfiche, or computer.

Notices and posters

All covered employers must display certain OSHA posters in a conspicuous place. A copy of that poster can be found at **www.osha.gov/Publications/poster.html**. Additionally, employees have the right to review the employer's OSHA Form 300. A summary of this form (Form 300A) must be posted in a location that is visible to employees. Form 300A must be posted by Feb. 1 the year after the year that is covered by the form and it must remain posted until April 30 of that year. A copy of Form 300A can be located at **www.osha.gov/recordkeeping/new-osha300form1-1-04.pdf#Page=8**.

Employee Rights and Responsibilities

Employees have the following rights under the OSH Act:

- To question unsafe conditions and request a federal inspection

- To assist OSHA inspectors on a limited basis

- To bring an action to compel the secretary of labor to seek injunctive relief in cases involving imminent danger to employees

- To gain access to information about his or her own health records and about exposure to dangerous substances

Employees can refuse to work in a hazardous work environment where they reasonably believe there is a real danger of death or injury and there is no time to take administrative action to eliminate the danger.

Employees have the duty to comply with all OSHA standards, rules, regulations, and orders. There are no penalties for employees if they fail to comply with the terms of the OSH Act.

Enforcement Agency and Procedures

The OSH Act is enforced by the Occupational Safety and Health Administration (OSHA), which is a part of the Department of Labor.

The Review Commission of OSHA has the authority to assess all civil penalties. The secretary of labor is authorized (after presenting proper credentials to business owner or agent in charge) to do the following:

- To enter any establishment or business where work is being performed by an employee.

- To inspect and investigate during regular working hours and at other reasonable times (within reasonable limits and manner) the actual place of employment and the conditions of the workplace. This includes, but is not limited to machines, apparatus, devices, equipment, and materials therein. The secretary may also question the owner, workers, operators, and agents privately.

If the secretary finds that an employer is in violation of the OSH Act, a citation shall be issued that sets out the nature of the violation, which will include a specific reference to the portion of the act that was violated. The citation will also set a time for the violation to be fixed.

The employer will have 15 days from his receipt of the citation to contest either the citation itself or the amount of the penalty. Also, an employee or representative of employees can file a notice with the secretary of labor stating that the period of time given to fix the violation is unreasonable.

If either of the above occur, the Review Commission will provide the employer with an opportunity for a hearing. After the hearing, an order shall be issued, which will become final 30 days after the hearing.

If the employer does not contest the citation within the 15-day time period and no employee files a statement with the commission, the citation and its corresponding assessment shall become a final order not subject to review by any court or agency.

Penalties for Violations

Civil

Civil penalties for violating the OSH Act can range from $0 to $70,000. Penalties increase as the likelihood of the violation resulting in serious harm to the employee grows. Willful violations or repeated violations of the OSH Act carry a civil penalty of no less than $5,000 or more than $70,000 for each violation. Citations for other-than-serious violations (those violations not considered serious) carry civil penalties up to $7,000 for each violation.

Employers who refuse or fail to correct the violation within the time frame set by the citation shall be assessed a penalty of not more than $7,000 for each day that the failure to correct the violation continues.

Violations of the posting requirements under the OSH Act carry a civil penalty of $7,000 for each violation.

Criminal

An employer who willfully violates the OSH Act and causes the death of an employee may be subject to a fine of no more than $10,000. In addition to the fine, the employer may face up to six months of imprisonment. However, if a violation is the employer's second conviction, the punishment shall be no more than $20,000 and the possible period of imprisonment could be up to one year.

An employer or anyone else who makes a false statement, representation, or certification in any application, record, report, plan, or other document filed or required to be kept in accordance with the OSH may be subject to a criminal fine of up to $10,000 and up to six months of imprisonment.

 Employers should remember that certain penalties under the OSH Act are assessed for each individual act. Therefore, multiple violations can cost employers a lot more than they may initially realize. The facts of *Chao v. Occupational Safety and Health Review Commission*, 480 F.3d 320 (5th Cir. 2007) demonstrate the possible severity of penalties for multiple violations.

In *Chao*, two related companies that shared facilities, Jindal and Saw Pipes, committed a total of 141 willful violations over a two-year period. The violations related to an intentional and knowing failure to record work-related accidents and illnesses.

The secretary of labor sought a penalty of between $8,000 and $9,000 for each willful violation. The companies contested the proposed penalties and the administrative law judge handling the case resolved the matter by grouping the individual violations of each company together and treating each company as if it had only committed one willful violation. Relying on the penalty provisions of the OSH Act that provide for a penalty between $5,000 and $70,000 for each willful violation, the administrative law judge assessed a penalty of $70,000 against each company.

The secretary appealed the decision to the Fifth Circuit Court of Appeals. The Fifth Circuit noted that the language of the statute requires that where the commission has found multiple violations, "a penalty between $5,000 and $70,000 for each violation" must be assessed (emphasis added).

 ...cntd.

The OSH Act creates a mandatory minimum penalty of $5,000 for each willful violation. The administrative law judge's decision to group the willful violations together and only assess a single $70,000 fine per company was, therefore, contrary to the clear language of the statute and improper. The Fifth Circuit vacated the opinion of the administrative law judge as to the amount of the penalties and sent the case back to him so that the correct penalty could be assessed. This penalty must take into account the mandatory $5,000 fine per violation established.

Helpful Web Sites

Information on record keeping
www.osha.gov/recordkeeping/index.html

OSHA information for small businesses
www.osha.gov/dcsp/smallbusiness/index.html

OSHA small business handbook
www.osha.gov/Publications/smallbusiness/small-business. html

Link to interactive training on occupation safety and health topics
www.osha.gov/dts/osta/oshasoft/index.html

OSHA safety and health topics — addresses individual industries and specific workplace hazards
www.osha.gov/SLTC/index.html

Links to various laws, rules, regulations, and interpretations dealing with OSHA
www.osha.gov/comp-links.html

State law considerations

OSHA does not prevent states from asserting jurisdiction over employers under state law that deals with occupational safety or health. If a state wants to take on responsibility for enforcement of any federal standard, the state will be required to submit a state plan for developing and enforcing said standards. The plan will have to be approved by the secretary of labor. The State Statutes Table in Appendix B provides information on states that have plans.

Chapter 15

Personal Responsibility and Work Opportunity Reconciliation Act

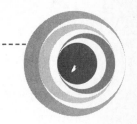

COMMON TERMS AND DEFINITIONS	
Income:	Any periodic form of payment due to a person. This includes wages, salaries, wages, commissions, bonuses, worker's compensation, disability, and pension payments.
Multi-state employers:	Employers who have the same business in more than one state.

History and Purpose

The Personal Responsibility and Work Opportunity Reconciliation Act (PRWORA) was signed into law in 1996 as part of the Welfare Reform Act. Title III of the PRWORA helps state agencies in charge of child support enforcement track down parents who are working and not paying child support. Title III requires states that receive Temporary Assistance to Needy Families block grants from the federal government to operate child support enforcement programs and implement certain data systems to monitor and enforce the payment of child support.

PRACTICALLY SPEAKING Instead of mandating that employers comply with federal reporting requirements for child support, the PRWORA creates an incentive for states to set certain standards for the collection of child support. While the PRWORA is a federal law, it is important to understand that employers submit to state requirements and not PRWORA. While the requirements of the states are set by the federal law, employers must look to state law to determine what they must comply with as far as child support withholding requirements are concerned.

Employers Subject to the PRWORA

- Private employers

- State and local governments

- The federal government

- Labor organizations

- Temporary and placement agencies that pay the employees from the fees collected from the employer

Protected Class of Employees

All newly hired employees are covered by Title III, including those that were fired and then rehired. There are exceptions to this general rule covered in the exceptions section of this chapter.

Employer Compliance and Requirements

Title III requires states to establish certain data systems to facilitate the collection from those individuals who owe child support. Specifically, Title III requires states develop a state-maintained directory of new hires and a unit to collect and disburse child support payments. The system that is set up is meant to facilitate withholding of child support payments from the paychecks of employees who owe child support.

All employers are required to report the name, address, and Social Security number of each new employee to their state's state directory of new hires office. The employer must also include its own name, address, and tax ID number when filing the report. The common method for reporting new hires is via the federal W-4 form. The W-4 can be sent out by first class mail, magnetically, or electronically. The report must be filed within 20 days of the date the employee is hired or (if the employer chooses to submit the report magnetically or electronically) by two transmissions a month. The transmissions must be between 12 and 16 days apart. Multi-state employers must choose a state to report to and report all new hires to the directory of new hires in that state.

Employers who receive a notice of withholding for child support are required to withhold that amount every month from the employee's income.

Exceptions to the general rule

Employees are not subject to the reporting requirements of Title III if they perform intelligence or counterintelligence for federal or state agencies and if their department head determines that reporting to the state could possibly place the employees in danger.

Penalties for Violations

State law governs penalties for violations of Title III. States have the option of fining employers $25 for each time they hire an employee but fail to send in a new hire report. Employers also can be fined up to $500 if they deliberately do not file the report at an employee's request.

CASE STUDY: HOW CLEAR IS THE LAW?

Hector deJesus
Lawyer & licensed health care
risk manager
The Law Firm of Hector M. deJesus, P.A.

The most egregious case I have handled dealt with a blatant act of pregnancy discrimination, where an employee told a company that a female colleague was pregnant. Within two weeks, the pregnant woman was fired. The current trend seems to be courts deciding cases in favor of employees; previously, the legal system leaned heavily in favor of employers, even in the face of laws that are enacted to protect employees. This trend seems to be changing back in favor of employees.

There is a corporate trend of diversity training, but I believe that the training is not having the required effect on lower level managers, who are most likely to have the greatest contact with employees. Upper management seems to understand what is required by law and actions that are prohibited, but the managers who deal with employees from day to day could benefit from either longer training periods or even continuing education classes to address the changes in employment law that occur frequently.

The best way for employers to avoid having a discrimination complaint or suit brought against them would be to ensure that all levels of supervisors and/or management buy in to the company's strict no tolerance guidelines for any type of prohibited behavior. Most employment law cases settle before they ever reach a courtroom. This is mostly attributable to the fact that employees are usually in need of the money and employers usually want to avoid the monetary and time cost of a long, drawn out court battle. It is also helpful if small businesses have an attorney on retainer to address small problems before they become full-blown complaints. In closing, federal employment law is a thrilling and fascinating area, yet poses challenges for employers, employees, and those representing them due to the ever-changing laws and sometime inconsistent court decisions.

Law is a second career for Hector deJesus. He first worked as a naval corpsman with the U.S. Navy and Marines. After his tour of duty ended, he attended nursing school and spent 12 years working in the health care industry, in both supervisory and management roles. He then attended law school and is currently working as a solo practitioner in a

> *variety of areas, including representing clients who have been a victim of employment discrimination. deJesus began his work in the employment arena when he received a case that dealt with a violation of the ADA. For the past two years, he has dealt with employment law cases, most of which have fallen under Title VII.*

Helpful Web Sites

1. Basic information regarding employers' requirements under the statute
   www.acf.hhs.gov/programs/cse/fct/irspam.htm

2. Basic information regarding the background of the PRWORA
   www.acf.hhs.gov/programs/cse/new/prwora.htm

3. Information geared toward ensuring that employers are in compliance with the act, including forms, publications and training materials
   www.acf.hhs.gov/programs/cse/newhire/employer/publication/publication.htm

4. Information specifically for private employers
   www.acf.hhs.gov/programs/cse/newhire/employer/private/index.htm

State law considerations

Each state has laws regarding the reporting of new hires. You can find information regarding each state law and the contact information for your state's child support enforcement offices at: **www.acf.hhs.gov/programs/cse/newhire/emplohyer/contacts/nh_matrix.htm**

Chapter 16

The Pregnancy Discrimination Act (PDA)

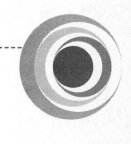

History and Purpose

The Pregnancy Discrimination Act (PDA) was passed in 1978 as an amendment to Title VII of the Civil Rights Act of 1964. The PDA was enacted to address employment discrimination on the basis of pregnancy. It applies to both women already in the workforce as well as those attempting to enter the workforce. The PDA was Congress' response to the Supreme Court's decision in General Electric v. Gilbert, 429 U.S. 125 (1976). In Gilbert, the court held that denying benefits for pregnancy-related disability did not amount to discrimination based on sex and was, therefore, not prohibited under Title VII of the Civil Rights Act of 1964. Congress passed the PDA to reverse this decision and bring pregnancy, childbirth and related medical conditions under the protection of Title VII.

Protected Class of Employees

The PDA protects all employees and job applicants of a covered employer.

Employers Subject to the PDA

The PDA applies to the following:

- Any company that has 15 or more employees

- Federal, state, and local governments

- Employment agencies

- Labor organizations

Prohibited Discriminatory Employer Acts

Employers subject to the PDA are prohibited from discriminating against pregnant women in employment-related matters. These include hiring, firing, seniority rights, job security, and the receipt of benefits. The protections of the PDA apply to current employees and potential employees. Prohibited actions may include refusing to hire a woman due to her being pregnant as long as she is able to perform the required job duties of the position for which she is interviewing.

Employers are barred from demoting or otherwise penalizing an employee on the basis of her pregnancy so long as she is able to perform her job. If the pregnant employee is temporarily unable to perform her job due to her pregnancy, an employer must treat the employee as a temporarily disabled employee. If this happens, the employer is required to provide other work assignments or modify the work that the employee is required to perform. In the event that the employee cannot work, the employer must provide either disability leave or leave without pay.

EVERYDAY
ILLUSTRATION   Mary, a sales representative for Acme Com-
                pany, is five months pregnant. Last week,
Mary missed two days of work due to a pregnancy-related
illness. When Mary returned to work, her boss, Joe, told her that
it was probably best for her to take an unpaid leave of absence
from Acme Company until after the birth of the child. Mary told
Joe her doctor had found no serious complications related to
her pregnancy or the illness and had told her she could continue
working in her normal job position. Mary also pointed out that
she had only missed two days of work. Joe ignored these facts
and placed Mary on unpaid leave, saying, "It is the best decision
for you and your baby at this time."

Under these facts, Joe has violated the PDA and Mary has a
claim against Joe and Acme Company for impermissibly discriminating under Title VII of the Civil Rights Act.

When an employee starts maternity leave, the employer must keep her position open for three months, the same length of time the position would
be held open for an employee on sick or disability leave. Pregnant employees are also entitled to receive health insurance coverage provided by
the employer at the same costs and under the same terms as for any other
medical condition. This means that employers already offering health insurance plans and temporary disability to employees must extend this coverage to include coverage for women during pregnancy, childbirth, and
related conditions.

PRACTICALLY
SPEAKING   Employers must provide the same health coverage and dis-
             ability benefits to pregnant employees that they provide to
other employees and ensure that this coverage covers pregnancy, childbirth, and related conditions. However, the PDA does not require employers
to provide health coverage or disability benefits to pregnant women if the
employers do not provide such coverage to their other employees.

If fringe benefits are provided to employees for other medical conditions, they must also be provided to pregnant employees. Also, pregnant employees must be treated the same as other employees on issues such as seniority, vacation, pay increases, and disability benefits. Issues regarding pregnancy leave are covered in the chapter dealing with the Family Medical Leave Act.

 As an employer, it is crucial that you have a stated nondiscriminatory reason for refusal to hire a pregnant applicant. In early 2007, maternity clothes retailer Mothers Work settled a pregnancy discrimination suit with the EEOC for $375,000. Mothers Work had been charged with violating the PDA by refusing to hire pregnant applicants. The company was also charged with firing an assistant manager for being pregnant and complaining about the company's policies toward pregnant employees and applicants.

Helpful Web Sites

General facts about pregnancy discrimination
www.eeoc.gov/facts/fs-preg.html

State law considerations

Each state has its own anti-discrimination law, which will encompass discrimination against law. State anti-discrimination laws are located in Appendix B.

Chapter 17

Title VII of the Civil Rights Act of 1964

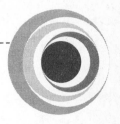

COMMON TERMS AND DEFINITIONS

Bona fide occupational qualification: An employer has to show that the discriminatory behavior is reasonably necessary to the normal operation of the particular business or enterprise.

Constructive discharge: Where the working conditions are so severe that a reasonable person would quit.

National origin: Country where a person was born or the country where his or her ancestors were born.

Race and/or color: This includes people classified as African Americans, Whites, Latinos, Asians, and Native Americans.

Religion: Religious beliefs and all aspects of religious observance and practice.

History and Purpose

The Civil Rights Act of 1964 was enacted in response to the turmoil of the civil rights movement and stands as a landmark piece of American legislation. The Civil Rights Act of 1964 secured a number of rights for minorities and contained several different titles, each of which provides a different set of rights to protected classes of citizens. Title VII, the relevant portion of the Civil Rights Act for our purposes, prohibits employer discrimination on the basis of race, color, religion, sex (including pregnancy), or national origin. (42 U.S.C. § 2000e-2).

Protected Class of Employees

Title VII covers employees who fall into one of the "protected classes" established by the statute. There are five protected classes: color, race, national origin, sex, and religion.

PRACTICALLY SPEAKING   To be entitled to Title VII protection, employees must be part of one of the protected classes designated in the statute. Discrimination not based on a protected class does not fall under the scope of Title VII. For example, Title VII does not prevent an employer from discriminating against an employee based on his or her weight. Weight does not fall into one of the five protected classes established by Title VII.

Employers Subject to Title VII

Title VII applies to all employers with at least 15 employees for at least 20 calendar weeks in the current or prior year. This includes private employers, and local, state, and federal government employers. Labor unions and employment agencies are also covered by Title VII.

The following employers are excluded from Title VII:

- Bona fide membership clubs

- Indian tribes

- Religious organizations (partial exclusion)

Employers and Title VII — What You Need to Know

To be in compliance with Title VII, employers must refrain from taking discriminatory or adverse actions when dealing with current and prospective employees. Employers are prohibited from taking action against current or prospective employees because of their race, national origin, sex, or religion.

PRACTICALLY SPEAKING Title VII prohibits employers from discriminating against an employee because of race, national origin, sex, or religion. It also prohibits employers from making employment decisions regarding that employee based on race, national origin, sex, or religion. For example, an employer who decides to penalize an employee based only on the fact that the employee is Hispanic violates Title VII. Similarly, an employer who refuses to hire an applicant simply because that applicant is from Iran violates Title VII.

Following are examples of the types of adverse employment actions prohibited when they are based on the employee's race, national origin, sex, or religion:

- Discharge

- Demotion

- Lack of promotion

- Harassment and retaliation

- Loss of benefits

- Loss of a distinguished title

- Diminished job responsibilities

- Constructive discharge

Prohibited Discriminatory Employer Actions

There are three main ways that employers can discriminate against current and prospective employees:

- Disparate treatment, also known as intentional discrimination. Disparate treatment occurs when current or prospective employees are discriminated against or treated differently because they are part of a protected class.

- Disparate impact on a protected group. Disparate impact occurs when an employer's practices, although meant to be neutral, have a negative impact on members of a protected class.

- Harassment aimed directly at a protected class.

EVERYDAY ILLUSTRATION The concept of disparate impact is illustrated by the following example. Acme Company is a beauty salon. As a matter of company policy, Acme Company hires only employees able to lift a 60 pound bag. If the effect of this policy is that only men are hired by Acme Company, the company's act of instituting the policy could be said to have a disparate impact on women that may violate Title VII.

Harassment by an employer can be based on any of the protected classes (for example, race, religion, sex, and national origin). There are two main types of sexual harassment — quid pro quo and hostile environment.

Quid pro quo harassment occurs when an employee is required to accept sexually harassing conduct as a condition of employment or suffers negative employment action due to not accepting the sexually harassing conduct. Sexually harassing conduct can consist of unwelcome sexual advances, requests for sexual favors, and any other verbal or physical conduct of an unwanted nature.

A hostile work environment exists when an employee is subjected to what that employee views as verbal or physical behavior of a sexual nature and when the conduct unreasonably interferes with the employee's performance or creates an intimidating, hostile, or offensive working environment.

Employer Liability

Generally, employers are liable for the illegal conduct of their employees toward one another. However, this liability does not arise automatically. The following situations are examples of when an employer will be liable for the conduct of employees:

- Co-worker harassment: Liability only arises if the situation was known or should have been known to the employer and the employer fails to take reasonable steps to correct the issue.

- Supervisor harassment: Liability arises when there is a hostile environment created by a supervisor with direct or higher authority over the harassed employee.

- Independent contractor harassment: Liability arises out of the independent contractor subjecting an employee to harassing conduct.

NOTE: Same-sex harassment can also create employer liability if the harassment is due to the employee's gender.

NOTE: Racial and/or ethnic jokes, slurs, and communications can form the basis for a violation as long as they create a hostile working environment as defined earlier.

Defenses

An employer can try to prove that reasonable care was taken to promptly prevent and correct the issue and that the employee did not take advantage of the preventative or cooperative opportunities to avoid the situation. It is worth noting that having an anti-harassment policy will not be allowed as a defense to a Title VII action.

Retaliation

Retaliation occurs when an employee suffers "real harm" as a result of exercising rights under Title VII. Employers must also refrain from discriminating against or creating a hostile work environment for current or former employees due to any of the following reasons:

- Filing charges with EEOC

- Assisting, testifying, or participating in a hearing

- Opposing any of the employer's illegal employment practices

<u>Employer Compliance and Requirements</u>

Reasonable Accommodations

Employers are under the duty to reasonably accommodate a current or prospective employee's religious holidays and practices. The only exception is if complying with this requirement causes an undue hardship on the employer's business.

Reporting

Private employers with 100 or more employees and certain federal contractors are required to file annual reports with the EEOC.

Posting

Employers must post notices regarding Title VII and prohibition of discrimination. These notices must be placed in places easily viewed by employees.

Record keeping

Employers who fall within the scope of the act must keep records on employees for at least one year. If an employee is fired, the employer must keep the records for a year after the firing takes place.

Enforcement Agency and Procedures

For an employee to file a Title VII claim, he or she must first follow the required procedures for filing a charge with the EEOC. Generally, an employee wanting to file a charge with the EEOC must do so within 180 days from the date the discrimination happens. Certain states have expanded this time limit.

The EEOC is vested with general enforcement powers, including the authority to fully investigate claims and to issue subpoenas. If the EEOC finds there is "reasonable cause" to believe the claim is true, an attempt must be made by the EEOC to resolve the issues using alternative dispute resolution.

NOTE: If the parties do not reach a resolution and the Justice Department decides not to litigate the case, the EEOC will issue a right to sue to the employee.

A right-to-sue letter is issued by the EEOC in the event that:

- EEOC does not believe "reasonable cause" exists to believe that the claim is true

- EEOC does not have jurisdiction over the charge

- Employee filing the claim cannot be found

- Employee filing the claim is uncooperative

- Filing party asks for the right-to-sue letter before the investigation is complete

If the right-to-sue letter is issued, the employee filing the charge has 90 days to sue from the date they receive the right-to sue-letter.

Special consideration for government employees

The Justice Department is the department vested with the authority to sue in local and state claims. The EEOC will issue a right-to-sue letter if the department chooses not to pursue the claim. Federal employees will be subjected to an internal process before they can file charges with the EEOC.

CASE STUDY: PREVAILING ON TITLE VII CLAIMS

Jennifer M. Smith
Associate Professor of Law
Florida A&M University College of Law
Tallahassee, Florida

How does employment litigation arise?

Many employment cases arise from employers' failure to adequately educate their workforce, as well as their failure to seriously address employee complaints.

However, one of the most blatant cases of retaliation of which I am aware was a case in which the plaintiff filed claims under Title VII and the Whistleblower (Protection) Act. In this case, the employer accidentally produced documents showing that the employer intentionally retaliated against the plaintiff because of the claims that he filed. The case settled. Thus, intentional acts of unlawful behavior still exist in the workplace.

Recent Developments

It is very difficult to prevail on Title VII claims, but much easier to win on retaliation claims. Recently, the Supreme Court ruled that two plaintiffs in two separate cases could bring retaliation claims against their employers under anti-discrimination statutes, even though the statutes do not men-tion a retaliation cause of action. These statutes are the Age Discrimination in Employment Act (ADEA) and Section 1981 of the Civil Rights Act of 1866, which is a Reconstruction era civil rights statute prohibiting race discrimination.

Employment laws could be stronger to offer more protection for employees, but judicial interpretation of employment laws has been weakening the laws. For example, the Supreme Court's recent interpretation of the Equal Pay Act's statute of limitations has severely limited the ability of employees to bring claims because of time limitations.

Diversity Training

Diversity training often helps corporations learn how to protect themselves better. For example, internal investigations often no longer result in a written report. Nevertheless, you generally find the same unlawful things happening in the workplace, even where there has been diversity training. I believe, however, that diversity training is helpful. Some corporations have even hired chief diversity officers. When such a position is created and it has real value in the corporation – and it is not just a title and an office – then it sends a signal that these corporations value a diverse workforce.

For employers who want to stay out of court, they should take employee complaints seriously and take action — (for example, termination/demotion/removal of the perpetrator) — if the investigation reveals that unlawful activity has taken place. You are your best monitor of your workplace, and frankly, the first monitor of your workplace.

Settlement

Most employment cases settle before going to trial. Even if you have sound evidence of unlawful activity, employment cases are still hard to win for plaintiffs. These cases are also expensive to litigate, and most plaintiffs' cases are taken on a contingency fee basis.

For small and large companies, hiring an attorney immediately upon receiving a notice of (a) charge being filed is recommended. It would be a good idea for smaller companies to have an attorney on permanent retainer, but often smaller companies cannot afford to do so.

Conclusion

There are many laws in the employment arena and many changes occurring with these laws. Good attorneys will be diligent in ensuring they keep up with the ever-evolving, complex area of employment law.

Smith received her J.D. from the University of Miami School of Law and her bachelor's of science from Hampton University in Hampton, Va. Before joining FAMU College of Law, Smith was a partner with the international law firm of Holland & Knight LLP. During her time with Holland & Knight, she was a trial lawyer who represented clients in a variety of litigation matters, including employment law. She has experience as lead counsel in jury trials, arbitrations and administrative hearings. Smith began handling employment matters in the mid-1990s and has represented both corporations and employees.

Penalties for Violations

Under Title VII, a prevailing employee may be entitled to equitable remedies, compensatory, and/or punitive damages. Unlike section 1981, there are limits set on how much an employee can be awarded in compensatory or punitive damages.

Whether an employee can be awarded compensatory and/or punitive damages is determined by the type of discriminatory behavior in which the employer was engaged. For instance, compensatory and punitive damages can be awarded in disparate treatment suits, but not in disparate impact suits.

Compensatory damage awards can consist of loss of future earnings and emotional pain, suffering, inconvenience, mental anguish, loss of enjoyment of life, and other non-monetary losses. Punitive damages are usually awarded in situations where the employer discriminates with malice or with reckless indifference. The court will look at whether the employer knew it was violating federal law, not necessarily whether the employer knew it was engaging in discrimination.

Punitive and compensatory damage limits

The award limits are set for a combined award of punitive and compensatory damages. The award limit directly corresponds with the number of employees. The guidelines for limiting awards are as follows:

- Employers with between 14 and 100 employees: $50,000

- Employers with between 101 and 200 employees: $100,000

- Employers with between 201 and 500 employees: $200,000

- Employers with more than 500 employees: $300,000

Equitable remedies

The court can enjoin the employer from the discriminatory practices it engages in and can order the reinstatement or hiring of employees (with or without back pay).

In regard to back pay and employee reinstatements, the complaining party must show that had it not been for the employer's discriminatory actions, the employee would have gotten the job or not been suspended and/or discharged. Future earnings are also part of the equitable remedies available under Title VII.

Attorney's fees and expert witness fees can be awarded to the prevailing party. An award of attorney's fees is within the court's discretion.

 **DELVING DEEPER** Title VII prohibits all types of intentional discrimination based on a protected trait. This includes discrimination directed at nonminorities. It is possible that employers attempting to avoid actions that create a disproportionately adverse impact (disparate impact) on one protected class will step into the trap of intentionally discriminating against others. The recent case of *Ricci v. DeStefano*, 129 S. Ct. 2658 (2009) highlights such a problem.

In *Ricci*, white firefighters sued the city and city officials, alleging the city violated Title VII by refusing to accept the results of an exam used to promote firefighters. The city refused to accept the results because it believed the results could have a disproportionately adverse impact on minority firefighters. The Supreme Court held that the city's refusal to accept the results violated Title VII because such refusal amounted to intentional

...cntd.

discrimination against nonminority firefighters. The court found that such intentional discrimination was not justified by the city's attempt to avoid an unintentional, disproportionately adverse impact on minority firefighters without more evidence that such an adverse impact would occur.

Even though the city's action may have been well-intentioned, the employment decision was based on race. Thus, the refusal of the exam results violated Title VII. The city's good-faith belief that such actions were necessary to avoid Title VII's adverse impact provisions was no defense.

Helpful Web Sites

Full Text of Title VII
   www.eeoc.gov/laws/statutes/titlevii.cfm

Compliance Assistance
   www.eeoc.gov/policy/docs/race-color.html

State law considerations

Each state has its own anti-discrimination law, some of which are stricter than federal laws. Appendix B has a list of state's anti-discrimination laws and their major guidelines.

Chapter 18
Uniformed Services Employment and Reemployment Rights Act

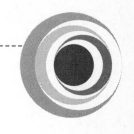

COMMON TERMS AND DEFINITIONS

Notice: Written or verbal notification of an obligation or intention to serve in the uniformed services. The notice can either be provided by the employee or by the division of the uniformed service that the employee is serving under.

Qualified (in regards to employment position): Having the ability to perform the required tasks of a position.

Reasonable efforts: Actions, including employer-sponsored training, that do not cause the employer any undue hardship.

Secretary: Secretary of labor or any person designated by the secretary of labor to carry out a role.

Seniority: Longevity in employment combined with benefits of employment governed by an individual's longevity in employment.

Undue hardship:	Actions that require significant difficulty or expense when viewed in relation to the following: (a) nature and cost of action; (b) overall financial resources of the facility or facilities providing the action (including the total number of employees, the effect on expenses and profits, and the overall impact of the action on the facility); (c) the overall financial resources of the employer (including the overall size of business, the number of employees, and the number, type, and location of its facilities); and (d) the type of business the employer is in (including the makeup, structure, and functions of the employer's workforce).
Uniformed service:	Includes service in the armed forces and active duty, active duty for training, inactive duty training, initial active duty training, and funeral honors duty that is performed by the National Guard and Reserves.

History and Purpose

The Uniformed Services Employment and Reemployment Rights Act (USERRA) was enacted in 1994 to help members of the uniformed services become re-employed upon returning from active duty. Under USERRA, it is illegal to engage in discriminatory employment practices against a person who is involved in the uniformed services. Through USERRA, Congress encourages employers to rehire employees who have served in the armed forces.

PRACTICALLY SPEAKING The USERRA seeks to ensure that those individuals who sacrifice their time to serve the United States as part of the armed services are not disadvantaged in their civilian careers due to their service.

Employers Subject to the USERRA

All private and government employers are subject to the USERRA. The USERRA also applies to any foreign entities controlled by U.S. corporations. The determination of whether a foreign company is controlled by a U.S. corporation depends on the degree to which operations of the two entities are interrelated, the overlap between management, whether there is centralized control of labor relations in the two entities, and whether there is common ownership or financial control between the two entities. A foreign entity controlled by an American employer shall be exempt from the USERRA only if complying with the USERRA violates the law of the country in which the foreign entity is based.

Protected Class of Employees

The USERRA covers all employees (including part-time and probationary employees) who are members of the uniformed services, including the Army, Navy, Marine Corps, Air Force, Coast Guard, and U.S. Public Health Service Commissioned Corps. Members of the National Reserves and the National Guard are also covered. While the USERRA seeks to protect civilian job rights for past, current, and future members of the uniformed services, it does not give such individuals preference in any employment matter over those who are covered by the USERRA.

Prohibited Discriminatory Employer Actions

Employers may not take the following actions against current, past, or intended members of the uniformed services:

- Refuse to hire, rehire, promote, or retain individuals based on their service in the uniformed service.

- Deny any benefit to individuals based on their service in the uniformed service.

Additionally, the USERRA prohibits an employer from retaliating against a protected employee for:

- Filing an action to enforce a right or benefit given by the USERRA.

- Testifying or making a statement in any proceeding under the USERRA.

- Assisting or participating in an investigation, or exercising a right provided by the USERRA.

Employer Compliance and Requirements

Notice

Employers must provide employees who are uniformed service members with a notice of the rights, benefits, and obligations such employees are provided under the USERRA. Employers can provide this notice by posting the "Your Rights Under USERRA" in the company location where such notices are normally posted. A copy of the notice is available at the DOL Web site: **www.dol.gov/vets/programs/userra/USERRA_Federal.pdf**.

Guidelines for reinstatement of employees

Individuals whose term of service was less than 91 days are entitled either to be reinstated in the position they would have held if they had never reported for service, or in the same position they held before they reported for service. An employer must make reasonable effort to bring individuals up to the new job requirements. Employers can only select the second option (reinstatement to same job position) if the individual is unable to perform the duties of the new position.

PRACTICALLY SPEAKING An employee's position that she would have held before her reporting purposes may not be the same position she held when she reported. The positions employees would have held but didn't due to their reporting for service include any jobs the employee would have been promoted to or transferred to had they remained at the company. If an employee can be prepared and placed in this new position through reasonable effort on the part of the employer, he or she must be placed in that position. If such placement would require more than reasonable efforts, the employee must be reinstated in his or her old job.

Consider the following example: Sue, a member of the National Guard Reserves, works as a page in Acme Company's office. It is company policy to automatically promote an individual who has worked as a page for 100 days to the position of assistant. The 100-day period is required as a safeguard to ensure that only those employees with a real interest in working at Acme Company attain the position of assistant. After working as a page for 92 days, Sue must report for military duty over a two-month period on account of her service in the National Guard Reserves. After serving two months, Sue reports back to Acme Company. Assuming Acme Company can inform and train Sue for the position of assistant through reasonable efforts, Acme Company must reinstate Sue as an assistant.

Individuals whose term of service was more than 90 days must be rehired for the position that they would have been in had they never reported for service, or they must be rehired for a position with the same benefits, status, seniority, and pay. Individuals who do not possess the qualifications for the new position after a reasonable effort by the employer to train them must be rehired in the same position they were in or a position with similar pay, status, and seniority.

An individual must be reinstated to another position that offers the same or similar seniority, status, pay, and benefits if he or she does not qualify for the position — due to a disability brought on (or made worse) by serving — that would have been held had the individual reported for duty.

If more than one individual is entitled to be rehired and more than one of them has returned to work, the first person to have left the position will have first claim to be rehired for that position. Subsequent individuals are entitled to re-employment in a position similar in status, seniority, and pay. If subsequent individuals are disabled, the rules governing disabled uniformed service individuals discussed earlier will apply.

Employee Rights and Responsibilities

An individual who served in the uniformed services and meets the following criteria will be entitled to the reinstatement rights and benefits of the USERRA:

- Individual must have had a civilian job
- Individual must have provided the employer with advance notice that she or he was leaving for duty in the uniformed services (unless giving notice was impossible or unreasonable)
- Individual's total period of time in the service must not be more than five years
- Individual cannot have been released from service due to dishonorable discharge
- Individual must have reported back to the civilian job within the required time frames

PRACTICALLY SPEAKING   If an employee's term of active duty is longer than five years while working for a particular employer, he or she will not qualify for the right and benefits of the USERRA.

The length of time that employees have to exercise the right of reinstatement is based on the length of their military service. No consideration is given to the type of job performed for the military when calculating the time period during which an employee must seek reinstatement. The statute sets time limits for employees to return to work based on the number of days the employee was in service.

The following list provides an overview of the applicable time frames.

- Employees in service for fewer than 31 days must return to work at the beginning of the first regular work week after returning home and getting an 8-hour rest period.

- Employees in service between 31 and up to 180 days must apply for re-employment within 14 days after completing term of service.

- Employees in service for more than 181 days must apply for re-employment not more than 90 days after completing term of service.

- Employees with service-related injuries or illnesses have up to two years to apply for re-employment.

- If reapplying for work is deemed impossible or unreasonable (by no fault of the employee) within the above time frames, then the employee must apply for re-employment as soon as possible.

If an individual fails to report to work or fails to apply for re-employment or employment within the time frames, it will not automatically bar him or her from the rights and benefits of the USERRA. The failure will subject the employee to the established policy and guidelines of the employer that deal with absence from scheduled work.

An employee who returns from a term of service is guaranteed to receive accrued pension plan benefits. He or she may also decide to keep employer-sponsored health coverage for up to 24 months. The employee would be responsible for up to 102 percent of the health coverage premiums unless the term of service was less than 31 days; in that case, the employee would only be responsible for the regular employee rate.

Exceptions to general rule

An employer is not required to re-employ a person if the employer's circumstances have changed so much that re-employment is impossible or unreasonable; if re-employment would impose an undue hardship on the employer; or if the employment left was temporary and the employee was aware that the employment was not to be for a significant length of time.

Enforcement Agency and Procedures

Individuals who feel as if their rights under the USERRA have been violated can file a complaint with the secretary of the Department of Labor, who will then investigate the claim. The complaint must be in writing and include the name and address of the employer along with a summary setting out the reasons why the claim is being filed.

The secretary must make a reasonable effort to get the employer to comply with the law if investigation found the claim to be valid. If the employer refuses to comply, the secretary will notify the employee of the results of the investigation and provide him or her with a notice of entitlement to proceed, which will allow the individual to proceed with the enforcement procedures outlined below.

An employee who receives notice that efforts to resolve a complaint were unsuccessful can request that the claim be forwarded to the attorney general. Upon finding that the claim is valid, the attorney general can represent the employee and file suit under the USERRA.

Also, an individual can file suit against a state or private employer if they did not apply to the secretary of labor for help, did not request that the attorney general review the case, or if they have been refused representation by the attorney general. Jurisdiction over the suit shall be given to the district courts of the United States for suits against both a state and a private employer. Even if the employer being filed against is a state government, the courts within that state will have jurisdiction to hear the suit.

Employees who receive a notice of entitlement to proceed may ask the secretary to forward the claim to be litigated in front of the Merit Systems Protection Board. The complaint will then be forwarded to the Office of Special Counsel. The Office of Special Counsel can then act as attorney for the employee or decide not to file an action.

The employee will then be able to file suit and have the case heard by the Merit Systems Protection Board. The board will have the power to order the federal employer to comply and/or compensate the employee for any loss wages or benefits, and for reasonable attorney, expert witness, and other litigation expenses if private counsel is utilized. Any order issued by the board can be appealed to the U.S. Court of Appeals.

Penalties for Violations

Employees that win an action under the USERRA may be entitled to the following:

- Employer being ordered to comply with the provisions of USERRA.

- Compensation for lost wages or benefits incurred by the employee due to the employer's failure to comply with the act.

- Compensation for liquidated damages equal to the amount of lost wages or benefits. (This is only if the court determines that the employer willfully failed to comply with the act.)

- Reasonable attorney fees, expert witness fees, and other litigation expenses if private counsel was hired to file suit.

Employers are subject to temporary or permanent injunctions, temporary restraining orders, and contempt orders if required to ensure that an individual's rights are protected.

DELVING DEEPER

In addition to reinstatement, employees who prevail in lawsuits related to the USERRA suits — especially employees who were highly compensated before leaving to service in the uniformed services — can be entitled to large amounts of damages. These damages become even larger when the employer is found to have willfully violated the USERRA. When considering whether to reinstate a former employee, employers should remember that a decision to violate the USERRA can be extremely costly. This decision can be especially costly when an individual's pay is based off commission estimates or asset growth.

In March 2009, Michael Serricchio, a former financial advisor for Prudential Securities (later renamed Wachovia Securities), was awarded $779,000 in back pay, damages, and attorney fees by a federal judge after a jury determined that Serricchio's employer violated the USERRA by refusing to reinstate him to the position he held before he was called to active duty. *Serricchio v. Wachovia Securities, LLC*, 606 F. Supp. 2d 256 (D. Conn. 2009). The judge also ordered Wachovia to reinstate Serricchio as a financial advisor.

During trial, the parties presented evidence to establish the amount of back wages and benefits to which Serricchio was entitled. As a financial advisor, Serricchio's wages were based on the return he was able to generate on the assets under his management. Serricchio's expert calculated his back wages by taking the hare of assets under his control when he left for military service and applying an estimated growth rate of those

DELVING DEEPER ...cntd.

assets based on expectations of the branch at which Serricchio worked. This helped determine Serricchio's rate of return, resulting in back pay of $1,052,009. Wachovia's expert used a similar calculation but used a growth rate based on the S&P 500 index, which resulted in a much smaller growth rate and, therefore, a smaller rate of return on the assets. This method resulted in back pay of $285,512.

The judge determined that neither approach was perfect. Serricchio's approach was imperfect because it assumed the assets would grow at the same rate indefinitely. Wachovia's approach was imperfect because it resulted in Serricchio's commissions falling significantly (from $80,000 to $35,000) and this result was inconsistent with the USERRA's purpose of reinstating veterans into positions equivalent to the position the veteran would have held had he never left. A drop in earnings of $45,000 would not approximate the job Serricchio had before he left for active duty.

The judge rejected both models and opted for a middle-ground model used at one point in the trial that estimated back wages of $680,312. From this number, the judge subtracted mitigated earnings equal to the amount of earnings Serricchio earned in a replacement position during the relevant period. This resulted in back wage damages of $389,453. The judge then doubled this amount because of a finding that Wachovia's actions violating USERRA were willful.

Helpful Web Sites

USERRA Fact Sheet
www.dol.gov/vets/programs/userra/userra_fs.htm

Broad overview of the USERRA
www.dol.gov/compliance/guide/userra.htm

Department of Labor site regarding the USERRA
www.dol.gov/vets/programs/userra/main.htm

State law implications

Federal or state laws that grant broader rights and benefits will not supersede the USERRA. The USERRA does overrule any state law that would reduce or limit the rights and benefits granted by the USERRA. For instance, state statute of limitations will not apply to actions under the USERRA.

Chapter 19
Worker Adjustment and Retraining Notification Act

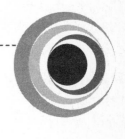

COMMON TERMS AND DEFINITIONS	
Operating unit:	Organizationally or operationally distinct product, operation, or specific work function within or across facilities at the single site.
Part-time workers:	Employees who have worked less than half of the 12-month period in the prior year or employees who average fewer than 20 hours a work week.
Reasonable expectation of recall:	When an employee understands that employment with a company has been temporarily interrupted but that he or she will be recalled to the same or a similar job.
Single site of employment:	Either a single location or a group of locations that are somehow connected.

History and Purpose

The Worker Adjustment and Retraining Notification Act (WARN) was enacted in 1988 to protect workers, their families, and their communities from unannounced layoffs and give them time to prepare for the move from their current job to a new job. The WARN requires certain companies to provide certain individuals with 60 days notice of plant closings and mass layoffs. The WARN provides standards for how, when, and to whom notice of layoffs should be provided.

Protected Class of Employees

Employees covered by the WARN include managers, supervisors, and salaried and hourly workers of employers subject to the WARN. Assuming that they work for a covered employer, the following categories of employees are covered by the WARN and are entitled to notice:

- Employees fired or laid off for more than six months

- Employees who have their working hours reduced by 50 percent within a six-month period due to a plant closing or a layoff

- Employees who are reasonably expected to lose employment due to a plant closing or a layoff

- Employees laid off or on leave but who have a reasonable expectation of recall

- Part-time employees

However, the following employees are not covered by the WARN and are, therefore, not entitled to WARN notice:

- Strikers or workers locked out due to a labor dispute

- Temporary workers aware of the temporary nature of the assignment when hired

- Business partners, consultants, or contract employees paid by another employer or who are self-employed

- Federal, state, and local government employees

Employers Subject to the WARN

The WARN applies to employers who have at least 100 employees, including private for-profit employers and private nonprofit employers. The WARN also applies to quasi-public entities separately organized from the government that operate in a commercial context. When counting employees, employers can exclude employees who worked fewer than six months during the last 12 months and employees who average less than 20 hours a week.

> ### EVERYDAY ILLUSTRATION
> Acme Company has 200 employees. One hundred of these employees are full-time workers who average 40 hours a week. Of the full-time employees, five were hired two months ago and the rest have worked for Acme Company for over two years. One hundred of Acme Company's employers are part-time workers who average 15 hours a week. In light of these facts, Acme Company is not covered by the WARN because it is considered to have only 95 employees for purposes of the WARN. Acme Company will not be required to provide WARN notice.

Employer Compliance and Requirements

Generally, employers are required to provide employees with 60 days advance notice of plant closings and mass layoffs. This notice is usually given to the workers, their labor representatives, the state's dislocated worker unit, and the local government.

Plant closing

An employer must provide WARN notice when closing a plant or other operating site if the closing affects at least 50 employees during any 30-day period. When calculating the number of employees affected, employers may exclude employees who worked fewer than six months in the prior 12 months and employees who work an average of fewer than 20 hours a week.

Mass layoffs

An employer must provide WARN notice of any mass layoff that will affect 500 employees at an employment site during a during a 30-day period. An employer must also provide WARN notice of any mass layoff that will affect 50 to 499 employees if they make up at least 33 percent (one-third) of the employer's active workforce. When calculating the number of employees affected, employers may exclude employees who worked fewer than six months in the prior 12 months and employees who work an average of fewer than 20 hours a week.

PRACTICALLY SPEAKING Employees who have worked fewer than six months over the previous 12 months and employees who work an average of less than 20 hours a week are not counted for purposes of determining whether an employer must give notice. However, they are entitled to WARN notice if the employer must give WARN notice.

Aggregate layoffs

When employment losses happen in stages, the number of employment losses at each stage may not be enough to trigger WARN notice. However, an employer is required to give WARN notice if the number of employment losses for each group of workers alone is not sufficient to trigger WARN notice, but the total number of the employment losses when added together reaches the threshold requirements during any 90-day period.

PRACTICALLY SPEAKING Job losses during a 90-day period will not be aggregated if they are the result of separate and distinct company decisions. This provision is meant to prevent employers from laying off workers in stages in an attempt to fall under the number thresholds and avoid WARN notice. Without this provision, a company could lay off 49 employees at a plant, wait 31 days and then lay off another 49 employees.

Requirements of the Notice

The employer must select the appropriate person within their company to prepare and deliver the notice to the affected employee and the required entities. Usually, the on site plant manager, personnel director, or a labor relations representative will provide the employees with the required notice.

When a company is being sold, the seller company and the buyer company will both be responsible for providing WARN notice if the sale involves a reduction in workforce that qualifies under the above mentioned thresholds. The seller will be responsible for providing WARN notice of plant closings and mass layoffs during the period of time up to and including the effective date and time of the sale. The buyer will be responsible for providing WARN notice of any plant closings and mass layoffs from the time he or she assumes ownership. No WARN notice is required if the sale does not result in a plant closing or mass layoff that reaches the above thresholds.

Timing of notice

An employer must notify employees 60 days in advance of their layoff. An employer can designate a two-week window in which layoffs are taking place. Notice can be served by any reasonable delivery method — for example, U.S. mail or hand delivery. Verbal notices or those placed in paychecks do not satisfy the notice requirement.

Contents of notice

When giving notice to an employee who is not in a union, an employer must include the following:

- Clear and specific language that is easily understood.

- Statement informing employees if the layoff is permanent, temporary, or a total plant closing.

- Date when the plant closing or layoffs will begin and date for when the employee will be released.

- Bumping rights existence.

- Name and number of a company official to contact for further information.

When giving notice to a state's dislocated worker unit and the head of the local government, an employer must include the following information in the notice:

- Name and address of where layoffs or plant closing is happening and the telephone number of a company contact person.

- Statement explaining if the loss of employees is temporary or permanent, or if the entire plant is being closed.

- Date of the first job losses and a schedule of the remaining employee releases.

- Job titles of positions included in the layoff or plant closing and the total number of employees in each category.

- Bumping rights existence.

- Name of each union/employee representative and name and address of the CEO of each union.

Employers can choose an alternative form of notice with less documentation but are still required to be able to provide the above documentation upon request. Failure to provide the information is considered to be a failure to give notice.

When providing notice to a union representative, the notice must include everything being reported to the state with the exception of the last two requirements.

Exceptions from 60-Day Notice

Temporary facilities

The WARN does not require an employer to provide notice if the plant closing results in the closing of a temporary facility. Employers are also not required to provide WARN notice if the mass layoff or plant closing is the result of the completion of a specific project and the employees were hired with the understanding that they were to be employed only for the limited duration of the specific project.

Specific Employees

WARN does not require an employer to provide notice to strikers or employees who are part of a bargaining unit involved in labor negotiations that result in a lockout if the strike or lockout is the equivalent of a plant closing or mass layoff. Employees who are not part of the bargaining unit involved in the negotiations are still entitled to WARN notice.

Natural disasters

The WARN does not require an employer to give 60 days of advanced notice when the plant closing or mass layoff is a result of a natural disaster or an unforeseeable business circumstance. An employer actively engaged in seeking capital or business who in good faith believes that providing WARN notice would prevent it from obtaining such capital or business is also excluded from providing WARN notice 60 days in advance. In these situations, an employer must give notice as soon as possible and comply with additional notice requirements.

Enforcement Agency and Procedures

A WARN action by employees, labor representatives, and units of the local government must be brought in the U.S. district courts. The DOL will only provide assistance in helping individuals, employers, and local governments in comprehending the law. The DOL has no enforcement powers in the context of WARN.

Penalties for Violations

Employers are liable to employees for damages equal to back pay and benefits for the period of the violation (up to 60 days). The damages will be reduced by any wages the employee receives over that time period. A court can also grant reasonable attorney's fees as part of costs.

Violations of the notice requirement to local governments will result in a civil penalty of up to $500 day for each day of noncompliance. An employer can avoid this penalty by taking care of the liability to each employee within three weeks after the layoffs or closings.

Helpful Web Sites

1. Guide to assist employers in understanding the basic provisions of the act
   www.doleta.gov/layoff/pdf/EmployerWARN09_2003.pdf-

2. WARN provisions in the event of a natural disaster
   www.doleta.gov/layoff/pdf/WARN_Natural_Disaster_Fact_Sheet.pdf

3. The Department of Labor's information page regarding the WARN
   www.dol.gov/compliance/laws/comp-warn.htm

4. Contact information for each state's dislocated workers unit
   www.doleta.gov/layoff/

5. Guide to assist employees
   www.doleta.gov/layoff/pdf/WorkerWARN2003.pdf

6. WARN fact sheet
   www.doleta.gov/programs/factsht/warn.htm

Conclusion

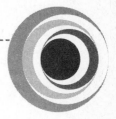

The Department of Labor alone enforces more than 180 employment laws, many of which can be overwhelming to read and interpret. By using this book as a guide, you the employer will be able to figure out what exactly your obligations are to your employees, and how to legally protect yourself and your company. It is not uncommon for a small business owner to be unfamiliar with the federal legalese surrounding employment, which is why this book provides a reference and background of each of the major laws that directly affect small businesses. While reading this book, you were able to lay your foundation and become familiar with the laws that are important to you overall.

Appendix A
Federal Agencies and Contact Information

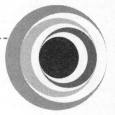

The following charts contain contact information for the federal agencies that have oversight over federal employment statutes.

DEPARTMENT OF HEALTH AND HUMAN SERVICES
200 Independence Avenue, S.W.
Washington, D.C. 20201
202-619-0257
877-696-6775 (toll free)
www.hhs.gov
Note: The ACF is a division of the Department of Health and Human Services. The ACF enforces PRWORA. - www.acf.hhs.gov

DEPARTMENT OF JUSTICE
950 Pennsylvania Avenue, NW
Washington, D.C. 20530-0001
202-514-2000
202-353-1555 (Office of the Attorney General)
www.usdoj.gov
Note: The Office of Special Counsel for Immigration Related Unfair Employment Practices is the division of the DOJ that enforces IRCA. Employer Hotline: 800-255-8255

DEPARTMENT OF LABOR
200 Constitution Ave., NW
Washington, D.C. 20210
866-4US-ADOL
www.dol.gov
Note: The following agencies within the department are vested with enforcement powers over certain employment statutes.
1. Employee Benefits Security Administration enforces COBRA and ERISA: www.dol.gov/ebsa
2. The Employment and Training Administration issued the regulations that enforce WARN: www.doleta.gov
3. The Occupational Safety and Health Administration enforces the OSH act and SOX: www.osha.gov/index.html
4. The Veterans Employment and Training Service enforces USERRA: www.dol.gov/vets
5. The Wage and Hour Division enforces the EPPA, FLSA, and FMLA: www.dol.gov/esa/whd

EQUAL EMPLOYMENT OPPORTUNITY COMMISSION
131 M Street, N.E.
Washington, D.C. 20507
202-663-4900
800-669-4000
www.eeoc.gov
Enforces the following: ADA, ADEA, EPA, GINA, OWBPA, PDA, and TITLE VII

FEDERAL TRADE COMMISSION
600 Pennsylvania Avenue, NW
Washington, D.C. 20580
202-326-2222
877-382-4357
www.ftc.gov
Enforces the FCRA

INTERNAL REVENUE SERVICE
1500 Pennsylvania Avenue, NW
Washington, D.C. 20220
800-829-4933 (for businesses)
800-829-1040 (for individuals)
www.irs.gov
Enforces COBRA and ERISA in conjunction with the EBSA

NATIONAL LABOR RELATIONS BOARD
1099 14TH St. N.W.
Washington, D.C. 20570
202-273-1991
866-667-6572
www.nlrb.gov
Enforces NLRA

SECURITIES AND EXCHANGE COMMISSION
100 F Street, N.E.
Washington, D.C. 20549
202-551-6000
888-SEC-6585
www.sec.gov
Enforces certain sections of SOX

CITIZENSHIP AND IMMIGRATION SERVICES
U.S. Department of Homeland Security
Washington, D.C. 20528
202-282-8000
800-375-5283
www.uscis.gov/portal/site/uscis
Enforces certain portions of IRCA

Appendix B
State Statutes Tables

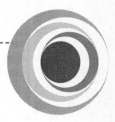

Below you will find tables for each state and the main national territories. Each table will provide the following information:

- Web site and contact information for the state's department of labor.

- A general statement of each state law that has a corresponding federal statute, with a citation to the state law.

The coverage information section is a general statement of what the law entails. There are many exceptions and nuances to each state law, so look up the statute to get a complete picture of what your state requires. Note that ERISA and SOX preempt state law, so no information is provided.

ALABAMA

Alabama Employment Agencies and State Employment Laws		
Department of Labor	**www.alalabor.state.al.us**	
	RSA 6th Floor, P.O. Box 303500 Montgomery, AL 36130-3500 334.342.3460	

	www2.dir.state.al.us Department of Industrial Relations has important job market information regarding the state of Alabama.	
Federal Statute	Corresponding State Statue coverage	State Statute (AL Code Section)
ADEA	Age discrimination (40 and over)	§ 25-1-20
ADA	Covers discrimination against disabled individuals by state employer.	(Same as above)
COBRA	Provides continuation coverage for victims of domestic abuse who lose coverage as a result of divorce, separa- tion, custody change, or termination of coverage of insured.	§27-55-3(4)
EPPA	Refer to Department of Labor Web site listed above.	
ERISA	N/A	
EPA	N/A	
FRCA	N/A	
FLSA	No minimum wage law.	
FMLA	Covers all state employees and a majority of local employees. Provides sick leave for illness, injury, or death of family member. Also provides maternity and bodily injury leave.	
GINA	N/A	
IRCA	N/A	
NLRA	Private: Illegal for union membership or payment of dues to be a job require- ment. Also, protects the right to orga- nize, join, and not join a union or strike. Public: Employers under duty to receive wage/hour and working condition proposals.	Private: §25-7-30, §25-7-6 Public: §11-43-143
OSHA	N/A	
OWBPA	N/A	

PRWORA	Employers must report new employees within seven days of hire or rehire to the following: Department of Industrial Relations New Hire Unit 649 Monroe St, Room 2683 Montgomery, AL 36131 334.353.8491	§25-11-1
PDA	State employees can use sick time for pregnancy disability under specific conditions.	AL Acts of 2005-526
SOX	N/A	
TITLE VII - TITLE VII	N/A	
USERRA	Covers active members of the following: National Guard, Naval Militia, Alabama State Guard, or U.S. Reserves.	§31-2-13, § 31-12, §31-12-7
WARN	**www.doleta.gov/layoff/rapid_coord. cfm** — Offers a link to state WARN offices.	

ALASKA

Alaska Employment Agencies and State Employment Laws		
Department of Labor	**www.labor.state.AK.us** Department of Labor & Workforce Dev. P.O. Box 11149, Juneau, AK 99822-2249 907.465.2700	
Federal Statute	Corresponding State Statue coverage	State Statute [AK Stat.]
ADEA	Covers age discrimination no matter the size of the employer.	§18.80.010 et seq.
ADA	Prohibits discrimination based on physical and mental disabilities. There is no employer size requirement.	§18.80.010 et seq.
COBRA	N/A	
EPPA	Refer to Department of Labor Web site listed above.	
ERISA	N/A	

EPA	Prohibits discrimination based on gender.	§18.80.10 et seq.
FCRA	Follows federal law.	§12.62.160(b)
FLSA	Minimum wage is $7.15.	§23.10.065
FMLA	Covers public agencies with 21 or more employees during a 20-week period the two weeks before leave requests that are also within a 50-mile radius. Covers the following employees: Those who have worked a minimum of 35 hours (a week) for a consecutive six-month period or worked a minimum of 17.5 hours (a week) in the preceding year.	§23.10500 et seq.
GINA	N/A	
IRCA	N/A	
NLRA	Private: N/A; also, no right-to-work laws. Public: Employees have the right to organize for collective bargaining purposes. Noncertified school employees will not be covered. The public employer is required to negotiate and enter into agreements, with employee organization, in regard to pay rates, hours worked, and other employment terms.	§23.40.075
OSHA	The state laws are administered by the Division of Labor Standards and Safety Department of Labor and Workforce Development.	§18.60.010
OWBPA	See Title VII	
PRWORA	All employees and all employers are covered. The required information must be reported within 20 days of hire/rehire.	§25.27.075

PDA	The state law covers all employers, unions, and employment agencies. It prohibits discrimination based on sex, pregnancy, childbirth, and related medication conditions including marital status or parenthood.	§18.80.010, et seq., 29.25.080
SOX	N/A	
TITLE VII-TITLE VII	State law prohibits employers of any size discriminating against employees on the basis of age, sex, religion, national origin, ancestry, color, race, marital status, changes in marital status, including pregnancy, and childbirth.	§18.810.010 et seq.
USERRA	Employees who are also part of state militia are protected when ordered for active duty by the governor. Employers are prohibited from discriminating against members of the National Guard or naval militia.	§26.05.340, 075, §39.20.340, 345, 350.
WARN	**www.doleta.gov/layoff/rapid_coord. cfm** — Offers a link to state WARN offices.	

ARIZONA

Arizona Employment Agencies and State Employment Laws		
Department of Labor	**www.ica.state.AZ.us**	
	Arizona Industrial Commission 800 West Washington Street Phoenix, AZ 85007 602.542.4515	
Federal Statute	Corresponding State Statue coverage	State Statute {AZ Rev. Stat. Ann.}
ADEA	Private employers with 15 or more employees are prohibited from discriminating against people over age 40.	§41-1463, et seq.

ADA	Private employers with 15 or more employees are prohibited from discriminating against employees/applicants who are disabled.	§41-1463, et seq.
COBRA	The state law will cover all disability insurance policies with the exception of disability income, accidental death/dismemberment policies, or single term nonrenewable policies.	§20-1377
EPPA	Refer to state Department of Labor Web site listed above.	
ERISA	N/A	
EPA	Prohibits discrimination on the basis of gender by private companies with 15 or more employees.	§41-1463, et seq.
FRCA	Follows federal law.	§44-1693(d)
FLSA	Minimum wage is $6.90.	§23-362
FMLA	State law covers all state employers and employers with 50 or more employees. The following individuals are entitled to leave: All state employees, employees that are victims of crime, or an immediate family member of someone who is killed or incapacitated.	§13-4439
GINA	Employers with 15 or more employees are prohibited from discriminating against individuals based on genetic test results.	§41-1463, et seq.
IRCA	N/A	
NLRA	Private: Agricultural employees have the right to organize. Public: Public employee salaries are fixed by law.	§23-1381, et seq. §23-350, §9-284
OSHA	Agency that administers: Division Of Occupational Safety and Health/Industrial Commission. Laws are the same as federal.	§23-401, §23-427(A)
OWBPA	N/A	

PRWORA	All employers must report all employees within 20 days of hire or rehire.	§23-722.01
PDA	Employers with 15 or more employees or state employers are prohibited from discriminating on the basis of sex, maternity, and pregnancy. State employees get 40 hours of sick time for pregnancy.	§41-1443
SOX	N/A	
TITLE VII	Prohibits discrimination against employees based on national origin, race, color, religion, age, disability, or genetic test results. Employers must have 15 or more employees for the state law to apply.	§41-1463
USERRA	National Guard has the right to assume active duty, attend camps, drills, and so forth. When called by governor for state duty, service members will get the same protection as if they were on federal active duty. Employers are not allowed to discriminate against an employee due to his or her status as a National Guard member.	§26-167-168, §38-610, §38-298
WARN	**www.doleta.gov/layoff/rapid_coord. cfm** — Offers links to state WARN offices.	

ARKANSAS

Arkansas Employment Agencies and State Employment Laws		
Department of Labor	**www.arkansas.gov/labor**	
	Arkansas Department of Labor 10421 West Markham Little Rock, AR 72205 501.682.4500	

Federal Statute	Corresponding State Statute coverage	State Statute [AR Stat. Ann.]
ADEA	See Title VII	
ADA	See Title VII	
COBRA	Employee will receive 120 days of coverage if covered three months prior to separation.	§23-56-1114
EPPA	Refer to the state Department of Labor-Web site listed above.	
ERISA	N/A	
EPA	See Title VII	
FCRA	Follows federal law.	
FLSA	Minimum wage is $6.25.	§11-4-210(a)
FMLA	Applies to state employees, public school teachers, and staff.	§21-4-201
GINA	See Title VII	
IRCA	N/A	
NLRA	Private: Right to work. Public: Right to join or not join unions.	(1)§11-3-301 (2) AR Const. Amendment 34
OSHA	N/A	
OWBPA	N/A	
PRWORA	Report new hire within 20 days of hire/rehire.	§11-10-901
PDA	Covers state employers with 15 or more employees.	§16-123-101
SOX	N/A	
TITLE VII	Prohibits discrimination on basis of race, religion, national origin, gender, disability, genetic tests.	§11-5-401
USERRA	Covers individuals who are members of the state's National Guard or state militia.	§12-62-801 - §12-62-808
WARN	N/A	

CALIFORNIA

California Employment Agencies and State Employment Laws		
Department of Labor	**www.dir.CA.gov/dlse** **www.labor.CA.gov**	
	California Labor and Workforce Development Agency 445 Golden Gate Ave., 10th FL San Francisco, CA 94102 916.263.1811	
Federal Statute	Corresponding State Statue coverage	State Statute [CA Stat.]
ADEA	See Title VII	
ADA	See Title VII	
COBRA	CAL-COBRA covers employers with two to 19 employees not covered by federal law.	§10128.50-10128.58 CA Ins. Code
EPPA	Refer to the state labor department Web site listed above	
ERISA	N/A	
EPA	See Title VII	
FCRA	Follows federal law.	CA Civil Code §1785.13.6, §1785.20.5, §1786, §1786.18(a)(7)
FLSA	Minimum wage is $8.	
FMLA	Public and private employers with more than 50 employees.	CA Govt Code §12945.2
GINA	See Title VII	
IRCA	N/A	
NLRA	Private: No right to work; agricultural employees can join or not join union. Public: Can participate or not participate in employee organization.	1. CA labor Code §110 2. CA Govt code §3502-§3522
OSHA	Same as federal with some additional restrictions added in record keeping, penalties, and knowledge.	Generally CA Labor Code §6300
OWBPA	N/A	

PRWORA	Report new hire/rehires within 20 days.	CA Unemm. Ins. Code §1088.5
PDA	Employers with five or more employees. (See Title VII)	CA Govt Code §43.3
SOX	N/A	
TITLE VII	Prohibits discrimination and harassment on the basis of race, religion, color, age, disability, gender, and genetic tests.	CA Govt Code §12940
USERRA	Individuals in the U.S. Reserves, National Guard, or Navy.	CA Govt Code §19771
WARN	**www.doleta.gov/layoff/rapid_coord. cfm** — Offers links to state WARN offices.	

COLORADO

Colorado Employment Agencies and State Employment Laws		
Department of Labor	**www.COworkforce.com**	
	Colorado Department of Labor and Employment 633 17th Street, 2nd FL Denver, CO 80202-3660 888.390.7936	
Federal Statute	Corresponding State Statue coverage	State Statute [CO Rev. Stat.]
ADEA	See Title VII	
ADA	See Title VII	
COBRA	Covers all employers and generally gives 18 months after termination of coverage with exceptions.	§10-16-108
EPPA	Refer to state Department of Labor Web site listed above.	
ERISA	N/A	
EPA	See Title VII	
FCRA	Follows federal law.	§12-14-.3-105.3

FLSA	Minimum wage rate is $7.02.	§8-6-108.5
FMLA	Covers state employers and state employees with at least one year of service.	4 Code of CO Regs §801
GINA	N/A	
IRCA	N/A	
NLRA	Private: No right to work law. The Labor Peace Act will cover all private employers with eight or more employees. Public: N/A	§8-3-101
OSHA	N/A	
OWBPA	N/A	
PRWORA	Report new hires/rehires within 20 days.	§26-13-125
PDA	Covers all employers no matter the size.	§24-34-402
SOX	N/A	
TITLE VII	Prohibits discrimination or harassment based on ancestry, national origin, race, religion, disability, and gender.	
USERRA	Individuals who belong to state National Guard or U.S. Reserves entitled to 15 days.	§28-3-506
WARN	**www.doleta.gov/layoff/rapid_coord. cfm** — Offers links to state WARN offices.	

CONNECTICUT

Connecticut Employment Agencies and State Employment Laws		
Department of Labor	**www.CT.gov/dol**	
	Connecticut Department of Labor 200 Folly Brook Blvd. Wethersfield, CT 06109-1114 860.263.6000	

Federal Statute	Corresponding State Statue coverage	State Statute [CT Gen. Stat.]
ADEA	§26-13-125	
ADA	§26-13-125	
COBRA	All employers covered — generally for an 18-month period.	§31-51o
EPPA	Refer to state Department of Labor Web site listed above.	
ERISA	N/A	
EPA	See Title VII	
FCRA	Follows federal law.	§54-142n, §540142o
FLSA	Minimum wage rate is $7.65.	§31-58(j)
FMLA	Private employers with 75 or more employees and state agencies.	§31-51kk
GINA	See Title VII	
IRCA	N/A	
NLRA	Private: All private employers covered with exception of farmers; no right to work law. Public: Covers state, local employees, and teachers; strikes are illegal.	§31-101, §5-270
OSHA	N/A	
OWBPA	See Title VII	
PRWORA	Report new hires/rehires within 20 days.	§31-254(b)
PDA	Covers employers with three or more employees, labor organizations, employment agencies. (See Title VII)	§46a-60, §46a-64
SOX	N/A	
TITLE VII	Prohibits discrimination on the basis of ancestry, national origin, race, color, religion, age, disability, martial status, genetic information, and sex (includes sexual harassment).	§46a-60, §46a-81c
USERRA	Covers employees who are in the National Guard, U.S. Reserves, and state military.	§27-53, §5-255
WARN	N/A	

DELAWARE

Delaware Employment Agencies and State Employment Laws		
Department of Labor	**www.Delewareworks.com**	
	Delaware Department of Labor 4425 N. Market St., 4th FL Wilmington, DE 19802 302.451.3423	
Federal Statute	Corresponding State Statue coverage	State Statute [DE Code. Ann.]
ADEA	See Title VII	
ADA	See Title VII	
COBRA	N/A	
EPPA	Refer to state Department of Labor Web site listed above.	
ERISA	N/A	
EPA	See Title VII	
FRCA	Follows federal law.	
FLSA	Minimum Wage is $7.15.	§9-902a
FMLA	Covers state employees who are full time and have been working for one continuous year.	§19-5116, §19-5501, §19-5551
GINA	See Title VII	
IRCA	N/A	
NLRA	Private: N/A Public: Employees can organize and bargain, but are barred from striking.	Public: Title 19 §1301
OSHA	N/A	
OWBPA	See Title VII	
PRWORA	Report hires/rehires within 20 days.	§13-2208
PDA	Private employers with more than four employees and all state and local government employees. (See Title VII)	§19-710
SOX	N/A	

TITLE VII	Prohibits discrimination based on national origin, race, color, age, genetic tests, disability, sex, and pregnancy-related conditions.	§19-710
USERRA	Covers National Guard members called to state duty.	§20-905, §29-5105
WARN	**www.doleta.gov/layoff/rapid_coord. cfm** — Offers links to state WARN offices.	

D.C.

District of Columbia Employment Agencies and State Employment Laws		
Department of Labor	**www.DOES.DC.gov**	
	D.C. Employment Services Department 613 New York Ave., NE Suite 300 Washington, DC 20002 202.671.1900	
Federal Statute	Corresponding State Statue coverage	State Statute [DC Code Ann.]
ADEA	See Title VII	
ADA	See Title VII	
COBRA	Covers employees of employers with less than 20 employees not covered by federal COBRA.	§32-731
EPPA	Refer to state Department of Labor Web site listed above.	
ERISA	N/A	
EPA	See Title VII	
FRCA	Follows federal law.	
FLSA	Minimum wage rate is $7. Employers are required to pay federal minimum wage rate plus $100 if higher.	§32-1003

FMLA	Covers all district employers with 20 or more employees. Employees must have at least one year of service equaling 1,000 hours in 12 months to qualify.	§32-501, §32-1201
GINA	See Title VII	
IRCA	N/A	
NLRA	Private: Covered by federal law. Public: Employees have right to form or join a labor organization and to exercise collective bargaining (court personnel not included).	Public: §1.617.01
OSHA	N/A	
OWBPA	See Title VII	
PRWORA	New hires/rehires must be reported within 20 days.	§46-116.01
PDA	Covers all employers. (See Title VII)	§2-1401.05
SOX	N/A	
TITLE VII	Prohibits discrimination/harassment based on race, color, religion, national origin, sex (includes pregnancy), age, personal appearance, sexual orientation, family responsibilities, smoking, political affiliations, genetic information, or disability by employers no matter what the size.	§2-1401, §7-1703.03
USERRA	N/A	
WARN	**www.doleta.gov/layoff/rapid_coord. cfm** — Offers links to state WARN offices.	

FLORIDA

Florida Employment Agencies and State Employment Laws		
Department of Labor	**www.floridajobs.org**	

	Agency for Workforce Innovation The Caldwell Building 107 East Madison St., Suite 100 Tallahassee, FL 32399-4120 800.342.3450	
Federal Statute	Corresponding State Statue coverage	State Statute [FL Stat.]
ADEA	See Title VII	
ADA	See Title VII	
COBRA	Covers employers with fewer than 20 employees for hospital, medical and HMO plans. Covers employees for 18 months after termination or reduction in hours.	§627.6692
EPPA	Refer to state Department of Labor Web site listed above.	
ERISA	N/A	
EPA	See Title VII	
FCRA	Follows federal law.	
FLSA	Minimum wage is $6.69.	
FMLA	Covers state agencies, victims of domestic violence, employers with 50 or more employees. Employee must have worked for employer for at least three months.	§110.221
GINA	N/A	
IRCA	N/A	
NLRA	Private: N/A Public: Public employees have the right to organize and enter into collective bargaining agreements. Public employees are barred from striking.	Private: N/A Public: §447.201, §447.401(4)
OSHA	N/A	
OWBPA	See Title VII	
PRWORA	Hires and rehires must be reported within 20 days.	§409.2576

PDA	Covers employers with 15 or more employees. (See Title VII)	
SOX	N/A	
TITLE VII	Prohibits discrimination on the basis of ancestry, national origin, race, color, religion, age, handicap, marital status, sex, sickle cell trait, AIDS, and other related diseases. Prohibits sexual harassment.	§760.01, §383.15, §448.075
USERRA	Public and private employers are prohibited from discriminating against individuals because they belong to the state National Guard or Reserves.	§250.481
WARN	**www.doleta.gov/layoff/rapid_coord. cfm** — Offers links to state WARN offices.	

GEORGIA

Georgia Employment Agencies and State Employment Laws		
Department of Labor	**www.dol.state.GA.us**	
	Georgia Department of Labor Sussex Place, Room 600 148 Andrew Young International Blvd, NE Atlanta, GA 30303 404.656.3011	
Federal Statute	Corresponding State Statue coverage	State Statute [GA Code Ann]
ADEA	See title VII	
ADA	See title VII	
COBRA	All employers are covered.	§33-24-21.1
EPPA	Refer to state Department of Labor Web site listed above.	
ERISA	N/A	
EPA	See Title VII	
FRCA	Follows federal law.	§35-3-34(b)

FLSA	Act preempted by federal law.	§34-4-3(a)
FMLA	Covers public school teachers and staff.	§20-2-850
GINA	N/A	
IRCA	N/A	
NLRA	Private: N/A Public: Employees do not have the right to enter into collective bargaining; firefighters are exempt.	Private: N/A Public: §25-5-3 §45-19-1
OSHA	N/A	
OWBPA	See title VII	
PRWORA	New hires and rehires must be reported within 10 days of employment.	§19-11-9.2
PDA	Covers public employers with 15 or more employees. (See Title VII)	§45-19-20 §31-1-9
SOX	N/A	
TITLE VII	Prohibits private employers from discriminating on basis of age, sex, or disability. Public employers are prohibited from discrimination on the basis of national origin, race, color, religion, age, disability, or sex.	§34-5-1, §34-1-6, §34-6A-1
USERRA	Covers permanent private employers.	§38-2-279, §38-2-280
WARN	**www.doleta.gov/layoff/rapid_coord. cfm** — Offers links to state WARN offices.	

HAWAII

Hawaii Employment Agencies and State Employment Laws		
Department of Labor	**www.hawaii.gov/labor**	
	Hawaii Department of Labor and Industrial Relations 830 Punchbowl Street Honolulu, HI 96813 808.586.8842	

Federal Statute	Corresponding State Statue coverage	State Statute [HI Rev. Stat]
ADEA	See Title VII	
ADA	See Title VII	
COBRA	Covers all employers.	§393-15
EPPA	See Title VII	
ERISA	N/A	
EPA	See Title VII	
FRCA	Follows federal law.	§378-2.5(a)(b)
FLSA	Minimum wage rate is $7.25.	§387-2
FMLA	Public employers and private employees with 100 or more employees who have had at least six months of service.	§398
GINA	See Title VII	
IRCA	N/A	
NLRA	Private: All employers not covered by federal labor law are covered and have the right to organize, bargain, and strike Public: Employees can join any labor organization and bargain collectively.	Private: §377-1 Public: §89-1Las
OSHA	Follows federal law.	§396-1
OWBPA	See Title VII	
PRWORA	All hires/rehires must be reporting within 20 days of employment.	§576D-16C
PDA	Covers all public and private employers no matter what the size. (See Title VII)	§378-1, §367-3
SOX	N/A	
TITLE VII	Statute prohibits discrimination on basis of ancestry, race, color, religion, age, sex, disability, genetic information, sexual orientation, martial status, arrest, or court record. Lie detector tests are prohibited as a condition of employment by any employer no matter the size.	§378-1
USERRA	Covers private employees who are members of the National Guard.	§121-43

| WARN | www.doleta.gov/layoff/rapid_coord.cfm — Offers links to state WARN offices. | |

IDAHO

Idaho Employment Agencies and State Employment Laws		
Department of Labor	**www.labor.Idaho.gov**	
	Idaho Department of Labor 317 W. Main St. Boise, ID 83735-0001 208.332.3579 800.843.3193	
Federal Statute	Corresponding State Statue coverage	State Statute [ID Code]
ADEA	See Title VII	
ADA	See Title VII	
COBRA	N/A	
EPPA	Refer to state Department of Labor Web site listed above.	
ERISA	N/A	
EPA	See Title VII	
FRCA	Follows federal law.	
FLSA	As of 07/24/08, minimum wage is $6.55.	§44-1502, §44-1503
FMLA	N/A	
GINA	See Title VII	
IRCA	N/A	
NLRA	Private: Covers agricultural workers. Public: Teachers and firefighters have the right to organize and bargain collectively.	Private:§22-4101 Public: §31-1271, §44-1801
OSHA	N/A	
OWBPA	See Title VII	
PRWORA	All hires/rehires must be reported within 20 days.	§72-1601

PDA	Private employers, government agencies, labor organization, and employment agencies with five or more employees are covered. (See Title VII)	§67-5901
SOX	N/A	
TITLE VII	Covers state agencies and private employers with five or more employees and bars them form discriminating on the basis of race, national origin, color, sex, religion, and disability.	§67-5901
USERRA	Covers permanent employees who are members of the state's National Guard or Reserves.	§46-224, $45-216
WARN	**www.doleta.gov/layoff/rapid_coord. cfm** — Offers links to state WARN offices.	

ILLINOIS

Illinois Employment Agencies and State Employment Laws		
Department of Labor	**www.state.IL.us/agency/idaho.gov**	
	Illinois Department of Labor 160 N. LaSalle Street, 13 Fl, Suite C-1300 Chicago, IL 60601 317.232.2655	
Federal Statute	Corresponding State Statue coverage	State Statute [IL Comp. Stat.]
ADEA	See Title VII	
ADA	See Title VII	
COBRA	Covers all employers, and all employees for nine months after termination.	§367e
EPPA	Refer to state Department of Labor Web site listed above.	
ERISA	N/A	
EPA	See Title VII	
FRCA	Follows federal law.	20 §2635/7

FLSA	As of 07/01/08, minimum wage is $7.75.	§105/4(a)
FMLA	Covers state agencies and their employees who are full time.	§303.148, §303.90
GINA	See title VII	
IRCA	N/A	
NLRA	Private: N/A Public: Public and school employees have the right to organize and enter into collective bargaining.	Private: N/A Public: 5-315/1
OSHA	N/A	
OWBPA	See Title VII	
PRWORA	New hires and rehires must be reported within 20 days of employment.	§405/1801.1
PDA	Covers employers with 15 or more employees. (See Title VII)	
SOX	N/A	
TITLE VII	Prohibits discrimination due to ancestry, national origin, race, color, religion, age, disability, sex, sexual orientation, marital status, arrest records, citizenship status, military status, and victims of domestic abuse. Also covers discrimination on the basis of genetics.	§82-55/1
USERRA	Employers are barred from discrimination against individuals on the basis of military status. Covers employers with 15 or more employees.	§5/1-501
WARN	**www.doleta.gov/layoff/rapid_coord. cfm** — Offers links to state WARN offices.	

INDIANA

Indiana Employment Agencies and State Employment Laws		
Department of Labor	**www.IN.gov/labor**	

	Indiana Department of Labor Indiana Government Center South 402 W. Washington Street, RM W195 Indianapolis, IN 46204 317.232.2655	
Federal Statute	Corresponding State Statue coverage	State Statute [IN Code]
ADEA	See Title VII	
ADA	See Title VII	
COBRA	Covers employers that have between three and 50 employees.	§27-8-15-31.1
EPPA	Refer to state Department of Labor Web site listed above.	
ERISA	N/A	
EPA	See Title VII	
FRCA	Follows federal law	
FLSA	Minimum wage is $5.15 or federal wage if employer has two or more employees.	§22-2-2-4
FMLA	Covers state employers and employers with 50 or more employees.	§1-9-4, §1-9-8
GINA	See Title VII	
IRCA	N/A	
NLRA	Private: Employees have right to organize. Public: Educational employees have right to organize and enter into collective bargaining.	Private: 22-6-1-2 Public: §20-29-1-1
OSHA	Follows federal law.	§22-8-1.1, §22-8-1.1-43.1
OWBPA	See Title VII	
PRWORA	Employers must report hires/rehires within 20 days.	§22-4.1-4.2
PDA	Employers with six or more employees are covered. (See Title VII)	§22-9-1.1
SOX	N/A	

TITLE VII	Prohibits discrimination on the basis of ancestry, national origin, race, color, religion, age, disability, and off-duty use of tobacco products.	§22-9-1-1, §22-5-4-1
USERRA	Covers permanent employees who are members of the state's National Guard or Reserves.	§10-17-4-1
WARN	N/A	

IOWA

Iowa Employment Agencies and State Employment Laws		
Department of Labor	**www.iowaworkforce.org/labor**	
	Iowa Workforce Development 1000 East Grand Avenue Des Moines, IA 50319-0209 515.242.5870	
Federal Statute	Corresponding State Statue coverage	State Statute [IA Code]
ADEA	See Title VII	
ADA	See Title VII	
COBRA	Covers all employers and employees for up to nine months after termination.	§509B.3
EPPA	Refer to state Department of Labor Web site listed above.	
ERISA	N/A	
EPA	See Title VII	
FRCA	Follows federal law.	
FLSA	Minimum wage is $7.25.	§91D-1
FMLA	Covers all state government, agencies, and state employees. (See Title VII)	§70A-1
GINA	See Title VII	
IRCA	N/A	

NLRA	Private: N/A; workers to have right to organize. Public: Employees have the right to organize and to bargain collectively.	Private: §22-6-1-2 Public: §20.1
OSHA	Follows federal law.	§875-2.1(88)
OWBPA	See Title VII	
PRWORA	All hires/rehires must be reported within 15 days of employment.	§252G.1
PDA	All employers no matter the size are covered.	§135.30A
SOX	N/A	
TITLE VII	Employers are prohibited from discrimination and harassment on basis of national origin, race, color, creed religion, age, disability, sex, and genetic test results.	§216.6
USERRA	Covers employees of the National Guard or Reserves and applies to public and private employers.	§29A.28
WARN	**www.doleta.gov/layoff/rapid_coord. cfm** — Offers links to state WARN offices.	

KANSAS

Kansas Employment Agencies and State Employment Laws		
Department of Labor	**www.dol.KS.gov**	
	Kansas Department of Labor 401 S.W. Topeka Blvd. Topeka, KS 66603-3182 785.296.5000	
Federal Statute	Corresponding State Statue coverage	State Statute [KS Stat. Ann.]
ADEA	See Title VII	
ADA	See Title VII	

COBRA	Covers all employers and covers employees for nine months after termination.	§40-2209
EPPA	Refer to state Department of Labor Web site listed above.	
ERISA	N/A	
EPA	See Title VII	
FRCA	Follows federal law.	
FLSA	As of 01/01/10, minimum wage is $7.25.	§4-1203(ab)
FMLA	Covers all state employers and employees.	Admin Regs1-9-5, 1-9-6
GINA	See Title VII	
IRCA	N/A	
NLRA	Private: Workers have the right to orga-nize, strike, and bargain collectively. Public: Workers generally have right to organize and bargain collectivell, but do not have the right to strike.	Private: §44-614, §44-615 Public: §75-4321
OSHA	N/A	
OWBPA	See Title VII	
PRWORA	Employers must report hires/rehires within 20 days.	§75-5742
PDA	See Title VII	
SOX	N/A	
TITLE VII	Covers the state and employers with at least four people and prohibits discrimi-nation on the basis of ancestry, national origin, race, color, religion, age, disabil-ity, sex, or any genetic testing.	§44-1001
USERRA	Covers private employers.	§48-222
WARN	**www.doleta.gov/layoff/rapid_coord. cfm** — Offers links to state WARN offices.	

KENTUCKY

Kentucky Employment Agencies and State Employment Laws		
Department of Labor	**www.labor.KY.gov**	
	Kentucky Department of Labor 1047 U.S. Hwy 127 South, Suite 4 Frankfort, KY 40601-4381 502.564.3070	
Federal Statute	Corresponding State Statue coverage	State Statute [KY Rev. Stat.]
ADEA	See Title VII	
ADA	See Title VII	
COBRA	Covers all employers not covered by federal law due to number of employees. Provides 18 months of coverage after termination.	§304.18-110
EPPA	Refer to state Department of Labor Web site listed above.	
ERISA	N/A	
EPA	See Title VII	
FRCA	Follows federal law.	§367.310
FLSA	Minimum wage rate is $6.55.	§337.275(1)
FMLA	Provides adoption leave for public and private employees and covers all state employers and employees.	§337.015
GINA	N/A	
IRCA	N/A	
NLRA	Private: N/A Public: Police and firefighters can organize and bargain collectively, but all public employees are barred from striking.	Private: N/A Public: §345.010
OSHA	Follows federal law.	§338.011
OWBPA	See Title VII	
PRWORA	Employers must report hires/new hires within 20 days.	§405.435

PDA	See Title VII	
SOX	N/A	
TITLE VII	Employers with eight or more employees prohibited from discrimination on basis of national origin, race, color, religion, age, sex (includes pregnancy and related conditions).	
USERRA	Covers employees who are members of the state's National Guard.	§38.250, §61.394, §61.375
WARN	**www.doleta.gov/layoff/rapid_coord. cfm** — Offers links to state WARN offices.	

LOUISIANA

Louisiana Employment Agencies and State Employment Laws		
Department of Labor	**www.LAworks.net**	
	Louisiana Department of Labor P.O. Box 94094 Baton Rouge, LA 70804-9094 207.623.7900	
Federal Statute	Corresponding State Statue coverage	State Statute [LA Rev. Stat.]
ADEA	See Title VII	
ADA	See Title VII	
COBRA	Covers all employees and employers not covered by federal COBRA. Provides them with 12 months of coverage.	§22.215.7
EPPA	Refer to state Department of Labor Web site listed above.	
ERISA	N/A	
EPA	See Title VII	
FRCA	Follows federal law.	
FLSA	N/A	
FMLA	Covers employers will more than 25 employees.	§23.341

GINA	See Title VII	
IRCA	N/A	
NLRA	Private: Right to organize and collective bargain. Public: N/A	Private: §23.822 Public: N/a
OSHA	N/A	
OWBPA	See Title VII	
PRWORA	Employers must report hires/new hires within 20 days.	§46.236.14
PDA	See Title VII	
SOX	N/A	
TITLE VII	Covers employers with 20 or more employees and prohibits discrimination based on national origin, race, religion, age, color, sex (includes pregnancy and related conditions), and genetic information.	§23.301
USERRA	Covers employees called to active duty in National Guard, state militia, or any other military force.	§29.38 §42.392
WARN	**www.doleta.gov/layoff/rapid_coord. cfm** — Offers links to state WARN offices.	

MAINE

Maine Employment Agencies and State Employment Laws		
Department of Labor	**www.state.ME.us/labor**	
	Maine Department of Labor 45 Commerce Street Augusta, ME 04330 207.623.7900	
Federal Statute	Corresponding State Statute coverage	State Statute [ME Rev. Stat. Ann, title 24A]
ADEA	See Title VII	

ADA	See Title VII	
COBRA	Covers all employers not covered by federal COBRA. Generally will provide coverage for one year after termination.	§2809-A
EPPA	Refer to state Department of Labor Web site listed above.	
ERISA	N/A	
EPA	See Title VII	
FRCA	Follows federal law.	
FLSA	Minimum wage is $7.	§663
FMLA	Covers private employers with 15 or employees, all state employers, and local government employers with 25 or more employees. Covers employees who have worked for one consecutive year.	§26-7-VI-A-843
GINA	See Title VII	
IRCA	N/A	
NLRA	Private: N/A Public: State, local, and university employees have right to organize and bargain collectively. Employees are barred from strikes.	Private: N/A Public: 9-A§961
OSHA	N/A	
OWBPA	See Title VII	
PRWORA	Employers must report new hires/re-hires within seven days.	19-A§2154
PDA	See Title VII	
SOX	N/A	
TITLE VII	Covers all employers and prevents them from discrimination on basis of ancestry, national origin, race, color, religion, age, disability, sex (includes pregnancy/related conditions), and genetic test results.	

| USERRA | Covers employees who are members of National Guard, Reserves, state military forces. | Tit. 37-B §342 |
| WARN | **www.doleta.gov/layoff/rapid_coord. cfm** — Offers links to state WARN offices. | |

MARYLAND

Maryland Employment Agencies and State Employment Laws		
Department of Labor	**www.dllr.state.MD.us**	
	Maryland Department of Labor and Industry 500 N. Calvert Street, Suite 401 Baltimore, MD 21202 410.767.2357	
Federal Statute	Corresponding State Statue coverage	MD State Statute (varied)
ADEA	See Titile VII	
ADA	See Titile VII	
COBRA	Covers all employees and provides employees with 18 months of protection.	MD Ann. Insurance code §15-401 and §15-409
EPPA	Refer to state Department of Labor Web site listed above.	
ERISA	N/A	
EPA	See Title VII	
FRCA	Follows federal law.	§14-1203(a)(5)
FLSA	Minimum wage is $6.15.	MD Labor and Empl. Code Ann. §3-413
FMLA	Covers state employers and employees.	MD Code State Pers. & Pens. §9-1001
GINA	See Title VII	
IRCA	N/A	

NLRA	Private: Collective bargaining allowed. Public: State employees will have the right to organize and bargain collectively.	MD Code Ann. §4-101 Public: State Pers. & Pens. Code §3-301
OSHA	Same as federal law.	MD Code Ann. Lab. & Empl. §5-101
OWBPA	See Title VII	
PRWORA	Employers must report hires/rehires within 20 days.	MD Code Lab. & Empl. §8-626.1
PDA	See Title VII	
SOX	N/A	
TITLE VII	Covers state agencies, local governments and private employers with 15 or more employees and prohibits them from discriminating based on national origin, race, color, religion, disability, age, sex (includes pregnancy/related conditions), marital status, and genetic information.	MD Code. Ann. 49B§1
USERRA	Covers National Guard employees.	MD Code Pub. Safety §13-705 and §13-707
WARN	**www.doleta.gov/layoff/rapid_coord. cfm** — Offers links to state WARN offices.	

MASSACHUSETTS

Massachusetts Employment Agencies and State Employment Laws		
Department of Labor	**www.Mass.gov/eolwd** **www.state.ma.us**	
	Massachusetts Department of Labor and Work Force Development One Ashburton Place, Rm 2112 Boston, MA 02108 617.626.7100	
Federal Statute	Corresponding State Statue coverage	State Statute [MA Gen. Laws]
ADEA	See Title VII	

ADA	See Title VII	
COBRA	Covers employers with two to 19 employees. Provides 18 months of coverage after termination.	Ch. 175§110G
EPPA	Refer to state Department of Labor Web site listed above.	
ERISA	N/A	
EPA	See Title VII	
FRCA	Follows federal law.	Ch. 93§52, Ch. 151B§4
FLSA	Minimum wage rate is $8.	Ch. 151§1
FMLA	Covers all public and private employers with six or more employees. Covers employees that have finished probationary period or at least been employed for three months.	Ch. 149 §105D
GINA	See Title VII	
IRCA	N/A	
NLRA	Private: Covers all employees with exception of agricultural, domestic, and those working for parents/spouses. Public: Employees have the right to organize and bargain collectively, but do not have the right to strike.	Private: Ch.150A §1 Public: Ch. 150E§1
OSHA	N/A	
OWBPA	See Title VII	
PRWORA	Employers must report hires and rehires within 14 days.	62E§2
PDA	19-A§2154	
SOX	N/A	
TITLE VII	Covers state employers and private employers with more than six employees. Employers are prohibited from discrimination against employees on the basis of ancestry, national origin, race, religion, color, age, sex (includes related/related matters), arrest records, disability, sexual orientation, marital status, and genetic information.	151B§1

| USERRA | Covers permanent employees who are members of the U.S. Reserves. | 52A §149 |
| WARN | **www.doleta.gov/layoff/rapid_coord. cfm** — Offers links to state WARN offices. | |

MICHIGAN

Michigan Employment Agencies and State Employment Laws		
Department of Labor	**www.Michigan.gov/cis**	
	Michigan Department of Labor and Economic Growth P.O. Box 30004 Lansing, MI 48909 517.335.0400	
Federal Statute	Corresponding State Statute coverage	State Statute [MI Comp. Laws Ann.]
ADEA	See Title VII	
ADA	See Title VII	
COBRA	N/A	
EPPA	Refer to state Department of Labor Web site listed above.	
ERISA	N/A	
EPA	See Title VII	
FRCA	Follows federal law.	§37.2205
FLSA	Minimum wage is $7.40.	§408.384(1)
FMLA	N/A	
GINA	N/A	
IRCA	N/A	

NLRA	Private: Covers all private employers with exception of those that fall under the Railway Labor Act, and all employees with exception of agricultural, domestic, employees of parent/spouse, and managerial positions. Public: Employees have right to organize and bargain collectively.	Private: §423.1 Public: §423.201
OSHA	Generally same as federal; there are certain informational posting requirements regarding the state law.	§408.1001
OWBPA	See Title VII	
PRWORA	Employers must report hires/rehires within 20 days.	§552.626
PDA	19-A§2154	
SOX	N/A	
TITLE VII	Covers all employers and bars them from discriminating on the basis of national origin, race, color, religion, age, disability, height, weight, arrest record, marital status, and sex (pregnancy/related conditions). Also prohibits sexual harassment.	
USERRA	Covers employees who are members of state or U.S. military/naval services.	§32.273, §34.351
WARN	**www.doleta.gov/layoff/rapid_coord.cfm** — Offers links to state WARN offices.	

MINNESOTA

Minnesota Employment Agencies and State Employment Laws		
Department of Labor	**www.doli.state.MN.us**	
	Minnesota Department of Labor and Industry 443 Lafayette Road North St. Paul, MN 55155 651.284.5070	

Federal Statute	Corresponding State Statute coverage	State Statute [MN Stat.]
ADEA	See Title VII	
ADA	See Title VII	
COBRA	Covers all employers, and gives employees up to 18 months of coverage.	§62A.16
EPPA	Refer to state Department of Labor Web site listed above.	
ERISA	N/A	
EPA	See Title VII	
FRCA	Follows federal law.	§13C.02
FLSA	Minimum wage is $6.14.	§177.24(a)
FMLA	Covers all employers with 21 or more employees at one site. Covers employees with at least one year of employment.	§181.940
GINA	N/A	
IRCA	N/A	
NLRA	Private: Covers all employers except public employers and those covered by the Railway Labor Act. Also covers all employees except family-based business, agricultural labor, and domestic. Public: All employees have right to organize and bargain collectively; employees in occupations essential to the facilitation of government are barred from striking; however, the remainder may strike under certain circumstances.	Private: §179.01 Public: §179A.01
OSHA	Follows federal law.	§182.65
OWBPA	See Title VII	
PRWORA	Employers must report hire/rehires within 20 days.	§256.998
PDA	19-A§2154	
SOX	N/A	

TITLE VII	Covers all employers and prevents them from discriminating on basis of national origin, race, color, religion, creed, age, disability, sexual prefer-ence, membership activity, public assistance, marital status, sex (pregnancy/related conditions) and sexual harassment.	§ 363A.03, §181.938
USERRA	Covers employees who are members of state or federal military service.	§43A.183, §192.261, 262
WARN	**www.doleta.gov/layoff/rapid_coord. cfm** — Offers links to state WARN offices.	

MISSISSIPPI

Mississippi Employment Agencies and State Employment Laws		
Department of Labor	**www.mdes.MS.gov**	
	Mississippi Department of Employment Security P.O. Box 1699 Jackson, MS 39215-1699 225-342-3111	
Federal Statute	Corresponding State Statue coverage	State Statute [MS Code Ann.]
ADEA	See Title VII	
ADA	See Title VII	
COBRA	Covers all employers and gives employ-ees 12 months of coverage.	§83-9-51
EPPA	Refer to state Department of Labor Web site listed above.	
ERISA	N/A	
EPA	See Title VII	
FRCA	Follows federal law.	
FLSA	N/A	
FMLA	Covers most public employers and generally full-time employees.	§24-3-91

GINA	N/A	
IRCA	N/A	
NLRA	Private: N/A Public: N/A	Private: N/A Public: N/A
OSHA	N/A	
OWBPA	See Title VII	
PRWORA	Employers must report hire/rehires within 15 days.	§43-19-46
PDA	See Title VII	
SOX	N/A	
TITLE VII	Covers state employers only and prohibits discrimination on basis of race, color, religion, sex, national origin, disability, age, or political affiliations.	§33-1-5, §25-9-103, §71-7-33
USERRA	Covers permanent employees who are members of the U.S. Reserves.	§33-1-19, §33-1-121
WARN	**www.doleta.gov/layoff/rapid_coord. cfm** — Offers links to state WARN offices.	

MISSOURI

Missouri Employment Agencies and State Employment Laws		
Department of Labor	**www.dolir.MO.gov/lirc**	
	Missouri Department of Labor and Industrial Relations P.O. Box 599 3315 W. Truman Boulevard Jefferson City, MO 65102-0599 573.751.7500	
Federal Statute	Corresponding State Statue coverage	State Statute [MO Rev. Stat]
ADEA	See Title VII	
ADA	See Title VII	

COBRA	Covers employers not covered by federal COBRA and provides employees with nine months of coverage after termination.	§376.428
EPPA	Refer to state Department of Labor Web site listed on previous page.	
ERISA	N/A	
EPA	See Title VII	
FRCA	Follows federal law.	
FLSA	Minimum Wage is $6.65.	§290.502
FMLA	Covers state government employers and employees.	§105.271
GINA	See Title VII	
IRCA	N/A	
NLRA	Private: N/A Public: Covers public employees with exception of law enforcement officials and educators. All employees have the right to organize and bargain collectively. All public employees are prohibited from striking.	Private: N/A Public: §105.500
OSHA	N/A	
OWBPA	See Title VII	
PRWORA	Employers must report hires/rehires within 20 days.	§285.300
PDA	See Title VII	
SOX	N/A	
TITLE VII	Covers state and local governments and private employers with more than six employees. Bars discrimination on the basis of ancestry, national origin, race, color, religion, age, disability, sex, and genetic information.	§213.010, §290.145, §375.1306
USERRA	Covers employees who are part of the state military.	§40.490, §105.270, §41.942

WARN	www.doleta.gov/layoff/rapid_coord.cfm — Offers links to state WARN offices.	

MONTANA

Montana Employment Agencies and State Employment Laws		
Department of Labor	www.dli.MT.gov	
	Montana Department of Labor and Industry P.O. Box 1728 Helena, MT 59624-1728 406.444.9091	
Federal Statute	Corresponding State Statue coverage	State Statute [MT Code Ann.]
ADEA	See Title VII	
ADA	See Title VII	
COBRA	Covers all employers and provides employees with one year of coverage after termination.	§33-2-507
EPPA	Refer to state Department of Labor Web site listed above.	
ERISA	N/A	
EPA	See Title VII	
FRCA	Follows federal law.	§31-3-112
FLSA	Minimum wage rate is $6.25.	§39-9-409
FMLA	Covers only state government employers and permanent state employees.	§49-2-310
GINA	See Title VII	
IRCA	N/A	
NLRA	Private: N/A Public: Employees have right to organize, bargain collectively. The right to strike varies according to the occupation.	Private: N/A Public: §39-31-101
OSHA	N/A	

OWBPA	See Title VII	
PRWORA	Employers must report hires/rehires within 20 days.	§40-5-922
PDA	See Title VII	
SOX	N/A	
TITLE VII	Covers all employers and prohibits discrimination based on national original race, color, creed, religion, age, disability, marital status, or sex (pregnancy/ related conditions).	§49-2-101
USERRA	Generally covers employees who are in U.S. service positions, Reserves, or National Guard.	§10-1-603 §10-2-211
WARN	**www.doleta.gov/layoff/rapid_coord. cfm** — Offers links to state WARN offices.	

NEBRASKA

Nebraska Employment Agencies and State Employment Laws		
Department of Labor	**www.Nebraskaworkforce.com**	
	Nebraska Department of Labor 550 South 16th Street, Box 94600 Lincoln, NE 68509-4600 402.471.9000	
Federal Statute	Corresponding State Statute coverage	State Statute [NE Rev . Stat.]
ADEA	See Title VII	
ADA	See Title VII	
COBRA	Covers employees not covered by federal COBRA and provides employees with six months of coverage after termination.	§44-1640
EPPA	Refer to state Department of Labor Web site listed above.	
ERISA	N/A	

EPA	See Title VII	
FRCA	Follows federal law.	
FLSA	Minimum Wage is $6.55.	§48-1023(1)
FMLA	Covers state government employers and employees who have been with employer for past year on full-time basis.	NE Admin. & Regs. Titl 273 Ch. 9 §015
GINA	See Title VII	
IRCA	N/A	
NLRA	Private: N/A Public: Employees have collective bargaining rights, teachers can organize and bargain collectively.	Private: N/A Public: §48-837
OSHA	N/A	
OWBPA	See Title VII	
PRWORA	Employers must report hires/rehires within 20 days.	§48-2301
PDA	See Title VII	
SOX	N/A	
TITLE VII	Covers all public and private employers with 15 or more employees and bars discrimination on basis of national origin, race, color, religion, age, disability, marital status, genetic test results, sex (pregnancy/related conditions), and sexual harassment.	§48-1101, §48-236, §20-168
USERRA	Generally covers members of National Guard or U.S. Reserves.	§55-161
WARN	**www.doleta.gov/layoff/rapid_coord.cfm** — Offers links to state WARN offices.	

NEVADA

Nevada Employment Agencies and State Employment Laws		
Department of Labor	**www.laborcommissioner.com** **www.NV.gov**	

	Nevada Department Of Business and Industry 555 E. Washington, Ave., Suite 4100 Las Vegas, NV 89101-1050 702.486.2650	
Federal Statute	Corresponding State Statute coverage	State Statute [NV Rev. Stat]
ADEA	See Title VII	
ADA	See Title VII	
COBRA	Covers employers with fewer than 20 employees and covers employees for 18 months after termination.	§689B.245
EPPA	Refer to state Department of Labor Web site listed above.	
ERISA	N/A	
EPA	See Title VII	
FRCA	Follows federal law.	§598C.150(2)
FLSA	Minimum wage is $5.30 if employer provides health benefits, and $6.33 if employer does not provide benefits.	NV Const. Art. 15
FMLA	Covers state employers and permanent state employees.	§392.920
GINA	See Title VII	
IRCA	N/A	
NLRA	Private: N/A Public: Employees have the right to organize and bargain collectively.	Private: N/A Public: §288.010
OSHA	Follows federal law.	NV Rev. Stat. Chap 618
OWBPA	See Title VII	
PRWORA	Employers must report hire/rehire within 20 days.	§606.010
PDA	See Title VII	
SOX	N/A	

TITLE VII	Covers state employers and employers with 15 or more employees and prohibits them from discriminating on the basis of race, color, religion, national origin, age, disability, sexual orientation, and sex (pregnancy/related conditions).	§613.310
USERRA	Covers employees who are members of the state's National Guard.	§412.1395, §284.359
WARN	**www.doleta.gov/layoff/rapid_coord. cfm** — Offers links to state WARN offices.	

NEW HAMPSHIRE

New Hampshire Employment Agencies and State Employment Laws		
Department of Labor	**www.labor.state.NH.us**	
	New Hampshire Department of Labor State Office Park South 95 Pleasant Street Concord, NH 03301 603.271.3176	
Federal Statute	Corresponding State Statute coverage	NH State Statute
ADEA	See Title VII	
ADA	See Title VII	
COBRA	Covers most public and private employers and provides employees with 18 months of coverage after termination.	§415.18
EPPA	Refer to state Department of Labor Web site listed above.	
ERISA	N/A	
EPA	See Title VII	
FRCA	Follows federal law.	§359-B.5
FLSA	Minimum wage is $6.55.	§279.21

FMLA	Covers all state employers and all public and private employers with six or more employees. State employees and female employees are covered.	§354-A.7
GINA	See Title VII	
IRCA	N/A	
NLRA	Private: N/A Public: Employees have the right to organize and bargain collectively. Employees who strike can be disciplined.	Private: N/A Public: §273-A.1
OSHA	N/A	
OWBPA	See Title VII	
PRWORA	Employers must report hires/rehires within 20 days.	§282-A-7
PDA	See Title VII	
SOX	N/A	
TITLE VII	Covers state employers and employers with six or more employees and prohibits them from discriminating on the basis of race, color, religion, creed, national origin, disability, sex (pregnancy/related conditions), age, and genetic test results.	§354-A.1, §141-E.19, §275.37a
USERRA	Follows federal law.	§110-C:1, §112:9
WARN	**www.doleta.gov/layoff/rapid_coord. cfm** — Offers links to state WARN offices.	

NEW JERSEY

New Jersey Employment Agencies and State Employment Laws		
Department of Labor	**lwd.dol.state.nj.us/labor**	

	New Jersey Department of Labor John Fitch Plaza 13th Floor, Suite D P.O. Box 110 Trenton, NJ 08625-0110 609.772.3200	
Federal Statute	Corresponding State Statute coverage	State Statute [NJ Stat. Ann]
ADEA	See Title VII	
ADA	See Title VII	
COBRA	Covers employers with fewer than 50 employees. This does not apply to employees covered by federal COBRA. Provides employees with 18 months of coverage after termination.	§17B:27A-27, §17B:27A-19.16
EPPA	Refer to state labor department Web site listed above.	
ERISA	N/A	
EPA	See Title VII	
FRCA	Follows federal law.	
FLSA	Minimum wage is $7.15.	§34:11-56a4
FMLA	Covers private employers with 50 or more employees. Covers state employers. Employees who have at least one year of full-time service are eligible.	§34:11B-1
GINA	See Title VII	
IRCA	N/A	
NLRA	Private: N/A Public: Generally, employees will have collective bargaining rights under various conditions of employment. Employees do not have the right to strike, and managerial and confidential employees are not covered.	Private: N/A Public: §34:13A-5.3
OSHA	N/A	
OWBPA	See Title VII	
PRWORA	Employers must report hire/rehires within 20 days.	§2A-:17-56.61

PDA	See Title VII	
SOX	N/A	
TITLE VII	Covers all employers and bars them from discriminating on the basis of race, creed, color, ancestry, national origin, age, sex, disability, marital status, sexual orientation, and genetic information.	§10:5-1 and §34:6B-1
USERRA	Covers permanent employees.	
WARN	**www.doleta.gov/layoff/rapid_coord. cfm** — Offers links to state WARN offices.	

NEW MEXICO

New Mexico Employment Agencies and State Employment Laws		
Department of Labor	**www.dol.state.NM.us**	
	New Mexico Department Of Labor P.O. Box 1928 401 Broadway, N.E. Albuquerque, NM 87103-1928 505.841.8450	
Federal Statute	Corresponding State Statute coverage	State Statute [NM Stat. Ann.]
ADEA	See Title VII	
ADA	See Title VII	
COBRA	Covers all employers and provides employees six months of coverage upon termination.	§59A-18-16
EPPA	Refer to state Department of Labor Web site listed above.	
ERISA	N/A	
EPA	See title VII	
FRCA	Follows federal law.	§56-3-6
FLSA	Minimum wage is $6.55.	§50-4-22(A)

FMLA	Covers all state employers who have at least one year of full time service.	NM Admin Code§1.7.7
GINA	See Title VII	
IRCA	N/A	
NLRA	Private: N/A Public: N/A	Private: N/A Public: N/A
OSHA	Follows federal law.	§50-9-1
OWBPA	See Title VII	
PRWORA	Employers must report hire/rehires within 20 days.	§50-13-1
PDA	See Title VII	
SOX	N/A	
TITLE VII	Covers private employers with four or more employees and prohibits discrimination on basis of race, color, religion, ancestry, national origin, disability, sex (includes sexual harassment), sexual orientation, age, and genetic test results.	§28-1-1
USERRA	Covers permanent employees who leave a job to go to U.S. military, National Guard or Reserves.	§28-15-1, §20-4-7, §20-5-14
WARN	**www.doleta.gov/layoff/rapid_coord. cfm** — Offers links to state WARN offices.	

NEW YORK

New York Employment Agencies and State Employment Laws		
Department of Labor	**www.labor.state.NY.us**	
	New York Department of Labor State Office Bldg. #12 W.A. Harriman Campus Albany, NY 12240 518.457.5519	

Federal Statute	Corresponding State Statute coverage	State Statute [NY Lab. Law]
ADEA	See Title VII	
ADA	See Title VII	
COBRA	Covers all employers of employees not eligible for federal COBRA.	NY Ins. Law §3221(m)
EPPA	Refer to state Department of Labor Web site listed above.	
ERISA	N/A	
EPA	See Title VII	
FRCA	Follows federal law.	Art. 25 §380-j
FLSA	Minimum wage is $7.15.	NY Lab law art. 19 §652 (1)
FMLA	Covers public and private employers. Covers all employees.	Ch. 32 Art. 7 201
GINA	See Title VII	
IRCA	N/A	
NLRA	Private: Employees have right to organize, bargain collectively, and strike. Covers all employers and employees with exception of agriculture workers and family-based workers. Public: All employees have right to organize and bargain collectively. This will not include judges and confidential/ managerial employees. Employees do not have the right to strike.	Private: Art. 20 §700 Public: Art. 14 §200
OSHA	N/A	
OWBPA	See Title VII	
PRWORA	Employers must report hires/rehires within 20 days.	NY Tax §171-h
PDA	See Title VII	
SOX	N/A	

TITLE VII	Covers state employers and private employers with four or more employees and prohibits discrimination on the basis of race, color, creed, national origin, age, genetic results, marital status, sexual orientation, and disability.	NY Exec Law §290
USERRA	Covers permanent employees.	NY Mil. Law Ch. 36 §208-a
WARN	**www.doleta.gov/layoff/rapid_coord. cfm** — Offers links to state WARN offices.	

NORTH CAROLINA

North Carolina Employment Agencies and State Employment Laws		
Department of Labor	**www.nclabor.com**	
	North Carolina Department of Labor 4 West Edenton Street Raleigh, NC 27601-1092 919.733.7166	
Federal Statute	Corresponding State Statute coverage	State Statute [NC Gen. Stat.]
ADEA	See Title VII	
ADA	See Title VII	
COBRA	Covers all employers and provides employees with 18 months of coverage after termination.	§58-53-5
EPPA	Refer to state Department of Labor Web site listed above.	
ERISA	N/A	
EPA	See Title VII	
FRCA	Follows federal law.	
FLSA	Minimum wage is $6.15.	§95-25.3 (a)
FMLA	Covers state employers and state employees with at least one year of full-time work.	§95-241

GINA	See title VII	
IRCA	N/A	
NLRA	Private: N/A Public: Employers cannot enter labor contracts with unions, and strikes are prohibited.	Private: N/A Public: §95-97
OSHA	Follows federal law.	§95-126
OWBPA	See title VII	
PRWORA	Employers must report hires/rehires within 20 days.	§110-129.2
PDA	See title VII	
SOX	N/A	
TITLE VII	Covers all employers and bars discrimination on the basis of race, color, creed, national origin, age, disability, genetic information, marital status, and sex (pregnancy/related conditions).	§95-28.1, §95-151, §127a-20.1, §95-241, §143-422.1
USERRA	Covers employees who are part of the National Guard.	§127A-111, §127A-2o1
WARN	**www.doleta.gov/layoff/rapid_coord.cfm** — Offers links to state WARN offices.	

NORTH DAKOTA

North Dakota Employment Agencies and State Employment Laws		
Department of Labor	**www.nd.gov/labor**	
	North Dakota Department Of Labor State Capitol Building 600 East Boulevard, Department 406 Bismarck, ND 58505-0340 701.328.2660	
Federal Statute	Corresponding State Statute coverage	State Statute [ND Cent. Code]
ADEA	See Title VII	
ADA	See title VII	

COBRA	Covers all employers.	§26.1-36-23
EPPA	Refer to state Department of Labor Web site listed above.	
ERISA	N/A	
EPA	See Title VII	
FRCA	Follows federal law.	
FLSA	Minimum wage is $6.55.	§NC Cent. Code wage Orders
FMLA	Covers all state employers, but will not cover the political subdivisions of the state. Employees must have been employed for at least one year part-time.	§54-52.4-01
GINA	N/A	
IRCA	N/A	
NLRA	Private: Covers all private employers with exception of not-for-profit hospitals and employers covered by the Railway Labor Act. All employees are covered except agricultural, domestic, family, supervisors, and guards. Public: Only teachers will have the right to bargain collectively and organize. Strikes are illegal.	Private: §34-12-01 Public: §34-11
OSHA	N/A	
OWBPA	See Title VII	
PRWORA	Employers must report hires/rehires within 20 days.	§34-15-01
PDA	See Title VII	
SOX	N/A	
TITLE VII	Covers all employers and will prohibit discrimination on basis of race, color, religion, national origin, age, disability, receipt of public assistance, marital status, sex (pregnancy/related conditions), and sexual harassment.	
USERRA	Covers employees who are members of the National Guard or Reserves and work for public employers.	§37-01-25

WARN	**www.doleta.gov/layoff/rapid_coord.cfm** — Offers links to state WARN offices.	

OHIO

Ohio Employment Agencies and State Employment Laws		
Department of Labor	**www.com.state.OH.us**	
	Ohio Department of Commerce 77 South High Street 22nd Floor Columbus, OH 43215 614.644.2239	
Federal Statute	Corresponding State Statute coverage	State Statute [OH Rev. Code Ann.]
ADEA	See Title VII	
ADA	See Title VII	
COBRA	Covers all employers and provides employees with six months of coverage after termination.	§3923.32
EPPA	Refer to state Department of Labor Web site listed above.	
ERISA	N/A	
EPA	See Title VII	
FRCA	Follows federal law.	
FLSA	Minimum wage is $7.	§4111.02(A)(E)(G)
FMLA	Covers state employers and all employees who work 30 or more hours a week and are biological parents or legal guardians.	§124.134, §124.382
GINA	N/A	
IRCA	N/A	
NLRA	Private: N/A Public: Employees can organize and bargain collectively regarding their wages and terms of employment.	Private: N/A Public: §4117.01

OSHA	N/A	
OWBPA	See Title VII	
PRWORA	Employers must report hires/rehires within 20 days.	§3121.891
PDA	See Title VII	
SOX	N/A	
TITLE VII	Covers state employers and private employers with four or more employees and bars them from discriminating on the basis of race, color, religion, ancestry, national origin, age, disability, and sex (pregnancy/related conditions).	§4112.01
USERRA	Follows federal law.	§5903.01, .02, §124.29, §5923.05-.051
WARN	**www.doleta.gov/layoff/rapid_coord. cfm** — Offers links to state WARN offices.	

OKLAHOMA

Oklahoma Employment Agencies and State Employment Laws		
Department of Labor	**www.state.OK.us/okdol**	
	Oklahoma Department Of Labor 4001 N. Lincoln Blvd. Oklahoma City, OK 73105-5212 405.528.1500	
Federal Statute	Corresponding State Statute coverage	State Statute [OK Stat.]
ADEA	See Title VII	
ADA	See Title VII	
COBRA	Covers all employees for 30 days after termination of coverage.	Tit. 36 §64509
EPPA	Refer to state Department of Labor Web site listed above.	
ERISA	N/A	
EPA	See Title VII	

FRCA	Follows federal law.	House Bill 2492
FLSA	Minimum wage is $6.55.	Tit. 40 §197.2
FMLA	Covers state government employers and employees with one year of full-time service.	Tit. 74 §840-2.22
GINA	See Title VII	
IRCA	N/A	
NLRA	Private: N/A Public: Law enforcement, teachers and firefighters can organize and bargain collectively.	Private: N/A Public: Tit. 11 §51-101
OSHA	N/A	N/A
OWBPA	See Title VII	
PRWORA	Employers must report hires/rehires within 20 days.	40 §2-802
PDA	See Title VII	
SOX	N/A	
TITLE VII	State employers and private employers with 15 or more employees are prohibited from discriminating on the basis of race, color, national origin, age, religion, disability, genetic information, and sex (pregnancy/related conditions). Also bars sexual harassment.	25 §1301, 36 §3614.2
USERRA	Covers employees who are members of Reserves or the National Guard.	72 §48:1, 44 §208.1
WARN	**www.doleta.gov/layoff/rapid_coord.cfm** — Offers links to state WARN offices.	

OREGON

Oregon Employment Agencies and State Employment Laws		
Department of Labor	**www.oregon.gov/boli**	

	Oregon Bureau of Labor and Industries 800 NE Oregon St., #32 Portland, OR 97232 971.673.0761	
Federal Statute	Corresponding State Statute coverage	State Statute [OR Rev. Stat]
ADEA	See Title VII	
ADA	See Title VII	
COBRA	Covers all employers and provides employees with six months coverage after termination.	§734.600, §743.610
EPPA	Refer to state Department of Labor Web site listed above.	
ERISA	N/A	
EPA	See Title VII	
FRCA	Follows federal law.	
FLSA	Minimum wage is $7.95.	§653.000
FMLA	Covers all employers with 25 or more employees and covers employees who have worked at least 180 days.	§659A.15
GINA	See Title VII	
IRCA	N/A	
NLRA	Private: All employers are covered with exception of those covered by the Railroad Labor Act. Covers all employees with exception of those involved in the following industries: agriculture, domestic, supervisors, guard, and family workers. Public: Employees have right to bargain collectively regarding salary and other conditions of employment.	Private: §663.005 Public: §243.650
OSHA	Same as federal, although under state law, employers must keep written records of safety committee meetings.	§654.001
OWBPA	See Title VII	

PRWORA	Employers must report hires/rehires within 20 days.	§25.790
PDA	See Title VII	
SOX	N/A	
TITLE VII	Covers all employees and prohibits discrimination on the basis of race, color, national origin, religion, age, disability, marital status, and sex (pregnancy/related conditions).	§659A.030
USERRA	Covers employees who are members of any state militias.	§399.230, §399.290, §408.210
WARN	**www.doleta.gov/layoff/rapid_coord. cfm** — Offers links to state WARN offices.	

PENNSYLVANIA

Pennsylvania Employment Agencies and State Employment Laws		
Department of Labor	**www.dli.state.PA.us**	
	Pennsylvania Department of Labor and Industry 1700 Labor and Industry Bldg 7th and Forster Streets Harrisburg, PA 17120 717.787.5279	
Federal Statute	Corresponding State Statute coverage	State Statute [PA Stat.]
ADEA	See Title VII	
ADA	See Title VII	
COBRA	N/A	
EPPA	Refer to state Department of Labor Web site listed above.	
ERISA	N/A	
EPA	See Title VII	
FRCA	Follows federal law.	
FLSA	Minimum wage is $7.15.	Tit. 40 §333.104(a).(a1)

FMLA	N/A	
GINA	See title VII	
IRCA	N/A	
NLRA	Private: All employers are covered with exception of those covered by the Railway Labor Act. All employees are covered with exception of those working for family or in agriculture. Public: employees have right to collectively bargain and organize. Under certain circumstances, certain public employees have the right to strike and others are prohibited.	Private: Tit. §211.1 Public: Tit. 43 §1011.01
OSHA	N/A	
OWBPA	See Title VII	
PRWORA	Employers must report hires/rehires within 20 days	23 §4392
PDA	See Title VII	
SOX	N/A	
TITLE VII	Covers state employers and private employers with at least four employees and bars discrimination on basis of ancestry, age, national origin, race, color, religious affiliation, and sex (pregnancy/ related conditions).	
USERRA	Covers employees who are members of state National Guard or U.S. Reserves.	51 §7309, 51 §4102
WARN	**www.doleta.gov/layoff/rapid_coord. cfm** — Offers links to state WARN offices.	

RHODE ISLAND

Rhode Island Employment Agencies and State Employment Laws		
Department of Labor	**www.dlt.state.RI.us**	
	Rhode Island Department of Labor and Training 1511 Pontiac Avenue Cranston, RI 02920 401.462.8000	
Federal Statute	Corresponding State Statute coverage	State Statute [RI Gen Laws]
ADEA	See Title VII	
ADA	See Title VII	
COBRA	Covers all employers and will provide up to 18 months of coverage to terminated employees.	§27-19.1-1, §27-20.4-f
EPPA	Refer to state Department of Labor Web site listed above.	
ERISA	N/A	
EPA	See Title VII	
FRCA	Follows federal law.	
FLSA	Minimum wage is $7.40.	28-12-3
FMLA	Covers private employers with five or more employees, all state employers, and all local government employers that have 30 or more employees. Covers employees who have had one year of service working 30 or more hours a week.	§28-48-1
GINA	See Title VII	
IRCA	N/A	
NLRA	Private: Covers all employers and employees except family business workers and agricultural workers. Public: Employees have the right to organize and bargain collectively, but they do not have the right to strike.	Private: §28-7-1 Public: §28-9.4-3, §36-11-1

OSHA	N/A	
OWBPA	See Title VII	
PRWORA	Employers must report hires/rehires within 14 days.	
PDA	See Title VII	
SOX	N/A	
TITLE VII	Covers state employers and private employers with four or more employees. Prohibits discrimination on basis of race, color, religion, age, disability, sexual orientation, genetic information, and sex (pregnancy/related conditions).	§28-5-1, §23-6-10, §23-20.7.1
USERRA	Covers employees who are members of state or U.S. military.	§30-21-1, §30-11-1
WARN	**www.doleta.gov/layoff/rapid_coord. cfm** — Offers links to state WARN offices.	

SOUTH CAROLINA

South Carolina Employment Agencies and State Employment Laws		
Department of Labor	**www.llr.state.SC.us**	
	South Carolina Department Of Labor, Licensing, and Regulations P.O. Box 11329 Columbia, SC 29211-1329 803.896.4300	
Federal Statute	Corresponding State Statute coverage	State Statute [SC Code Ann.]
ADEA	See Title VII	
ADA	See Title VII	
COBRA	Covers all employers and provides employees with six months of coverage after termination.	§38-71-770
EPPA	Refer to state Department of Labor Web site listed above.	

ERISA	N/A	
EPA	See Title VII	
FRCA	Follows federal law.	
FLSA	N/A	
FMLA	Covers state government employers and all state employees.	§8-11-40, §8-11-155, §8-11-610
GINA	See Title VII	
IRCA	N/A	
NLRA	Private: N/A Public: N/A	Private: N/A Public: N/A
OSHA	Follows federa law.	§41-15-10
OWBPA	See Title VII	
PRWORA	Employers must report hires/rehires within 20 days.	§43-5-598
PDA	See Title VII	
SOX	N/A	
TITLE VII	Covers state employers and private employers with 15 or more employees, and bars discrimination based on national origin, disability, race, color, religion, age, and sex (pregnancy/related conditions).	§1-13-1
USERRA	Covers employees who are members of state or National Guard, or any other military duty.	§25-1-2310, §8-7-90, §25-1-2250
WARN	**www.doleta.gov/layoff/rapid_coord.cfm** — Offers links to state WARN offices.	

SOUTH DAKOTA

South Dakota Employment Agencies and State Employment Laws		
Department of Labor	**www.state.SD.us**	
	South Dakota Department of Labor 700 Governors Drive Pierre, SD 57501-2291 605.773.3682	
Federal Statute	Corresponding State Statute coverage	State Statute [SD Comp]
ADEA	See Title VII	
ADA	See Title VII	
COBRA	Covers employers with less than 20 employees and provides the employee with 18 months of coverage after termination.	§58-18.7.5, §58-18C-1
EPPA	Refer to state Department of Labor Web site listed above.	
ERISA	N/A	
EPA	See Title VII	
FRCA	Follows federal law.	
FLSA	Minimum wage $6.55.	§60-11-3
FMLA	Covers state government and state employees who have worked at least 12 months full time.	SD Admin Code §55.01
GINA	N/A	
IRCA	N/A	
NLRA	Private: Covers all employers and all employees with the exception of domestic, farm, and ranch workers, and supervisors. Employees have the right to organize, bargain collectively, and strike. Public: Employees have the right to organize and bargain collectively, but are prohibited form striking.	Private: §60-9A-1 Public: §3-18-1
OSHA	N/A	

OWBPA	See Title VII	
PRWORA	Employers must report hires/rehires within 20 days.	§25-7A-3.3
PDA	See Title VII	
SOX	N/A	
TITLE VII	Covers all employers and prohibits discrimination on basis of national origin, race, color, creed, religion, disability, and sex (pregnancy/related conditions).	§20-13-10
USERRA	Covers employees who are members of state guard.	§33-17-15.1, §3-6-19, §3-6-2
WARN	**www.doleta.gov/layoff/rapid_coord. cfm** — Offers links to state WARN offices.	

TENNESSEE

Tennessee Employment Agencies and State Employment Laws		
Department of Labor	**www.state.TN.us/labor**	
	Tennessee Department of Labor and Workforce Development Andrew Johnson Tower 710 James Robertson Parkway Nashville, TN 37243-0655 615.741.6642	
Federal Statute	Corresponding State Statute coverage	State Statute [TN Code.Ann]
ADEA	See Title VII	
ADA	See Title VII	
COBRA	Covers all employers and provides employees with coverage for the remainder of the relevant policy month plus three additional months.	§56-7-2312
EPPA	Refer to state Department of Labor Web site listed above.	
ERISA	N/A	

EPA	See Title VII	
FRCA	Follows federal law.	
FLSA	N/A	
FMLA	Covers all employers with 100 or more full-time workers at one job site and also state employees. Employees must have worked for a year.	§4-21-408, §8-5-806, §8-5-802
GINA	N/A	
IRCA	N/A	
NLRA	Private: N/A Public: Transit employees have right to bargain collectively and teachers have limited bargaining rights. Generally strikes are prohibited, with narrow exceptions.	Private: N/A Public: §7-56-101, §49-5-601
OSHA	Follows federal law. Workplace fatalities and major hospitalization accidents must be reported to the state agency.	§50-3-101
OWBPA	See Title VII	
PRWORA	Employers must report hires/rehires within 20 days.	§36-5-1101
PDA	See Title VII	
SOX	N/A	
TITLE VII	Covers all employers and bars discrimination on basis of national origin, race, creed, color, age, religion, disability, or sex (pregnancy/related conditions).	§4-21-101, §8-50-103
USERRA	Covers employees who are members of state guard.	§8-33-102, §58-1-106, §58-604
WARN	**www.doleta.gov/layoff/rapid_coord. cfm** — Offers links to state WARN offices.	

TEXAS

Texas Employment Agencies and State Employment Laws		
Department of Labor	**www.twc.state.TX.us**	
	Texas Workforce Commission 101 East 15th St. Austin, TX 78778 512.475.2670	
Federal Statute	Corresponding State Statute coverage	TX State Statute [varies]
ADEA	See Title VII	
ADA	See Title VII	
COBRA	Covers all employers and provides employees with six months of coverage after termination.	TX Ins. Code art. 3.51-6, art. 26.21(o)
EPPA	Refer to state Department of Labor Web site listed above.	
ERISA	N/A	
EPA	See Title VII	
FRCA	Follows federal law.	Bus. & Commerce Code Ch. 20 §20.05
FLSA	Minimum wage is $6.55.	TX. Labor Code Tit.2 §62.051
FMLA	Covers state employers and state employees who have a year of full-time service.	TX Govt §661.912, §661.206, §661.906
GINA	See Title VII	
IRCA	N/A	
NLRA	Private: N/A Public: Employees can join unions but states cannot enter into collective bargaining contracts. Fire departments and law enforcement have right to organize and public employees do not have the right to strike.	Private: N/A Public: Gov't code §617.001
OSHA	N/A	
OWBPA	See Title VII	

PRWORA	Employers must report hires/rehires within 20 days.	§234.101
PDA	See Title VII	
SOX	N/A	
TITLE VII	Covers state employers and private employers with 15 or more employees and prohibits discrimination based on national origin, race, color, religion, age, disability, genetic testing, sex (pregnancy/related conditions), and ancestry.	§21.051
USERRA	Covers employees who are members of state military forces.	
WARN	**www.doleta.gov/layoff/rapid_coord. cfm** — Offers links to state WARN offices.	

UTAH

Utah Employment Agencies and State Employment Laws		
Department of Labor	**www.laborcommision.utah.gov**	
	Utah Labor Commission P.O. Box 146610 Salt Lake City, UT 84114-6610 801.530.6800	
Federal Statute	Corresponding State Statute coverage	State Statute [UT Code Ann.]
ADEA	See Title VII	
ADA	See Title VII	
COBRA	Covers all employers except those covered by federal COBRA for up to six months after employee is terminated.	§31A-22-714
EPPA	Refer to state Department of Labor Web site listed above.	
ERISA	N/A	
EPA	See Title VII	
FRCA	Follows federal law.	

FLSA	Minimum wage is $6.55.	Regulation R610-1-3
FMLA	Covers state employers and follows the federal rules of eligibility.	§477-8-9, §477-7-4
GINA	See Title VII	
IRCA	N/A	
NLRA	Private: All employers are covered with exception of nonprofit hospitals and those covered by the Railway Labor Act. Provides all employees (with the exception of agricultural workers, domestics, family employees) the right to bargain collectively and join and organize unions. Public: Teacher organizations can organize and bargain collectively. All employees are barred from striking.	Private: §34-20-1 Public: §53A-7-101
OSHA	Mostly the same as federal; however, there are reporting requirements in regards to the State Occupational Safety and Health Agency.	§34A-6-101
OWBPA	See Title VII	
PRWORA	Employers must report hires/rehires within 20 days.	§35A-7-102
PDA	See Title VII	
SOX	N/A	
TITLE VII	Covers state employers and private employers with 15 or more employees and bars discrimination on basis of national origin, race, color, age, disability, and sex (pregnancy/related conditions).	
USERRA	Covers employees who are members of state military forces.	§39-1-38
WARN	**www.doleta.gov/layoff/rapid_coord.cfm** — Offers links to state WARN offices.	

VERMONT

Vermont Employment Agencies and State Employment Laws		
Department of Labor	**www.labor.vermont.gov**	
	Vermont Department of Labor 5 Green Mountain Drive P.O. Box 488 Montpelier, VT 05601-0488 802.828.4000	
Federal Statute	Corresponding State Statute coverage	State Statute [VT Stat. Ann]
ADEA	See Title VII	
ADA	See Title VII	
COBRA	Covers all employers and provides six months of coverage after an employee is terminated.	Tit. 8 §4090a
EPPA	Refer to state Department of Labor Web site listed above.	
ERISA	N/A	
EPA	See Title VII	
FRCA	Follows federal law.	
FLSA	Minimum wage rate is $7.68.	Tit. 21 §384(a)
FMLA	Covers employers with 10 or more employees who have worked with employer for at least one year at 30 hours a week.	Tit. 21 §470
GINA	See Title VII	
IRCA	N/A	

NLRA	Private: Covers employers with five or more employees, but does not cover employers subject to the Railway Labor Act or nonprofit hospitals and nursing homes. Covers all employees except family workers, agricultural workers, and domestics. Public: Employees have the right to organize and bargain collectively. State employees are barred from striking, but local government employees may strike under certain circumstances.	Private: Tit. 21 §1501 Public: Tit. 3 §901, Tit. 28 §1721
OSHA	Same as federal law.	Tit.21 §201, Tit. 28 §1415
OWBPA	See Title VII	
PRWORA	Employers must report hires/rehires within 20 days.	33 §4110
PDA	See Title VII	
SOX	N/A	
TITLE VII	Covers all employers and prohibits discrimination on basis of ancestry, national origin, race, color, religion, age, disability, and sex (pregnancy/related conditions).	Tit. 21 Ch. 5 §491, §494
USERRA	Covers employees who are members of U.S. Reserves and National Guard.	Tit. 21 §491
WARN	**www.doleta.gov/layoff/rapid_coord.cfm** — Offers links to state WARN offices.	

VIRGINIA

Virginia Employment Agencies and State Employment Laws		
Department of Labor	**www.doli.Virginia.gov**	
	Virginia Department of Labor and Industry Powers-Taylor Building 13 S. 13th Street Richmond, VA 23219 804.371.2327	
Federal Statute	Corresponding State Statute coverage	State Statute [VA Code]
ADEA	See Title VII	
ADA	See Title VII	
COBRA	Covers all employers on medical, hospital, and surgical plans. The terminated employee has 90 days.	
EPPA	Refer to state Department of Labor Web site listed above.	
ERISA	N/A	
EPA	See Title VII	
FRCA	Follows federal law.	
FLSA	Minimum wage is 6.55.	§40.1-28.10
FMLA	Covers all employers and all employees. The time off allowed will be dependent on the time spent with the company.	§51.1-1107
GINA	N/A	
IRCA	N/A	
NLRA	Private: N/A Public: Employer cannot bargain collectively and employees are barred from striking.	Private: N/A Public: 40.1-55
OSHA	Same as federal with additional requirements for access to medical records.	§40.1-49.3
OWBPA	See Title VII	

PRWORA	Employers must report hires/rehires within 20 days.	§63.2-1946
PDA	See Title VII	
SOX	N/A	
TITLE VII	Covers all employers and prohibits discrimination on the basis of national origin, race, color, religion, age, disability, marital status, and sex (pregnancy/related conditions).	§2.2-2639, §2.2-3900
USERRA	Covers employees who are members of the National Guard or any state military forces.	§44-93.2, §44-93.3, §2.2-2802
WARN	**www.doleta.gov/layoff/rapid_coord. cfm** — Offers links to state WARN offices.	

WASHINGTON

Washington Employment Agencies and State Employment Laws		
Department of Labor	**www.lni.WA.gov**	
	Washington Department of Labor and Industries P.O. Box 440001 Olympia, WA 98504-4001 360.902.4200	
Federal Statute	Corresponding State Statue coverage	State Statute [WA Rev Code]
ADEA	See Title VII	
ADA	See Title VII	
COBRA	State COBRA is optional except during a strike, when it will be required.	§48.21.075, §48.21.250
EPPA	Refer to state Department of Labor Web site listed above.	
ERISA	N/A	
EPA	See Title VII	
FRCA	Follows federal law.	§19.182.040

FLSA	Minimum wage is $8.07.	§49.46.020
FMLA	Covers employers with 100 or more employees. Generally follows federal statute regarding employee eligibility, although there are two exceptions.	§49.78.005, §49.12.270, §49.12.265
GINA	See Title VII	
IRCA	N/A	
NLRA	Private: N/A Public: Employees have the right to organize and bargain collectively.	Private: N/A Public: §41.56.010
OSHA	Follows federal law.	§49.17.01
OWBPA	See Title VII	
PRWORA	Employers must report hires/rehires within 20 days.	§26.23.040
PDA	See Title VII	
SOX	N/A	
TITLE VII	Covers state employers and private employers with eight or more employees and bars them from discriminating on basis of race, religion, national origin, age, disability, sex (pregnancy/related conditions), genetic information, and marital status.	§49.44.090, §49.44.180, §49.60.010
USERRA	Covers employees who are residents of the state and enter, or are members of state military services or U.S. armed forces.	§73. 16.033, §73.16.035, §38.24.040
WARN	**www.doleta.gov/layoff/rapid_coord.cfm** — Offers links to state WARN offices.	

WEST VIRGINIA

West Virginia Employment Agencies and State Employment Laws		
Department of Labor	**www.labor.state.WV.us**	
	West Virginia Division of Labor State Capitol Complex Building #6 1900 Kanawha Blvd. Charleston, WV 25305 304.558.7890	
Federal Statute	Corresponding State Statute coverage	State Statute [WV Code]
ADEA	See Title VII	
ADA	See Title VII	
COBRA	Covers employers that offer group health plans and gives terminated employees 18 months of coverage.	§33-16-3
EPPA	Refer to state Department of Labor Web site listed above.	
ERISA	N/A	
EPA	See Title VII	
FRCA	Follows federal law.	
FLSA	Minimum wage is $7.25.	§21-5C-2(a)
FMLA	Covers all state employers and all permanent hire employees.	§21-5D-1
GINA	See Title VII	
IRCA	N/A	
NLRA	Private: Covers employers with 15 or more employees, with exception of Railroad Labor Act employers. Covers all employees with exception of agricultural, domestics, supervisors, and family workers. Public: Employees have right to organize and bargain collectively (employers not bound to do so).	Private: §21-1A-1 Public: Case law
OSHA	N/A	

OWBPA	See Title VII	
PRWORA	Employers must report hires/rehires within 14 days.	§48-18-125
PDA	See Title VII	
SOX	N/A	
TITLE VII	Covers state employers and private employers with 12 or more employees.	§5-11-1, §21-3-19
USERRA	Covers employees who are in the state armed forces.	§15-iF-1
WARN	**www.doleta.gov/layoff/rapid_coord. cfm** — Offers links to state WARN offices.	

WISCONSIN

Wisconsin Employment Agencies and State Employment Laws		
Department of Labor	**www.dwd.state.WI.us**	
	Wisconsin Department Of Workforce Development 201 E. Washington Ave, #A400 P.O. Box 7946 608.266.6861	
Federal Statute	Corresponding State Statute coverage	State Statute [WI Stat.]
ADEA	See Title VII	
ADA	See Title VII	
COBRA	Covers all employers and provides terminated employees with 18 months of coverage.	§632.897
EPPA	Refer to state Department of Labor Web site listed above.	
ERISA	N/A	
EPA	See Title VII	
FRCA	Follows federal law.	

FLSA	Minimum wage is generally $6.50, with a few exceptions.	WI Admin. Code DWD 272.05, 272.03, 272.08
FMLA	Covers all employers with 50 or more employees. Employees must have been with same employer for past year to qualify.	§103.10
GINA	See Title VII	
IRCA	N/A	
NLRA	Private: covers all employers and all employees except domestics, executives, supervisors, and family workers. Public: state and local employees have right to bargain collectively and right to organize; state employees are barred from striking.	Private: §111.01 Public: §111.84, §111.77
OSHA	N/A	
OWBPA	See Title VII	
PRWORA	Employers must report hires/rehires within 20 days.	§103.05
PDA	See Title VII	
SOX	N/A	
TITLE VII	Covers all employers and bars discrimination on basis of ancestry, national origin, religion, race, color, age, disability, arrest records, marital status, and genetic testing.	§111.31
USERRA	Covers employees who are members of state military.	§113.45
WARN	**www.doleta.gov/layoff/rapid_coord. cfm** — Offers links to state WARN offices.	

WYOMING

Wyoming Employment Agencies and State Employment Laws		
Department of Labor	**www.doe.state.WY.us**	
	Wyoming Department of Employment 1510 East Pershing Blvd. Cheyenne, WY 82002 207.777.7261	
Federal Statute	Corresponding State Statute coverage	State Statute [WY Stat.]
ADEA	See Title VII	
ADA	See Title VII	
COBRA	Will cover employers that are not covered by federal COBRA.	§26-19-113
EPPA	Refer to state Department of Labor Web site listed above.	
ERISA	N/A	
EPA	See Title VII	
FRCA	Follows federal law.	
FLSA	Minimum wage is $6.55.	§27-4-202
FMLA	Covers all employers no matter the size.	§1-40-202
GINA	See Title VII	
IRCA	N/A	
NLRA	Private: N/A Public: firefighters can organize and bargain collectively.	Private: N/A Public: §27-10-101
OSHA	Same as federal law.	§27-11-101
OWBPA	See Title VII	
PRWORA	Employers must report hires/rehires within 20 days.	§27-1-115
PDA	See Title VII	
SOX	N/A	

TITLE VII	Covers state employers and private employers with more than two employees and prohibits discrimination on the basis of ancestry, national origin, creed, race, color, religion, disability, or sex (pregnancy/related conditions).	§27-9-101
USERRA	Covers employees who are members of state military.	§27-9-105
WARN	**www.doleta.gov/layoff/rapid_coord. cfm** — Offers links to state WARN offices.	

Bibliography

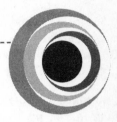

http://a257.g.akamaitech.net/7/257/2422/03jul20071500/edocket.acce

www.access.gpo.gov/nara/cfr/waisidx_07/29cfr1626_07.html

www.dol.gov/ebsa/pdf/cobraemployer.pdf

www.dol.gov/ebsa/faqs/faq_consumer_cobra.html

www.dol.gov/dol/allcfr/ebsa/Title_29/Part_2590/29CFR2590.606-1.htm

www.crbenefits.com/clients/pdf/04-11796.pdf

www.infinisource.net/infinisource/Benefit_Resources/caseLaw/Giddens.aspx

www.elinfonet.com/fedarticles/4/1

www4.law.cornell.edu/uscode/html/uscode29/usc_
sup_01_29_10_18_20_I_30_B.html

http://frwebgate2.access.gpo.gov/cgi-bin/waisgate.cgi?WAISdocID=815505303
686+0+0+0&WAISaction=retrieve

www.hmw.com/workcite/20060518.htm

www4.law.cornell.edu/usc-cgi/usc_cfr.cgi?title=29&section=1002

www.dol.gov/dol/allcfr/ESA/Title_29/Part_801/Subpart_D.htm

www.dol.gov/esa/regs/compliance/whd/whdfs36.pdf

www.dol.gov/esa/regs/statutes/whd/poly01.pdf

Federal Trade Commission
www.ftc.gov/os/statutes/fcradoc.pdf

U.S. Citizenship and Immigration Services. **www.uscis.gov/portal/site/uscis/ menuitem.eb1d4c2a3e5b9ac89243c6a7543f6d1a/?vgnextoid=02729c7755cb90 10VgnVCM10000045f3d6a1RCRD&vgnextchannel=02729c7755cb9010VgnV CM10000045f3d6a1RCRD** (accessed March 28, 2008).

www.hklaw.com/id24660/PublicationId2371/ReturnId31/contentid50894/ 1630.10, 29 CFR sec. July 1, 2007.

"2005 CFR Title 29, Volume 4."
http://www.access.gpo.gov/nara/cfr/waisidx_07/29cfr1625_07.html

"29 CFR 1630.05." July 1, 2007.
http://a257.g.akamaitech.net/7/257/2422/03jul20071500/edocket.acce

"3rd Circuit Extends Pregnancy Discrimination Act Proection to Cover Abortion." McGuire LLP. June 12, 2008.
www.mcguirewoods.com/news-resources/item.asp?item=3348

"42 U.S.C. 1981 ." Employment Law Information Network.
www.elinfonet.com/1981sum.php

Colb, Sherry F. "What's So Special About Genetic Discrimination? Congress Passes a Revealing Bill." Findlaw.com. May 14, 2008.
http://writ.news.findlaw.com/colb/20080514.html

"Company's RICO Case Can Proceed Against Union Waging Corporate Campaign, Judge Says ." Jackson Lewis. June 6, 2008.
www.jacksonlewis.com/legalupdates/article.cfm?aid=1400

"Compliance Assistance-Immigration Reform and Control Act." U.S. Department of Labor Employment Standards Administration.
www.dol.gov/esa/regs/compliance/ofccp/ca_irca.htm

"Compliance Manual Chapter 10: Compensation Discrimination." The U.S. Equal Employment Opportunity Commission. December 3, 2000.
www.eeoc.gov/policy/docs/compensation.html

"Congressional Findings and Purpose." U.S. Department of Labor-Occupational Safety and Health Administration. **http://www.osha.gov/pls/oshaweb/owadisp. show_document?p_table=OSHACT&p_id=3356**

Cornell University Law School-Legal Information Institute. "Topical Index: State Statutes 3/ LII-Legal Information Institute." Cornell University Law School. **http:// topics.law.cornell.edu/wex/state_statutes3#labor**

"Court Invalidates Group Termination Releases, Requiring Strict Compliance with OWBPA ." JacksonLewis.com. June 6, 2008. **www.jacksonlewis.com/legalup-dates/article.cfm?aid=1399**

"Discrimination: Immigration Status." **www.aflcio.org. www.aflcio.org/issues/job-seconomy/workersrights/rightsatwork_e/disc_immigrants.cfm**

"Disposing of Consumer Report Information? New Rule Tells How." Federal Trade Commission. **www.ftc.gov/bcp/conline/pubs/alerts/disposalalrt.shtm**

"DOL WHD: Compliance Assistance Material: The Family and Medical Leave Act." U.S. Department of Labor-Employment Standards Administration Wage and Hour Division. **www.dol.gov/esa/regs/compliance/whd/1421.htm**

"DOL WHD: Off-the-Clock Reference." US Department of Labor. **www.dol.gov/ esa/whd/offtheclock/index.htm**

"DOL-WHD Minimum Wage Laws in the States." U.S. Department of Labor, ESA- Wage and Hour Division. **www.dol.gov/esa/minwage/america.htm#Alaska**

EEOC. "Enforcemnt Guidance on O'Connor V. Consolidated Coin Caterers Corp." September 18, 1996. **www.eeoc.gov/policy/docs/oconnor.html**

"EEOC Settles Pregnancy Discrimination Case." Workplace Prof Blog. January 10, 2007. **http://lawprofessors.typepad.com/laborprof_blog/2007/01/eeoc_settles_ pr.html**

Elarbee Thompson. "Employers Bear Burden of Proof in Age Cases." www.en-voynews.com. **www.envoynews.com/elarbee/e_article001129002.cfm?x=b11,0,w**

Equal Emplohyment Opportunity Commission. EEOC. **www.eeoc.gov/facts/ ada17.html**

"Equal Pay and Compensation Discrimination." The U.S. Equal Employment Op-portunity Commission. **www.eeoc.gov/epa/index.html**

"Executive Order Requiring Federal Contractors to Use E-Verify Could Affect Mil-lions of Workers." Jackson Lewis. June 9, 2008. **www.jacksonlewis.com/legalup-dates/pa.cfm?paid=6&start=1**

"Facts About Pregnancy Discrimination." The U.S. Equal Employment Opportu-nity Commission. **www.eeoc.gov/facts/fs-preg.html**

"Federal Laws Prohibiting Job Discrimination Questions And Answers Federal Equal Employment Opportunity (EEO) Laws." The U.S. Equal Employment Opportunity Commission. **www.eeoc.gov/facts/qanda.html**

"FTC Bureau of Consumer Protection-Resources: Credit Guidance." Federal Trade Commission. **www.ftc.gov/bcp/menus/resources/guidance/credit.shtm**

"FTC Office of the Secretary- Fair Credit Reporting Act Links." Federal Trade Commission. **www.ftc.gov/os/statutes/fcrajump.shtm**

"H.R.3734." THOMAS(Library of Congress). **http://thomas.loc.gov/cgi-bin/query/F?c104:1:./temp/~c104VMXwib:e336343**

"Jackson Lewis - OSHA's Discretion to Cite Per-Instance Willful Recordkeeping Violations More Expensive for Employers." Jackson Lewis. April 4, 2008. **www.jacksonlewis.com/legalupdates/article.cfm?aid=1082.**

"Jackson Lewis - SOX Applied to Employee Working Overseas." Jackson Lewis. 2008. **www.jacksonlewis.com/legalupdates/article.cfm?aid=1364.**

"Jackson Lewis - Special Rules on Release Agreements for Workers Raise Questions and Create Litigation Risks." Jackson Lewis. **www.jacksonlewis.com/legalupdates/article.cfm?aid=992**

"Law.com - N.Y. Judge Applies SOX Protections to Ex-Partner of Global Firm's French Office." Law.com. **www.law.com/jsp/article.jsp?id=1202732109483#**

"NLRB Workplace Rights-Employer/Employees Not Covered." National Labor Relations Board. **www.nlrb.gov/Workplace_Rights/employees_or_employers_not_covered_by_nlra.aspx**

Office of the Assistant Secretary for Policy. "Compliance Assistance Employment Law Guide." U.S. Department of Labor. June 10, 2008. **www.dol.gov/compliance/guide/index.htm**

"OSHA's Discretion to Cite Per-Instance Willful Recordkeeping Violations More Expensive for Employers ." Jackson Lewis. March 7, 2007. **www.jacksonlewis.com/legalupdates/article.cfm?aid=1082**

"Pregnancy Discrimination." The U.S. Equal Employment Opportunity Commission. **www.eeoc.gov/types/pregnancy.html**

"Questions And Answers: Final Regulation On "Tender Back" and Related Issues Concerning ADEA Waivers." Equal Employment Opportunity Commission. **www.eeoc.gov/policy/regs/tenderback-qanda.html**

"Recent United States Supreme Court Decisions Broaden Employees' Ability to Bring Retaliation Claims." Cooley Godward Kronish, LLP. June 13, 2008. **www.cooley.com/news/alerts.aspx?id=41129920**

"Section 1981 of the Civl Rights Act of 1866." HRhero.com. **www.hrhero.com/topics/section1981.html**

"Sexual Harassment." The U.S. Equal Employment Opportunity Commission. **www.eeoc.gov/types/sexual_harassment.html**

"Solutions at Work- Getting to know Gina." Fisher & Phillips, LLP. **www.laborlawyers.com/shownews.aspx?Show=10579&Type=1122**

"SOX Applied to Employee Working Overseas." Jackson Lewis. April 30, 2008. **www.jacksonlewis.com/legalupdates/article.cfm?aid=1364**

"SOX Resources." **www.whistleblowers.org/html/sox__resources.html**

"Special Rules on Release Agreements for Workers Raise Questions and Create Litigation Risks." Jackson Lewis. **www.jacksonlewis.com/legalupdates/article.cfm?aid=992**

"State Occupational Safety and Health Plans." U.S. Deparment of Labor-Occupatiohnal Safety and Health Administration. **www.osha.gov/dcsp/osp/index.html**

Sulds, Johnathan L., and Johnathan L. Israel. "Discrimination by Associaton." **www.akingump.com/docs/publication/275.pdf**

"Supreme Court Extends Retaliation Claims to More Employees." Vedderprice.com. **www.vedderprice.com/docs/pub/2736173e-32e7-4da6-9516-e3946bd72ca4_document.pdf**

"Supreme Court: Willful Violation of Fair Credit Reporting Act Requires Knowing and Reckless Conduct." Jackson Lewis. **www.jacksonlewis.com/legalupdates/article.cfm?aid=1136**

"The Equal Pay Act of 1963." The U.S. Equal Employment Opportunity Commission. **www.eeoc.gov/policy/epa.html**

"The Personal Responsibility and Work Opportunity Reconciliation Act of 1996 (PRWORA) ." U.S. Department of Health andHuman Services- Office of Child Support Enforcement. **www.acf.hhs.gov/programs/cse/fct/irspam.htm**

"THE SARBANES OXLEY ACT 2002." **www.soxlaw.com/**

"The Sarbanes Oxley Act of 2002." The Securities Lawyer's Deskbook. **www.law.uc.edu/CCL/SOact/sec906.html**

"The Uniformed Services Employment and Reemployment Rights Act (USERRA)." U.S. Department of Labor- Office of Compliance Assistance Policy. **www.dol.gov/compliance/laws/comp-userra.htm**

"Title VII of the Civil Rights Act of 1964." The U.S. Equal Employment Opportunity Commission. **www.eeoc.gov/policy/vii.html**

U.S. Department of Labor. "The Americans with Disabilities Act." Equal Employment Opportunity Commission. **www.eeoc.gov/policy/ada.html**

"U.S. Department of Labor: Compliance Assistance: Fair Labor Standards." U.S. Department of Labor. **www.dol.gov/esa/whd/flsa/**

"U.S. GOVERNMENT PRINTING OFFICE VIA GPO ACCESS-29CFR1620.13." July 1, 1999. **http://frwebgate.access.gpo.gov/cgi-bin/get-cfr.cgi?TITLE=29&PART=1620&SECTION=13&YEAR=1999&TYPE=TEXT**

"US CODE: Title 38,CHAPTER 43—EMPLOYMENT AND REEMPLOYMENT RIGHTS OF MEMBERS OF THE UNIFORMED SERVICES." Cornell University Law School. **www.law.cornell.edu/uscode/html/uscode38/usc_sup_01_38_10_III_20_43.html**

"Using Consumer Reports: What Employers Need to Know." Federal Trade Commission. **www.ftc.gov/bcp/conline/pubs/buspubs/credempl.shtm**

"WARN Employers Guide." U.S. Department of Labor. **www.doleta.gov/layoff/pdf/EmployerWARN09_2003.pdf**

"WARN Natural Disaster Fact Sheet." U.S. Department of Labor. **www.doleta.gov/layoff/pdf/WARN_Natural_Disaster_Fact_Sheet.pdf**

Author Biographies

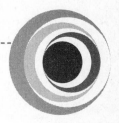

S hannon Johnson graduated from Mercer University School of Law in Macon, Ga., in 2000. She began practicing in 2001 and opened her law firm shortly thereafter. Johnson litigated a wide variety of cases before she left the practice of law in 2006 to begin a teaching and freelance writing career.

B erit Everhart received her bachelor of arts in English from the University of North Carolina at Chapel Hill in 2005. In 2009, she received her J.D. from Washington and Lee University School of Law in Lexington, Va. She is currently a candidate for a master of laws in taxation from New York University School of Law.

Index

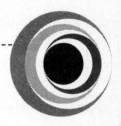

G

H

I

L

M

Q

R

S

T

U

W